R. Gupta's ®

OBJECTIVE

Computer Science

A COLLECTION OF HIGHLY USEFUL QUESTIONS FOR COMPETITIVE EXAMS

by
RPH Editorial Board

RAMESH PUBLISHING HOUSE, New Delhi

Published by
O.P. Gupta *for* Ramesh Publishing House

Admin. Office
12-H, New Daryaganj Road, Opp. Officers' Mess,
New Delhi-110002 ☏ 23261567, 23275224, 23275124

E-mail: info@rameshpublishinghouse.com
Website: www.rameshpublishinghouse.com

Showroom
● Balaji Market, Nai Sarak, Delhi-6 ☏ 23253720, 23282525
● 4457, Nai Sarak, Delhi-6, ☏ 23918938

Book Code: R-426

ISBN: 978-93-5012-593-9

25th Edition: 1704

CONTENTS

OBJECTIVE

Computer Science

1. All of the following are examples of real security and privacy risks EXCEPT:
   (*a*) hackers   (*b*) spam
   (*c*) viruses   (*d*) identity theft

2. The unit in CPU or processor, which performs arithmetic and logical operations is
   (*a*) control   (*b*) register
   (*c*) ALU   (*d*) cache memory

3. Which one of the following is volatile?
   (*a*) RAM   (*b*) EEPROM
   (*c*) EPROM   (*d*) ROM

4. A process known as ____________ is used by large retailers to study trends.
   (*a*) data mining   (*b*) data selection
   (*c*) POS   (*d*) data conversion

5. The result of an arithemtic and logical operations are stored in a/an
   (*a*) accumulator
   (*b*) instruction register
   (*c*) cache
   (*d*) ROM

6. A small amount of memory included in the processor for high speed access is called
   (*a*) Register   (*b*) Cache
   (*c*) RAM   (*d*) ROM

7. ____________terminals (formerly known as cash registers) are often connected to complex inventory and sales computer systems.
   (*a*) Data
   (*b*) Point-of-sale (POS)
   (*c*) Sales
   (*d*) Query

8. A bus is a/an
   (*a*) electronic track system
   (*b*) part of register
   (*c*) special memory
   (*d*) part of the CPU

9. A byte represents a group of
   (*a*) 10 bits   (*b*) 40 bits
   (*c*) 8 bits   (*d*) 22 bits

10. A co-processor is used to
    (*a*) enchance main memory
    (*b*) track errors in the CPU
    (*c*) improve performances of business applications
    (*d*) improve the speed of mathematical calculations

11. A(n) ____________ system is a small, wireless handheld computer that scans an item tag and pulls up the current price (and any special offers) as you shop.
    (*a*) PSS   (*b*) POS
    (*c*) inventory   (*d*) data mining

12. Intel 80286 belongs to
    (*a*) first generation microprocessors
    (*b*) second generation microprocessors
    (*c*) third generation microprocessors
    (*d*) fourth generation microprocessors

13. The power speed product of HMOS microprocessors is
    (*a*) one half of the power speed product of NMOS microprocessors
    (*b*) one fourth of the power speed product of NMOS microprocessors

(c) two times the power speed product of NMOS microprocessors

(d) same as that of NMOS microprocessors

14. A(n) hexadigit can be represented by

(a) three binary (consecutive) bits

(b) four binary (consecutive) bits

(c) eight binary (consecutive) bits

(d) sixteen binary (consecutive) bits

15. The Pentium processor contains

(a) tens of thousands of transistors

(b) hundred thousands of transistors

(c) thousands of transistors

(d) several millions of transistors

16. The proliferation of MOS technology for implementing microprocessor is attributed to

(a) its low power dissipation property and lower cost

(b) its operating speed

(c) its low capacitance

(d) nonavailability of suitable material for manufacturing microprocessors with other technology

17. The ability to recover and read deleted or damaged files from a criminal computer is an example of a law enforcement specialty called:

(a) robotics

(b) simulation

(c) computer forensics

(d) animation

18. The economics of RISC technology was improved by

(a) increasing cache memory size

(b) reducing memory requirement

(c) improving speed of processor

(d) adopting super-scalar architecture in processor design

19. In spite of the extra power needed for refreshing, DRAMs are widely used in computers because

(a) of the lower cost of bus

(b) of its lower cost relative to SRAMs

(c) of case of programming

(d) of its higher speed relative to SRAMs

20. Which of the following devices can be used to directly image printed text?

(a) OCR　　　　(b) OMR

(c) MICR　　　　(d) All of above

21. SOI technology has been successful with reference to

(a) SRAM　　　　(b) DRAM

(c) magnetic tape　　(d) core memory

22. Low-power, single-transistor cell and in-system re-writability are the features associated with

(a) SRAM　　　　(b) flash

(c) EEPROM　　　(d) ROM

23. Secondary storage device is needed to

(a) perform arithmetic and logical calculations

(b) store small volume of data

(c) print output results

(d) store large volumes of data and programs that exceed the capacity of the main memory (at reasonable costs)

24. Which one of the following does not fall under the category of secondary storage devices?

(a) Static Random Access Memory

(b) Hard disk

(c) Optical disk

(d) Winchester disk

25. Which one of the following medium is universal, portable and inexpensive but has its own limitation in terms of storage capacity and speed?

(a) Hard disk　　　(b) Winchester disk

(c) Floppy disk　　(d) Optical disk

26. Which one of the following features is common for all types of disks?

(a) Some physical property of the microscopic area of the disk surface is changed for recording
(b) Weight of the disk
(c) Size of the disk
(d) Colour of the disk

27. In a disk, each block of data is written into
(a) one sector
(b) three sectors
(c) two sectors
(d) two or more sectors

28. The output quality of a printer is measured by
(a) Dot per inch
(b) Dot per sq. inch
(c) Dots printed per unit time
(d) All of above

29. In the case of Winchester disk, the head
(a) contacts the recording surface occasionally
(b) never contacts the disk surface
(c) always contacts the recording surface
(d) contacts only the landing area while not recording

30. Out of the following types of floppy disks, which one has a metal hub?
(a) 5.25 inch floppy disk
(b) 8 inch floppy disk
(c) 3.5 inch floppy disk
(d) 7.25 inch floppy disk

31. In analog computer
(a) Input is first converted to digital form
(b) Input is never converted to digital form
(c) Output is displayed in digital form
(d) All of above

32. A floppy disk rotates at
(a) 1,000 rpm
(b) 2,000 rpm
(c) 100 rpm
(d) 360 rpm

33. The sector size of a floppy disk
(a) varies from 1 byte to 1000 bytes
(b) is fixed

(c) is unlimited
(d) varies from 128 bytes to 1024 bytes

34. In latest generation computers, the instructions are executed
(a) Parallel only
(b) Sequentially only
(c) Both sequentially and parallel
(d) All of above

35. Who designed the first electronics computer-ENIAC?
(a) Van-Neumann
(b) Joseph M. Jacquard
(c) J. Presper Eckert and John W Mauchly
(d) All of above

36. Who invented the high level language c?
(a) Dennis M. Ritchie (b) Niklaus Writh
(c) Seymour Papert (d) Donald Kunth

37. The access time of bubble memory is
(a) 300 milliseconds (b) 100 milliseconds
(c) 4 milliseconds (d) 20 milliseconds

38. The recording density that can be obtained in a magnetic tape using vertical recording technique is
(a) 1,00,000 bits/sq.cm
(b) 50,000 bits/sq.cm
(c) 10000 bits/sq.cm
(d) 2.5 million bits/sq.cm

39. Personnel who design, program, operate and maintain computer equipment refers to
(a) Console-operator (b) Programmer
(c) Peopleware (d) System Analyst

40. Which of the following encoding technique is used to record data in high density magnetic tape transport?
(a) Phase encoding
(b) Frequency modulation
(c) Return-to-zero encoding
(d) Modified frequency modulation

41. When did arch rivals IBM and Apple Computers Inc. decide to join hands?

(a) 1978   (b) 1984
(c) 1990   (d) 1991

42. For a storage requirement exceeding 1 GB, which one of the following system costs the least per megabyte?
(a) Optical disk   (b) Floptical disk
(c) Floppy disk   (d) Syquest disk

43. Which one of the following is not an input device?
(a) Joystick   (b) Mouse
(c) Keyboard   (d) Printer

44. The input device that is closely related to a touch screen is the
(a) light pen   (b) keyboard
(c) joystick   (d) mouse

45. The input device that is most likely to be used to play computer games is the
(a) keyboard   (b) joystick
(c) mouse   (d) touch screen

46. Which one of the following printers generates characters from a grid of pins?
(a) Inkjet   (b) Laser
(c) Daisy wheel   (d) Dot matrix

47. Human beings are referred to as Homosapiens, which device is called Sillico Sapiens?
(a) Monitor   (b) Hardware
(c) Robot   (d) Computer

48. An error in software or hardware is called a bug. What is the alternative computer jargon for it?
(a) Leech   (b) Squid
(c) Slug   (d) Glitch

49. Which of the following is NOT one of the four major data processing functions of a computer?
(a) gathering data
(b) processing data into information
(c) analyzing the data or information
(d) storing the data or information

50. ___________ tags, when placed on an animal, can be used to record and track in a database all of the animal's movements.
(a) POS   (b) RFID
(c) PPS   (d) GPS

51. The resolution offered by SVGA is
(a) 1024 × 768 pixels
(b) 720 × 348 pixels
(c) 1280 × 1024 pixels
(d) 640 × 350 pixels

52. The liquid crystal display works on the basis of the relation between
(a) temperature and volume
(b) light intensity and variation
(c) voltage and current
(d) polarisation and electric field

53. The UNIX operating system has been written in
(a) Assembly language
(b) C language
(c) Machine language
(d) PASCAL language

54. Which one of the software needs a compiler for its execution?
(a) dBASE IV   (b) ORACLE
(c) LOTUS   (d) FORTAN

55. Which one of the following is not considered to be a system software?
(a) Assembler
(b) Interpreter
(c) Compiler
(d) A COBOL program in a source code

56. Surgeons can perform delicate operations by manipulating devices through computers instead of manually. This technology is known as:
(a) robotics
(b) computer forensics
(c) simulation
(d) forecasting

57. A compiler breaks the source code into a uniform stream of tokens by
(a) syntactic analysis (b) lexical analysis
(c) code generation (d) error analysis

58. Which one of the following attributes is not applicable to an interpreter?
(a) Very expensive
(b) Consumes less time
(c) Simplicity
(d) None of the above

59. Which one of the following statements indicates the optimal usage of interpreter and compiler?
(a) Use the interpreter for both program development and execution
(b) Use the interpreter for program development and the compiler for execution
(c) Use the compiler for both program development and execution
(d) Use the compiler for program development and the interpreter for execution

60. Which one of the following tasks is not performed by a file utility program?
(a) Copying of a file
(b) Sorting of a file
(c) File deletion
(d) Linking the program library with main program

61. Technology no longer protected by copyright, available to everyone, is considered to be:
(a) proprietary
(b) open
(c) experimental
(d) in the public domain

62. Which one of the following languages is associated with real time processing?
(a) COBOL (b) RTL/2
(c) Ada (d) CORAL-66

63. ______________ is the study of molecules and structures whose size ranges from 1 to 100 nanometers.
(a) Nanoscience
(b) Microelectrodes
(c) Computer forensics
(d) Artificial intelligence

64. Which one of the following is not a DOS prompt?
(a) C > (b) B >
(c) A > (d) ENTER

65. Which one of the following in not an internal DOS command?
(a) BACKUP (b) COPY
(c) CLS (d) BREAK

66. Modern Computer are very reliable but they are not
(a) Fast (b) Powerful
(c) Infallible (d) Cheap

67. What is the name of the display feature that highlights are of the screen which requires operator attention?
(a) Pixel (b) Reverse video
(c) Touch screen (d) Cursor

68. Which one of the following file names is invalid in DOS?
(a) RIT . BAT (b) LISTEN . BIN
(c) RLUA . BAT (d) TALK . BAS

69. Which one of the following DIR commands lists a group of files?
(a) DIR INVOICE . BAS
(b) DIR RESCUE . BAS
(c) DIR PAY ROLL . BAS
(d) DIR TOOL? . BAS

70. IMB launched its first personal computer called IBM-PC in 1981. It had chips from Intel, disk drives from Tandon, operating system from Microsoft, the printer from Epson and the application software from everywhere. Can you name the country which contributed the video display?

(a) India   (b) China
(c) Germany   (d) Taiwan

71. Personal computers use a number of chips mounted on a main circuit board. What is the common name for such boards?
(a) Daughter board   (b) Motherboard
(c) Father board   (d) Breadboard

72. Which one of the following software resides in ROM?
(a) COMMAND . COM
(b) BIOS of MS-DOS
(c) Kernal of MS-DOS
(d) None of these

73. In most IBM PCs, the CPU, the device drives, memory expansion slots and active components are mounted on a single board. What is the name of this board?
(a) Motherboard
(b) Breadboard
(c) Daughter board
(d) Grandmother board

74. The UNIX operating system (available commercially) has been written in
(a) Pascal language
(b) C language
(c) Assembly language
(d) Machine language

75. Pick out the correct statement out of the four statements given below:
(a) UNIX has better security for files relative to MS-DOS
(b) MS-DOS has better file security system as compared to UNIX.
(c) UNIX and MS-DOS are comparable from the file security viewpoint
(d) None of the above

76. UNIX is
(a) only a multiprogramming system
(b) only a time sharing system
(c) neither a time sharing nor a multi-programming system
(d) both a time sharing and multi-programming system

77. What is meant by a dedicated computer?
(a) Which is used by one person only
(b) Which is assigned one and only one task
(c) Which uses one kind of software
(d) Which is meant for application software

78. The UNIX operating system
(a) uses six files to do the task mentioned
(b) uses two files to do the task mentioned
(c) uses three files to do the task mentioned
(d) uses only one file to read information from or write information on the terminal

79. The system unit of a personal computer typically contains all of the following except:
(a) Microprocessor   (b) Disc controller
(c) Serial interface   (d) Modem

80. A computer program that converts an entire program into machine language is called a/an
(a) Interpreter   (b) Simulator
(c) Compiler   (d) Commander

81. A computer program that translates one program instructions at a time into machine language is called a/an
(a) Interpreter   (b) CPU
(c) Compiler   (d) Simulator

82. A small or intelligent device is so called because it contains within it a
(a) Computer   (b) Microcomputer
(c) Programmable   (d) Sensor

83. A daemon wakes up
(a) once in hour
(b) once in 10 microseconds
(c) once in one minute
(d) once in 5 minutes

84. In UNIX, open files are
(a) shared between the parent and the child
(b) shared only by the child
(c) shared only by the parent
(d) None of the above

85. _____________ is the science that attempts to produce machines that display the same type of intelligence that humans do.
(*a*) Nanoscience
(*b*) Nanotechnology
(*c*) Simulation
(*d*) Artificial intelligence (AI)

86. The spooler operation
(*a*) is not at all included in multi-user version of dBASE IV
(*b*) is always included in single-user version of dBASE IV
(*c*) may not be included in single-user version of dBASE IV
(*d*) None of the above

87. _____________ is data that has been organized or presented in a meaningful fashion.
(*a*) A process   (*b*) Software
(*c*) Storage   (*d*) Information

88. The name for the way that computers manipulate data into information is called:
(*a*) programming   (*b*) processing
(*c*) storing   (*d*) organizing

89. Which one of the items given below is not an item of the Menu Bar?
(*a*) Root   (*b*) Tools
(*c*) Catalog   (*d*) Exit

90. Which of the following feature in Tools menu permits the user to follow an upgrade path from a wide range of DBMS programs and spread- sheets?
(*a*) Command . Com   (*b*) Import
(*c*) Create   (*d*) Macros

91. Computers gather data, which means that they allow users to _____________ data.
(*a*) present   (*b*) input
(*c*) output   (*d*) store

92. After a picture has been taken with a digital camera and processed appropriately, the actual print of the picture is considered:
(*a*) data   (*b*) output
(*c*) input   (*d*) the process

93. Computers use the _____________ language to process data.
(*a*) processing   (*b*) kilobyte
(*c*) binary   (*d*) representational

94. Which of the following items of the control center listed below simplifies data entry?
(*a*) Queries   (*b*) Data
(*c*) Forms   (*d*) Reports

95. Which one of the following in not considered to be a feature of the spreadsheet?
(*a*) Single view of data
(*b*) Limited access to external data
(*c*) Data tied to the model
(*d*) Difficult to do what-if projections

96. Four features of Lotus DBMS have been given below. One feature has been wrongly stated. The incorrect feature is
(*a*) transport access to multiple source of data
(*b*) tight links to lotus spreadsheet
(*c*) powerful SQL relational database system
(*d*) lacks graphical tools and database server

97. Computers process data into information by working exclusively with:
(*a*) multimedia   (*b*) words
(*c*) characters   (*d*) numbers

98. In the binary language each letter of the alphabet, each number and each special character is made up of a unique combination of:
(*a*) eight bytes   (*b*) eight kilobytes
(*c*) eight characters   (*d*) eight bits

99. In Lotus 1-2-3
(*a*) an individual cell can store a combination of data and text
(*b*) an individual cell can store either a data item or text

(c) an individual cell can be used only to store a single item of data. It cannot be used for storing text

(d) None of the above

100. The term bit is short for:

(a) megabyte   (b) binary language

(c) binary digit   (d) binary number

ANSWERS

1	2	3	4	5	6	7	8	9	10
(b)	(c)	(a)	(a)	(a)	(b)	(b)	(a)	(c)	(d)
11	12	13	14	15	16	17	18	19	20
(a)	(c)	(b)	(b)	(d)	(a)	(c)	(d)	(b)	(a)
21	22	23	24	25	26	27	28	29	30
(a)	(b)	(d)	(a)	(c)	(a)	(d)	(b)	(d)	(c)
31	32	33	34	35	36	37	38	39	40
(b)	(d)	(d)	(c)	(c)	(a)	(c)	(d)	(c)	(a)
41	42	43	44	45	46	47	48	49	50
(d)	(a)	(d)	(a)	(b)	(d)	(d)	(d)	(c)	(b)
51	52	53	54	55	56	57	58	59	60
(c)	(d)	(b)	(d)	(d)	(a)	(b)	(a)	(b)	(d)
61	62	63	64	65	66	67	68	69	70
(a)	(a)	(a)	(d)	(a)	(c)	(b)	(c)	(d)	(d)
71	72	73	74	75	76	77	78	79	80
(b)	(b)	(a)	(b)	(a)	(d)	(b)	(c)	(d)	(c)
81	82	83	84	85	86	87	88	89	90
(a)	(d)	(c)	(a)	(d)	(c)	(a)	(b)	(a)	(b)
91	92	93	94	95	96	97	98	99	100
(d)	(b)	(c)	(c)	(d)	(d)	(c)	(d)	(b)	(c)

1. The sampling rate, (how many samples per second are stored) for a CD is...?
(a) 48.4 kHz
(b) 22.050 Hz
(c) 44.1 kHz
(d) 48 kHz

2. Compact discs, (according to the original CD specifications) hold how many minutes of music?
(a) 74 mins
(b) 56 mins
(c) 60 mins
(d) 90 mins

3. While performing wide printing jobs, which one of the following options does not necessarily need modifications of printing width?
(a) Sending a code to the printer to switch condensed mode
(b) Selection of condensed mode
(c) Using wide paper
(d) Printing only a part of worksheet

4. While creating a format line, the symbol use for specifying width of data item is
(a) L
(b) W
(c) >
(d) <

5. The base 10 (or decimal - our normal way of counting) number 65535 is represented in hexadecimal as...?
(a) 0 × FFFFF
(b) 0 × FFFF
(c) 0 × FFF
(d) 0 × FFFFFF

6. Where is the headquarters of Microsoft located?
(a) Santa Clara, California
(b) Tucson, Arizona
(c) Richmond, Virginia
(d) Redmond, Washington

7. In what year was the "@" chosen for its use in e-mail addresses?
(a) 1976
(b) 1972
(c) 1980
(d) 1984

8. Out of the three statements (related to Wordstar) given below, the correct statement is
(a) We can invoke the non-document mode on a document file only by using a very complex procedure
(b) We cannot invoke the non-document mode on a document file
(c) We can invoke the non-document mode on a document file very easily
(d) None of the above

9. In Wordstar, the maximum permissible length of search string is
(a) 225
(b) 10
(c) 65
(d) None of the above

10. In Wordstar, the defalut value of top page margin setting is
(a) 6 lines
(b) 2 lines
(c) 4 lines
(d) 3 lines

11. What was the first ARPANET message?
(a) "lo"
(b) "hello world"
(c) "mary had a little lamb"
(d) "cyberspace, the final frontier"

12. Where is the headquarters of Intel located?
(a) Redmond, Washington
(b) Tucson, Arizona
(c) Santa Clara, California
(d) Richmond, Virginia

13. In which year was MIDI introduced?
(a) 1987 (b) 1983
(c) 1973 (d) 1977

14. '.BAK' extension refers usually to what kind of file?
(a) Backup file
(b) Audio file
(c) Animation/movie file
(d) MS Encarta document

15. Which one of the following scientific software packages does not have animation capabilities?
(a) Macphase (b) Covis
(c) Derive XM (d) O-Matrix

16. We can define hypertext definition in notebooks using
(a) Snap Master General Analysis 3.0
(b) Sigma 3.0
(c) Data Desk 5.0
(d) Macsyma 2.0

17. Which of the following software packages does not run in Mac and Power Mac platforms?
(a) IBM visualization data explorer
(b) Matlab symbolic math tool box
(c) HIQ 2.2
(d) Deltagraph pro 3.5

18. Which one of the following scientific packages finds application in geology, physics and biochemistry and is equipped with animation and visualisation (2D + 3D) capabilities?
(a) Math tensor 2.2
(b) AVS express 2
(c) Iris explorer 3.0
(d) Temple MVV

19. '.MPG' extension refers usually to what kind of file?
(a) WordPerfect Document file
(b) MS Office document
(c) Animation/movie file
(d) Image file

20. A string of eight 0s and 1s is called a:
(a) megabyte (b) byte
(c) kilobyte (d) gigabyte

21. A ________ is approximately one billion bytes.
(a) kilobyte (b) bit
(c) gigabyte (d) megabyte

22. The number of line types permitted in MATLAB graphics is
(a) 6 (b) 4
(c) 2 (d) 1

23. The number of point types permitted in MATLAB graphics is
(a) 6 (b) 10
(c) 5 (d) 4

24. Which one of the following scientific software packages was developed under contract with NASA?
(a) FAST drivers
(b) Tech plot 6.05
(c) NCAR graphics
(d) Argus Meshmaker 2.5

25. Which one of the following is a valid DOS command?
(a) RENAME A:SAMPLE.TXT
(b) LIST ???.???
(c) RECOVER A:
(d) LIST *.*

26. Which one of the following is an invalid statement?
(a) MSAV is an anti-virus detection and virus removal program
(b) DEFRAG may improve disk read-write speed

(c) RECOVER recovers readable information from bad/defective disk

(d) DISKCOMP compress files in a diskette

27. Which one of the following statements is incorrect?
   (a) The area above 1MB is called the expanded memory.
   (b) An OS can be loaded in high memory.
   (c) All the programs can use the extended memory.
   (d) None of these

28. A _________ is approximately a million bytes.
   (a) gigabyte
   (b) kilobyte
   (c) megabyte
   (d) terabyte

29. Which one of the following is not an internal DOS command?
   (a) PATH
   (b) COPY
   (c) XCOPY
   (d) VER

30. Which one of the following is not an internal DOS command?
   (a) MORE
   (b) REN
   (c) DATE
   (d) CLS

31. Which one of the following is not an internal DOS command?
   (a) TIME
   (b) RD
   (c) FORMAT
   (d) TYPE

32. _____________ is any part of the computer that you can physically touch.
   (a) Hardware
   (b) A device
   (c) A peripheral
   (d) An application

33. Which one of the following is not true?
   (a) MSBACKUP is used for backup as well as restore
   (b) REN and RENAME are similar commands
   (c) XCOPY is faster than COPY
   (d) None of the above

34. Mark the invalid statement
   (a) MKDIR and MD are similar commands
   (b) A 360KB diskette can be copied to 1.2MB diskette with DISKCOPY

(c) You have to format a new diskette before using it for any purpose

(d) None of the above

35. Which one of the following is true?
   (a) A mouse is connected to LPT2:
   (b) A mouse is connected to LPT1:
   (c) A mouse is connected to the serial port
   (d) None of these

36. Which one of the following is not true?
   (a) PRINT prints the files in background while we can execute another DOS command
   (b) PRINT is an external DOS command
   (c) More than one file can be sent to the print queue with a single PRINT command
   (d) None of the above

37. The components that process data are located in the:
   (a) input devices
   (b) output devices
   (c) system unit
   (d) storage component

38. Mark the most appropriate statement
   (a) TYPE can be used to display and modify any file
   (b) TYPE can be used to display any file
   (c) TYPE can be used to display a text file
   (d) TYPE can be used to display and modify a text file

39. All of the following are examples of input devices EXCEPT a:
   (a) scanner
   (b) mouse
   (c) keyboard
   (d) printer

40. DSHD stands for
   (a) Double Sided High Density
   (b) Double Sided Head Drive
   (c) Double Standard High Density
   (d) None of the above

41. How many FORMATTED TRACKS are there on 5.25 inch DSHD disk?
(a) 48
(b) 70
(c) 100
(d) 80

42. The specification of a floppy is identified by
(a) BPI
(b) TPI
(c) CPI
(d) FPI

43. A DSDD floppy diskette has a storage capacity of
(a) 48 TPI
(b) 80 TPI
(c) 64 TPI
(d) 96 TPI

44. The formatted capacity of a 5.25-inch DSDD floppy diskette is
(a) 720 KB
(b) 360 KB
(c) 1.44 MB
(d) 1.2 MB

45. The formatted capacity of a 3.5-inch micro-floppy diskette is
(a) 1.8 MB
(b) 1 MB
(c) 1.44 MB
(d) 1.2 MB

46. A floppy diskette is organised according to
(a) Head and side
(b) Sectors
(c) Tracks and sectors
(d) Tracks

47. In order to format a high density floppy into double density, use the command
(a) FORMAT A: /9
(b) FORMAT A: /D
(c) FORMAT A: /D/V
(d) FORMAT A: /4

48. The data for the "Hard Disk Type" is stored in the
(a) Boot Record
(b) CMOS RAM setup
(c) Main Memory
(d) Partition Table

49. A hard disk is logically organised according to
(a) Cylinders
(b) Tracks
(c) Cylinders and sectors
(d) Both (a) and (b)

50. Disk partitioning can be done by
(a) PARTITION COMMAND
(b) FDISK COMMAND
(c) SCANDISK COMMAND
(d) FORMAT COMMAND

51. The address of the first cell in the worksheet is
(a) 1A
(b) A
(c) A1
(d) 1

52. Which of the following is an example of an input device?
(a) scanner
(b) speaker
(c) CD
(d) printer

53. All of the following are examples of storage devices EXCEPT:
(a) hard disk drives
(b) printers
(c) floppy disk drives
(d) CD drives

54. The ____________, also called the "brains" of the computer, is responsible for processing data.
(a) motherboard
(b) memory
(c) RAM
(d) central processing unit (CPU)

55. In a blank worksheet, if you enter Profit and Loss Account in cell C1, then
(a) an error message will appear
(b) only "Profit an" will be displayed
(c) "Profit and Loss Account" will be displayed
(d) None of the above

56. The CPU and memory are located on the:
(a) expansion board
(b) motherboard

(c) storage device

(d) output device

57. Which one of the following cannot be used to enter a date?

(a) Mar-97 (b) 4-Mar-97

(c) 97 / 04 / 12 (d) 3 / 4 / 97

58. Word processing, spreadsheet, and photo-editing are examples of:

(a) application software

(b) system software

(c) operating system software

(d) platform software

59. Which one of the following is not a math function?

(a) SIGN() (b) COUNT()

(c) ABS() (d) INT()

60. Which one of the following is not a statistical function?

(a) COUNT() (b) MIN()

(c) PI() (d) all of the above

61. Which one of the following is not a database function?

(a) DAVERAGE() (b) DMIN()

(c) DISC() (d) DCOUNT()

62. Which one of the following is not a text function?

(a) VAR() (b) LEN()

(c) CHAR() (d) ABS()

63. Which one of the following is not a date function?

(a) TODAY() (b) DAYS360()

(c) DAY() (d) LEFT()

64. Mark the most appropriate statement

(a) RAND() returns a random number between −1 and 1

(b) RAND() returns a random number between 0 and 10

(c) RAND() returns a random number between 0 and 1

(d) RAND() returns a random number

65. Mark the most appropriate statement

(a) PV() is a financial function

(b) PV() is used to calculate the present value of an investment

(c) PV() is used to calculate the parent value

(d) None of these

66. Mark the most appropriate statement

(a) NOW() can be used to display the current date

(b) NOW() can be used to display the current time

(c) NOW() can be used to display the current date as well as the current time in the same cell

(d) None of these

67. = MOD(−3, 2) entered in a cell displays

(a) −1 (b) 1

(c) −1.5 (d) 0

68. The maximum number of arguments that can be used with MIN() is

(a) 3 (b) 2

(c) 30 (d) No limit

69. The addressing mode(s) that can be used in a formula is / are

(a) not applicable

(b) only absolute and relative

(c) absolute, relative and mixed

(d) only absolute

70. The function ROUND(1343.45, −2) returns

(a) 1343 (b) −1300

(c) −1343 (d) 1300

71. '.INI' extension refers usually to what kind of file?

(a) Image file

(b) System file

(c) Hypertext related file

(d) Image Color Matching Profile file

72. '.BAT' extension refers usually to what kind of file?

(a) Compressed Archive file

    (b) System file
    (c) Audio file
    (d) Backup file

73. Which one of the following statements is incorrect?
    (a) A macro can be used with more than one worksheet
    (b) A macro can be used to put the current time in a cell
    (c) A macro can be used to erase a range
    (d) None of the above

74. '.JPG' extension refers usually to what kind of file?
    (a) System file
    (b) Animation/movie file
    (c) MS Encarta document
    (d) Image file

75. '.MOV' extension refers usually to what kind of file?
    (a) Image file
    (b) Animation/movie file
    (c) Audio file
    (d) MS Office document

76. Windows is popular because of its
    (a) GUI features
    (b) Desktop Technology
    (c) Multitasking capacity
    (d) Being inexpensive

77. Windows is
    (a) a character user interface
    (b) an operating environment
    (c) an operating system
    (d) None of the above

78. Paint brush belongs to
    (a) Startup group
    (b) Application group
    (c) Accessories group
    (d) Main group

79. WINDOWS settings are recorded in
    (a) WINDOWS.INI   (b) WIN.INI
    (c) COMMAND.INI   (d) GROUPS.INI

80. All systems settings in WINDOWS are stored in
    (a) MAIN.INI   (b) CONTROL.INI
    (c) SYSTEM.INI   (d) SETTING.INI

81. PIF editor belongs to which group?
    (a) Main
    (b) Games
    (c) Accessories
    (d) None of the above

82. WINDOWS can work in which of the following modes?
    (a) Expanded
    (b) Extended
    (c) Enhanced & Standard
    (d) Compressed

83. Through a PIF file, one can
    (a) Load a DOS based application
    (b) Load a CONFIG.SYS file
    (c) Load a WINDOWS based application
    (d) None of the above

84. _default.pif is found in
    (a) WINDOWS directory
    (b) Root directory
    (c) DOS directory
    (d) None of the above

85. A file name with extension as VXD represents a
    (a) text file
    (b) normal application file
    (c) device drivers
    (d) picture file

86. Which one does not belong to Main group?
    (a) Control Panel   (b) PIF Editor
    (c) Character Map   (d) File Manager

87. PIF editor is a
    (a) Device driver
    (b) WINDOWS bases application
    (c) DOS based application
    (d) None of the above

88. '.TXT' extension refers usually to what kind of file?
- (a) Text File
- (b) Image file
- (c) Audio file
- (d) Adobe Acrobat file

89. '.TMP' extension refers usually to what kind of file?
- (a) Compressed Archive file
- (b) Image file
- (c) Temporary file
- (d) Audio file

90. Who created Pretty Good Privacy (PGP)?
- (a) Paul Zimmerman
- (b) Tim Berners-Lee
- (c) Marc Andreessen
- (d) Ken Thompson

91. RTF stands for
- (a) Real Time Files
- (b) Real Time Fonts
- (c) Rich Text Format
- (d) Rich Text Fonts

92. Combo Box, in a dialog box, is a / an
- (a) list box
- (b) combination of list box and check box
- (c) option button
- (d) combination of text box and list box

93. Who co-founded Hotmail in 1996 and then sold the company to Microsoft?
- (a) Shawn Fanning
- (b) Ada Byron Lovelace
- (c) Sabeer Bhatia
- (d) Ray Tomlinson

94. Who co-created the UNIX operating system in 1969 with Dennis Ritchie?
- (a) Bjarne Stroustrup
- (b) Steve Wozniak
- (c) Ken Thompson
- (d) Niklaus Wirth

95. Mark the most appropriate statement.
- (a) MailMerge can be used to print form letters and mailing labels
- (b) MailMerge can be used to print form letters
- (c) MailMerge can be used to print envelopes
- (d) All of the above

96. Creating form letters using MailMerge involves the
- (a) creation of the main document
- (b) creation of the main document and date source
- (c) insertion of merge fields in the main document and merging of the main document with the data source
- (d) Both (b) and (c)

97. Graphics is inserted in
- (a) frame
- (b) page
- (c) box
- (d) None of the above

98. A frame can include
- (a) text and graphics
- (b) tables and graphics
- (c) graphics
- (d) All of the above

99. Select the most appropriate statement
- (a) A frame can be resized
- (b) A frame is automatically repeated on everypage.
- (c) Both (b) and (c)
- (d) A frame can includ any type of text, and border and shade can be added to frame.

100. All the formatting data for the paragraph is stored
- (a) in the page setup
- (b) in the paragraph mark
- (c) in the style sheet
- (d) None of the above

ANSWERS

1	2	3	4	5	6	7	8	9	10
(c)	(a)	(d)	(c)	(b)	(a)	(b)	(c)	(c)	(d)
11	**12**	**13**	**14**	**15**	**16**	**17**	**18**	**19**	**20**
(a)	(c)	(b)	(a)	(d)	(d)	(a)	(c)	(c)	(b)
21	**22**	**23**	**24**	**25**	**26**	**27**	**28**	**29**	**30**
(c)	(b)	(c)	(a)	(c)	(d)	(c)	(c)	(c)	(a)
31	**32**	**33**	**34**	**35**	**36**	**37**	**38**	**39**	**40**
(c)	(a)	(d)	(b)	(c)	(d)	(c)	(c)	(d)	(a)
41	**42**	**43**	**44**	**45**	**46**	**47**	**48**	**49**	**50**
(d)	(b)	(a)	(b)	(c)	(c)	(d)	(b)	(c)	(b)
51	**52**	**53**	**54**	**55**	**56**	**57**	**58**	**59**	**60**
(c)	(a)	(b)	(d)	(c)	(b)	(c)	(a)	(b)	(c)
61	**62**	**63**	**64**	**65**	**66**	**67**	**68**	**69**	**70**
(c)	(d)	(d)	(c)	(b)	(c)	(b)	(c)	(c)	(d)
71	**72**	**73**	**74**	**75**	**76**	**77**	**78**	**79**	**80**
(b)	(b)	(d)	(d)	(b)	(a)	(b)	(c)	(b)	(c)
81	**82**	**83**	**84**	**85**	**86**	**87**	**88**	**89**	**90**
(a)	(c)	(a)	(a)	(c)	(c)	(b)	(a)	(c)	(a)
91	**92**	**93**	**94**	**95**	**96**	**97**	**98**	**99**	**100**
(c)	(d)	(c)	(c)	(d)	(d)	(a)	(d)	(c)	(b)

1. In order to paste text from the clipboard in the document being edited, press the key(s)
   - (a) Ctrl-A
   - (b) Ctrl-V
   - (c) Ctrl-X
   - (d) Ins

2. Which of the following devices can be used to directly image printed text?
   - (a) OCR
   - (b) OMR
   - (c) MICR
   - (d) All of above

3. In order to delete the selected sentence, we can press the following key
   - (a) Backspace
   - (b) Del
   - (c) Both (a) and (b)
   - (d) None of these

4. Select the most appropriate statement
   - (a) AutoText automatically inserts the text and/ or graphics on typing the Auto Text entry and pressing the spacebar
   - (b) AutoText is the standard feature of all word processors
   - (c) AutoText is used to insert commonly used text and graphics in a document
   - (d) None of the above

5. The output quality of a printer is measured by
   - (a) Dot per inch
   - (b) Dot per sq. inch
   - (c) Dots printed per unit time
   - (d) All of above

6. Select the most appropriate statement
   - (a) AutoCorrect automatically inserts the text and / or graphics on typing the AutoCorrect entry
   - (b) AutoText and AutoCorrect are similar
   - (c) AutoCorrect automatically inserts the text and / or graphics on typing the AutoCorrect entry and pressing the spacebar
   - (d) None of the above

7. Which one of the following statements is true?
   - (a) In case of multiple columns in a documents, all columns are of the same width
   - (b) Multiple columns cannot be viewed in the normal view mode
   - (c) A Word document can have a maximum of four columns
   - (d) None of the above

8. In analog computer
   - (a) Input is first converted to digital form
   - (b) Input is never converted to digital form
   - (c) Output is displayed in digital form
   - (d) All of above

9. Which one of the following statements is true?
   - (a) If you delete a paragraph mark, Word applies the formatting of the previous paragraph to the current paragraph
   - (b) In order to copy the selected text with the mouse, hold down the shift key and drag the insertion point to the new location
   - (c) Selected text can be moved to a new location in the document by dragging
   - (d) None of these

10. In latest generation computers, the instructions are executed
   (*a*) Parallel only
   (*b*) Sequentially only
   (*c*) Both sequentially and parallel
   (*d*) All of above

11. Who designed the first electronics computer-ENIAC?
   (*a*) Van-Neumann
   (*b*) Joseph M. Jacquard
   (*c*) J. Presper Eckert and John W Mauchly
   (*d*) All of above

12. After a table has been created, which of the following operations cannot be performed?
   (*a*) Split the table into two tables
   (*b*) Delete and insert columns
   (*c*) Insert rows in a table
   (*d*) None of the above

13. A sequence of instructions, in a computer language, to get the desired result is known as
   (*a*) a decision table
   (*b*) an algorithm
   (*c*) a program
   (*d*) None of the above

14. The first commerciallly available computer was
   (*a*) MARK-I   (*b*) ABACUS
   (*c*) UNIVAC-I   (*d*) ENIAC

15. Which type of errors is flagged by compilers?
   (*a*) Run-time errors
   (*b*) Logical errors
   (*c*) Syntax errors
   (*d*) None of the above

16. An algorithm is best described as
   (*a*) a branch of mathematics
   (*b*) a step-by-step procedure for solving a problem
   (*c*) a computer language
   (*d*) None of these

17. The abbreviation CAD stands for
   (*a*) Computer Aided Drawing
   (*b*) Computer Aided Design
   (*c*) Commonly Available Data
   (*d*) Computer And Data

18. Bug means
   (*a*) A logical error in a program
   (*b*) A difficult syntax error in a program
   (*c*) Documenting programs using an efficient documentation tool
   (*d*) None of the above

19. The part of a machine level instruction, which tells the central processor what has to be done, is
   (*a*) an operation code
   (*b*) an address
   (*c*) an operand
   (*d*) None of the above

20. The ALU of a computer responds to the commands coming from
   (*a*) Primary memory (*b*) Control section
   (*c*) External memory (*d*) Cache memory

21. Indicate which one of the following best describes the term SOFTWARE
   (*a*) Application programs only
   (*b*) Operating System programs only
   (*c*) Both (*a*) and (*b*)
   (*d*) None of the above

22. A language translator is best described as
   (*a*) a hardware component
   (*b*) a system software
   (*c*) an application software
   (*d*) None of the above

23. Indicate which one of the following in not true about an interpreter
   (*a*) An interpreter generates an object program from the source program
   (*b*) An interpreter is a kind of translator
   (*c*) An interpreter is a part of a source code
   (*d*) An interpreter analyses each source statement every time it is to be executed

24. Those errors that can be pointed out by the compiler are
(a) syntax errors   (b) logical errors
(c) semantic errors   (d) None of these

25. Which one of the following statements is not true?
(a) FORTRAN is extensively used to write programs for performing scientific computations
(b) A FORTRAN program written for the IBM-PC is totally different from a FORTRAN program written for the execution of SUN machine
(c) FORTRAN is a high-level language
(d) None of the above

26. C is
(a) a machine language
(b) a third generation high level language
(c) an assembly language
(d) None of the above

27. A program that converts a high level language program to a set of instructions that can run on a computer is called a
(a) compiler
(b) editor
(c) debugger
(d) None of the above

28. The function of a kernel in an operating system is to
(a) interpret the JCL commands
(b) interact with the hardware devices
(c) interact with the user
(d) None of the above

29. Indicate which one of the following is necessary to work on a computer
(a) An assembler
(b) An operating system
(c) A compiler
(d) None of the above

30. Indicate which one of the following is true about a PSEUDOCODE?

(a) It is an assembly language
(b) It is a machine language
(c) It is a high level language
(d) None of the above

31. The language used to describe the user's requirements to a computer's operating system is
(a) Assembly language
(b) COBOL
(c) JCL
(d) None of these

32. The act of retrieving existing data from memory is called
(a) Read-out   (b) Read from
(c) Read   (d) All of above

33. JCL stands for
(a) Just Command Language
(b) Jump Control Logic
(c) Job Control Language
(d) None of the above

34. The abbreviation EFT stands for
(a) Electronic File Transfer
(b) Electronic Forms Typing
(c) Electronic Funds Transfer
(d) Electronic Flow Table

35. The speed of a dot matrix printer is specified in terms of
(a) BPI   (b) CPS
(c) BPS   (d) CPI

36. The resolution of a laser printer is specified in terms of
(a) API   (b) CPI
(c) DPI   (d) LSI

37. The Stored Program concept was proposed by
(a) Pascal
(b) John Von Neumann
(c) Abacus
(d) Von Leibniz

38. Which one of the following allows users to continue to operate computers while printing is in progress?
- (a) Spooler
- (b) Job Control Program
- (c) OS Supervisor
- (d) None of these

39. Choose the odd one out of the following
- (a) FORTRAN
- (b) COBOL
- (c) PASCAL
- (d) ASSEMBLER

40. A computer cannot boot if it does not have a / an
- (a) loader
- (b) compiler
- (c) operating system
- (d) assembler

41. Indicate which one of the following, is a phase of the compilation process?
- (a) Code generation
- (b) Lexical analysis
- (c) Both of the above
- (d) None of these

42. Connecting different computers in an organised manner, within an office building can be termed as
- (a) MAN
- (b) WAN
- (c) ANN
- (d) LAN

43. All modern computer operate on
- (a) Information
- (b) Floppies
- (c) Data
- (d) Word

44. Operating System is
- (a) a collection of input-output devices
- (b) a collection of hardware components
- (c) a collection of software routines
- (d) None of these

45. An operating system
- (a) enables the programmer to draw a flowchart
- (b) provides a layered, user-friendly interface
- (c) links a program with the subroutines it refers to
- (d) none of the above

46. A characteristic of an on-line, real-time system is
- (a) off-line batch processing
- (b) no delay in processing
- (c) more that one CPU
- (d) None of these

47. Line printer speed is specified in terms of
- (a) DPM
- (b) CPM
- (c) COM
- (d) LPM

48. Job control statements are used to
- (a) allocate the CPU to a job
- (b) specify, to the operating system, the beginning and end of a job in a batch
- (c) read the input from the slow-speed card reader to the high speed magnetic disk
- (d) None of the above

49. Optical storage technique is used in
- (a) magnetic disk drives
- (b) hard disk drives
- (c) floppy drives
- (d) CD-ROM drives

50. The technique, which stores a program on a disk and then, transfers the program into main memory, as and when they are needed, is known as
- (a) Thrashing
- (b) Swapping
- (c) Spooling
- (d) None of the above

51. Batch processing means
- (a) a batch of computer programs
- (b) processing data in periodic intervals of time
- (c) entering a batch of records
- (d) None of the above

52. Education through computers is referred to as
- (a) CAD
- (b) CAM
- (c) CAI
- (d) None of the above

53. A database is
(a) a vast amount of data stored in a group of integer files
(b) a set of condensed Data highlighting specific information
(c) an arrangement of data in a particular order
(d) basic data for processing an application

54. The name given to a sequence of instructions in a computer language, to get the desired result, is
(a) a program
(b) a decision table
(c) a pseudocode
(d) an algorithm

55. The language understood by a computer without translation is called a/an
(a) Assembly language
(b) High level language
(c) Command language
(d) Machine language

56. A program to convert a high-level computer program into a set of instructions that will run on a machine is called a/an
(a) Compiler
(b) Editor
(c) Linker
(d) Debugger

57. 1Kbits is
(a) 512 bits
(b) 1024 bits
(c) 1000 bits
(d) None of the above

58. A sequence of steps written in a natural language to solve a given problem is called a/an
(a) Algorithm
(b) Binary code
(c) Program
(d) None of the above

59. Which one of the following describes the functions of a program?
(a) Specifying constants
(b) Specifying the locations of variables in the memory
(c) Specifying the various operations to be performed by the computer
(d) All of the above

60. Which one of the following is not an operating system?
(a) CP / M
(b) PC-DOS
(c) MS-DOS
(d) Z - 80

61. Mapping from assembly language instructions into machine language instructions is
(a) many - many
(b) one - many
(c) one - one
(d) many - one

62. A compiler is
(a) machine-independent and OS-dependent
(b) machine-dependent and OS-dependent
(c) machine-dependent and OS-independent
(d) machine-independent and OS-independent

63. The source program testing in respect of the correct format of instructions is performed at
(a) Execution phase
(b) Design phase
(c) Compilation phase
(d) None of the above

64. Instructions and memory address are represented by
(a) Character code
(b) Binary codes
(c) Binary word
(d) Parity bit

65. Which one of the following commands can be used to delete all the files with the extension name ".BAK" in the current directory while running a DBMS software?
(a) RUN ERASE *.BAK
(b) RUN DEL *.BAK
(c) ! DEL *.BAK
(d) All of the above

66. If AGE and SALARY are numeric fields in a database file, which one of the following commands is incorrect?
    (a) REPLACE AGE WITH AGE + 1 FOR AGE < 20 ALL
    (b) REPLACE ALL AGE WITH AGE + 1 WHILE AGE > 20
    (c) REPLACE ALL AGE WITH AGE + 1 FOR AGE < 20
    (d) All of the above

67. Which one of the following is invalid?
    (a) AVERAGE calculates average of a specified memory variable
    (b) A user defined message can be specified with WAIT
    (c) INPUT can create character, numeric or logical variable
    (d) None of these

68. Which of the following statements is false?
    (a) Contents of a variable can be searched with FIND and SEEK commands.
    (b) CONTINUE cannot be used to find the next matching record after using FIND / SEEK.
    (c) FIND and SEEK Commands need an indexfile.
    (d) None of the above

69. The Command that selects an index file / tag for a database file is
    (a) SELECT ORDER   (b) SELECT INDEX
    (c) SET ORDER   (d) None of these

70. The command to create a new database file based on two open database files is
    (a) UPDATE
    (b) SET RELATION
    (c) JOIN
    (d) None of the above

71. The command used to change the contents of a database file using contents of another file by linking them on a common key field is
    (a) CHANGE   (b) UPDATE
    (c) REPLACE   (d) JOIN

72. The most appropriate command to permanently remove all records from the current database file is
    (a) DELETE FILE   (b) DELETE ALL
    (c) ZAP   (d) PACK

73. Which one of the following is an invalid command in a DBMS package?
    (a) CLEAR
    (b) RUN
    (c) REPLACE
    (d) None of the above

74. To convert a numeric to a character string, use the function
    (a) ASC()   (b) CHR()
    (c) STR()   (d) VAL()

75. The function to remove leading and trailing spaces from a character expression is
    (a) LTRIM()   (b) TRIM()
    (c) RTRIM()   (d) ALLTRIM()

76. If NAME is a character field and AGE is a numeric field, which one of the following commands is invalid?
    (a) REPLACE NAME WITH [RAMA]
    (b) REPLACE NAME WITH "Rama"
    (c) REPLACE NAME WITH [RAMA], AGE WITH 150
    (d) None of the above

77. Which of the following code used in present day computing was developed by IBM Corporation?
    (a) ASCII   (b) Hollerith Code
    (c) Baudot Code   (d) EBCDIC Code

78. Who is largely responsible for breaking the German Enigma codes, created a test that provided a foundation for artificial intelligence?
    (a) Alan Turing   (b) Jeff Bezos
    (c) George Boole   (d) Charles Babbage

79. Who built the world's first binary digit computer: Z1...?
(a) Konrad Zuse
(b) Ken Thompson
(c) Alan Turing
(d) George Boole

80. Which one of the following is an invalid statement?
(a) A procedure can be entered in a procedure file or in the command file itself
(b) Each procedure begins with PROCEDURE <procedure name> Command
(c) A procedure normally ends with RETURN but we can skip the RETURN at the end of the procedure
(d) None of the above

81. Who developed Yahoo?
(a) Dennis Ritchie & Ken Thompson
(b) David Filo & Jerry Yang
(c) Vint Cerf & Robert Kahn
(d) Steve Case & Jeff Bezos

82. The command used to add a new field to an active database file is
(a) MODIFY REPORT
(b) MODIFY COMMAND
(c) MODIFY STRUCTURE
(d) MODIFY LABEL

83. Which command is used for closing the text file that has been created with SET ALTERNATE TO <file name> command?
(a) CLOSE DATABASES
(b) SET ALTERNATE OFF
(c) CLOSE ALTERNATE
(d) CLEAR ALL

84. The MODIFY command is used to
(a) modify a report format file
(b) modify the structure of a database file
(c) add a new field to every record of a data base file
(d) None of the above

85. The command to find out the number of records that meet a specified condition is

(a) JOIN
(b) UPDATE
(c) CONDITION
(d) None of the above

86. 'DTP' computer abbreviation usually means?
(a) Digital Transmission Protocol
(b) DeskTop Publishing
(c) Data Type Programming
(d) Document Type Processing

87. What do we call a network whose elements may be separated by some distance? It usually involves two or more small networks and dedicated high-speed telephone lines.
(a) URL (Universal Resource Locator)
(b) LAN (Local Area Network)
(c) WAN (Wide Area Network)
(d) World Wide Web

88. What do we call a collection of two or more computers that are located within a limited distance of each other and that are connected to each other directly or indirectly?
(a) Internet
(b) Intranet
(c) Local Area Network
(d) Wide Area Network

89. What is part of a database that holds only one type of information?
(a) Report
(b) Field
(c) Record
(d) File

90. The window which shows icons for things like the mouse, sound, and display is...?
(a) My Computer
(b) Explorer
(c) Control Panel
(d) Taskbar

91. To establish a link between two database files, one can use the command
(a) UPDATE
(b) JOIN
(c) SET RELATION
(d) BROWSE

92. Which one of the following statements is incorrect?

(a) Structural compound index files are automatically opened and updated

(b) Structural compound index files are automatically opened

(c) All open index files are automatically updated

(d) None of the above

93. Mark the invalid statement

(a) A report format file can use three database files

(b) A report format file can be used with more than one database file

(c) A report can be previewed while designing

(d) Indexed database files cannot be used with a report format file

94. When an interrupt occurs, the processor completes the current .... before jumping to the interrupt service subroutine

(a) procedure call it is executing

(b) instruction it is executing

(c) current macro it is executing

(d) microinstruction it is executing

95. We wish to test if the number present in an 8-bit register A is an odd number. For this purpose, we must

(a) AND the A register with mask 01H and test if Z flag is set to 0

(b) OR the A register with mask 01H and test if Z flag is set to 0

(c) AND the A register with mask 01H and test if Z flag is set to 1

(d) OR the A register with mask 01H and test if Z flag is set to 1

96. Parenthese are required to indicate the order of evaluation of arithmetic operations in

(a) Postfix expressions

(b) Infix expressions

(c) Prefix expressions

(d) Both (a) and (c)

97. On the Task bar the time is shown in the...?

(a) Start menu

(b) Scrollbar

(c) Desktop

(d) Notification area or Tray

98. Experts say the healthiest way to view a computer monitor is by...

(a) Placing it 18 to 30 inches away from your eyes

(b) Viewing from a darkened room

(c) Adjusting the screen for maximum contrast

(d) Using special glasses that filter out UV rays

99. If an even parity mechanism is being used for data transfer, which of the following data type has been received incorrectly?

(a) 03 H

(b) 00 H

(c) D0 H

(d) FF H

100. Which one of the following will be able to verify if a given string is a valid parenthesised arithmetic expression?

(a) A postfix expression evaluator

(b) A parser

(c) A lexical analyser

(d) None of these

ANSWERS

1	2	3	4	5	6	7	8	9	10
(b)	(a)	(c)	(c)	(b)	(c)	(b)	(b)	(c)	(c)
11	12	13	14	15	16	17	18	19	20
(c)	(d)	(c)	(c)	(c)	(b)	(b)	(a)	(a)	(b)

21	22	23	24	25	26	27	28	29	30
(c)	(b)	(a)	(a)	(b)	(b)	(a)	(b)	(b)	(d)
31	32	33	34	35	36	37	38	39	40
(b)	(d)	(c)	(c)	(b)	(c)	(b)	(a)	(d)	(c)
41	42	43	44	45	46	47	48	49	50
(c)	(d)	(c)	(c)	(b)	(b)	(d)	(b)	(d)	(b)
51	52	53	54	55	56	57	58	59	60
(a)	(c)	(c)	(a)	(d)	(a)	(b)	(a)	(c)	(d)
61	62	63	64	65	66	67	68	69	70
(c)	(b)	(c)	(c)	(d)	(d)	(a)	(b)	(c)	(c)
71	72	73	74	75	76	77	78	79	80
(b)	(c)	(d)	(c)	(d)	(d)	(d)	(a)	(a)	(d)
81	82	83	84	85	86	87	88	89	90
(b)	(c)	(c)	(c)	(d)	(b)	(c)	(c)	(b)	(c)
91	92	93	94	95	96	97	98	99	100
(c)	(d)	(d)	(b)	(c)	(b)	(d)	(a)	(c)	(b)

1. The minimum number of flip-flops required to implement a 16-bit ring counter is
(*a*) 4
(*b*) 16
(*c*) 8
(*d*) 65,536

2. Who invented the high level language c?
(*a*) Dennis M. Ritchie
(*b*) Niklaus Writh
(*c*) Seymour Papert
(*d*) Donald Kunth

3. The number of select input lines in an 8-to-1 multiplexer is
(*a*) 256
(*b*) 8
(*c*) 1
(*d*) None of the above

4. Personnel who design, program, operate and maintain computer equipment refers to
(*a*) Console-operator
(*b*) Programmer
(*c*) Peopleware
(*d*) System Analyst

5. The advantage of horizontally organised microcode over vertically organised microcode is that
(*a*) smaller number of control steps are required
(*b*) smaller number of storage locations are required
(*c*) generation of control signals is faster
(*d*) None of the above

6. The least negative value that the product of two 8-bit two's complement numbers can take is
(*a*) -2^{16}
(*b*) -2^{15}
(*c*) -2^{14}
(*d*) None of the above

7. The value 38 Hex is stored in register B of an 8-bit computer. The computer executes an instruction to complement all the bits of register B. Assuming two's complement representation, the decimal value in register B after the execution of the instruction is
(*a*) -56
(*b*) -57
(*c*) 57
(*d*) None of the above

8. A Toggle flip-flop can be constructed using a JK flip-flop by connecting the
(*a*) inverted form of toggle input to K
(*b*) toggle input to J
(*c*) toggle input to J and the inverted form of toggle input to K
(*d*) None of the above

9. Two 4-bit carry look a head adders A1 and A2 are cascaded in order to form an 8-bit adder. The carry output from adder A1 is given as carry input to adder A2. When wiring the circuit, the carry output from A1 is accidentally connected to the ground signal. Which one of the following situations reveals this fault?
(*a*) Addition of F0H and FFH
(*b*) Addition of 44H and 22H
(*c*) Addition of 0FH and 01H
(*d*) Addition of F4H and 22H

10. The fully associative cache memory of a computer has a blocks of 256 bytes each.

The cache is initially empty. The CPU requests for blocks 0, 2, 3, 1, 4, 0, 2, 3 and 1. Assuming the LRU replacement policy, the number of misses in this access sequence is

(a) 8 (b) 7
(c) 4 (d) 9

11. Which one of the following is not an advantage of a subroutine?
(a) Faster execution of programs
(b) Better documentation of programs
(c) Saving in memory storage
(d) Easy readability of programs

12. A page replacement policy is not necessary in
(a) write-through caches
(b) set associative caches
(c) directly mapped caches
(d) fully associative caches

13. Which of the following representations requires the least number of bits to store the number +255?
(a) 1's complement
(b) Two's complement
(c) Binary coded decimal
(d) Unsigned binary

14. In a stack computer, there is support for
(a) Zero address instructions
(b) PUSH and POP instructions only
(c) Zero address instructions, PUSH, and POP
(d) None of the above

15. In the instruction LOAD A, #32, the first operand is the destination operand and is in the register addressing mode. The second operand is the source operand and is in the immediate addressing mode. This means that the
(a) contents of location 32 will be moved to the address stored in register A
(b) contents of location 32 will be moved to register A
(c) value 32 will be moved into register A
(d) value in register A will be moved into the location 32

16. A printer device is connected to a computer. The status of the printer is indicated by bit 3 of the 8-bit status register. (Assume that LSB position is bit 0.) If bit 3 is 1, then the printer is ready, else the printer is not ready. In order to test if the printer is ready
(a) OR the status register with 08H and test for Z flag = 0
(b) AND the status register with 04H and test for Z flag = 1
(c) AND the status register with 08H and test for Z flag = 0
(d) None of the above

17. When did arch rivals IBM and Apple Computers Inc. decide to join hands?
(a) 1978 (b) 1984
(c) 1990 (d) 1991

18. Floating point division involves
(a) Floating point division of mantissas and fixed point addition of exponents
(b) Fixed point division of mantissas and fixed point addition of exponents
(c) Fixed point division of mantissas and fixed point subtraction of exponents
(d) Floating point division of mantissas and fixed point subtraction of exponents

19. In order to obtain the best possible speed up from a K-stage pipeline
(a) The clock signal to the individual stages must be skewed by an amount equal to the latch delay
(b) K must be equal to log2 n where n is the number of inputs handled by the pipeline
(c) The delay of individual stages must be made equal
(d) All of the above

20. The minimum hardware required to construct a 3-to-8 decoder is
(a) two 2-to-4 decoders

(b) two 2-to-4 decoders and a 1-to-2 decoder
(c) three 2-to-4 decoders
(d) depends upon the technology (TTL, CMOS etc.)

21. Two instructions 11 and 12 are of the form D1 = f(S1) and D2 = g(S2) respectively. Here, S1 is the set of source operands for I1 and S2 is the set of source operands for I2. D1 and D2 are the destination operands for I1 and I2 respectively. f and g are the fuctions (such as ADD, SUB, etc.). The instructions I1 and I2 can be executed concurrently if
(a) D1 does not belong to S2 and D2 does not belong to S1
(b) D1 is not the same as D2
(c) Both (a) and (b) above
(d) None of the above

22. What is the latest write-once optical storage media?
(a) Digital paper
(b) Magneto-optical disk
(c) WORM disk
(d) CD-ROM disk

23. A microprocessor, is a processor with a reduced
(a) instruction set
(b) power requirement
(c) MIPS performance
(d) None of the above

24. In a CPU, the current value of program counter is saved in a special register called previous context register before the control transfer to the subroutine. Such a CPU cannot support
(a) recursive subroutines
(b) branch instructions
(c) interrupts
(d) None of the above

25. In an 8-bit Booth's multiplication algorithm, the largest number of additions that will be ever required is

(a) 8
(b) 4
(c) 3
(d) 2

26. The most important advantage of a video disk is
(a) Compactness
(b) Potential capacity
(c) Durability
(d) Cost effectiveness

27. A computer-readable image has 256 × 256 picture elements. Each picture element has a grey level. There are at most 256 grey levels. In order to store one image, we require
(a) 8 KB
(b) 64 KB
(c) 128 KB
(d) None of the se

28. The Hamming distance between two n-bit binary numbers is defined as the number of bit positions they differ. If we have a function called onescount(x), which returns the number of 1's in the number x, then a correct way to compute the Hamming distance between two numbers x and y is
(a) onescount ($x|y$), where | is the bitwise OR operation
(b) onescount ($x\&y$), where & is the bitwise AND operation
(c) onescount(x) + onescount(y) - n
(d) onescount ($x@y$), where @ is the bitwise XOR operation

29. In a computer, fractions are represented using a 16-bit fixed left of the most significant bit. The representation for 0.625 in this notation is
(a) D0 in Hex
(b) AA in Hex
(c) C0 in Hex
(d) None of these

30. Two 4-bit two's complement numbers are added using a ripple carry adder. The range of the sum output is
(a) −256 to +256
(b) −256 to +255
(c) −512 to +511
(d) −128 to +127

31. Cycle stealing refers to
(a) overlapping of the memory refresh operation and memory read operations in dynamic memories
(b) reduction in the number of clock cycles for memory access in a cache memory
(c) reduction in instruction cycle time through instruction pipelining
(d) None of the above

32. Two negative numbers are added and the result is observed to be positve. The most likely reason for this phenomenon is
(a) incorrect representation of the input numbers
(b) an underflow due to limited precision of the adder
(c) a dynamic fault in the adder circuit
(d) a wiring fault in the adder circuit

33. A computer program includes a subroutine which is declared as an 'external' subroutine. This means that the subroutine
(a) resides on a different computer and will be downloaded dynamically at run-time
(b) uses external devices
(c) is defined elsewhere
(d) is defined in the kernel of the operating system

34. What is the number of read-write heads in the drive for a 9-trac magnetic tape?
(a) 9   (b) 16
(c) 18   (d) 27

35. Before a disk drive can access any sector record, a computer program has to provide the record's disk address. What information does this address specify?
(a) Track number   (b) Sector number
(c) Surface number   (d) All of above

36. The difference between a COMPARE instruction and a SUBTRACT instruction is
(a) SUBTRACT instruction does not set any flags

(b) COMPARE instruction does not set any flags
(c) COMPARE instruction leaves the registers unchanged
(d) COMAPRE instruction does not require the ALU

37. Which one of the following subroutines is unlikely to be a part of the kernel of an operating system?
(a) Maintenance of the real time clock
(b) Sorting algorithm
(c) Page swapping algorithm
(d) Process scheduling algorithm

38. In the IEEE 754 floating point representation standard, the base is
(a) 127   (b) 23
(c) 16   (d) None of these

39. The sum of two hexadecimal numbers 23D and 9AA gives the hexadecimal number
(a) BE5   (b) BF6
(c) BE7   (d) AF7

40. The simplified form of the expression AB + ABC' is
(a) A (B + C)   (b) AB
(c) A (B + C')   (d) None of these

41. In an 8-bit microcomputer, the locations 100 Hex and 101 Hex contain values F3 Hex and FE Hex respectively. A program fetches these two values, compares them on relative magniture, stores the larger of the two in location 102 Hex. Assuming two's complement representation, the value stored in location 102 is
(a) 102 Hex   (b) FE Hex
(c) F3 Hex   (d) None of these

42. The memory map of a microcomputer is as follows: the first 8 KB of the memory consists of EPROM memory and the remaining 56 KB of memory consists of RAM memory. The valid RAM locations are

(a) we cannot determine the memory map of the RAM without additional information

(b) 1FFF - FFFF

(c) 0000 - 1FFF

(d) None of the above

43. The basic reason why hierarchical memory organisation in computers can offer very small average access time is that

(a) due to advances in software technology, computer programs have become small enough to fit into cache memory

(b) the computer programs display a locality of reference

(c) the advances in semiconductor memory technology have led to the development of very high speed memories

(d) operating systems provide advanced memory management functions, which reduce the average access time considerably

44. Which one of the following is not a universal building block?

(a) Two-input NOR gate

(b) Three-input NAND gate

(c) Two-input multiplexer

(d) Two-input EXOR gate

45. A four bit register contains a number X. After two rotate-right operations and one rotate-left operation on the register, the value in the register is 6 (decimal). The number X is equal to

(a) 10 in octal (b) 12 in octal

(c) 14 in octal (d) 03 in octal

46. As compared to diskettes, the hard disks are

(a) More expensive (b) More portable

(c) Less rigid (d) Slowly accessed

47. The minimum number of JK flip-flops required to construct a sequential circuit, which has 23 states is

(a) 6

(b) 23

(c) There is insufficient information

(d) None of the above

48. Which one of the following strings is not described by the regular expression? $(0 + 1)1^* (10)^*$

(a) The empty string (b) 110

(c) 10 (d) 0

49. Which one of the following sets is not regular?

(a) The set of all binary strings, which begins with a 0 and end with a 1

(b) The set of all binary strings, which represents multiples of two

(c) The set of all binary strings, which have at least one occurrence of the pattern 101 in them

(d) None of the above

50. In order to correct a single error, the minimum number of check bits that must be added to 4 data bits is

(a) 3

(b) 2

(c) 4

(d) There is insufficient data to answer the question

51. The fundamental mode of operation of asynchronous sequential circuits implies that

(a) the flow table of the circuit cannot be reduced

(b) we cannot feed pulses as inputs to the circuit

(c) there exists a homing sequence for each of the states in the flow table

(d) None of the above

52. Which of the following is not an advantage of asynchronous circuits?

(a) Lesser power consumption

(b) Higher speed

(c) Smaller design effort

(d) No need to provide clock generation circuitry

53. The minimum number of bits required to represent numbers in the range -23 to +31 is
(a) 7
(b) 8
(c) 6
(d) 5

54. A dual-layer DVD is valued because it:
(a) Can hold more data
(b) Contains a backup of the data stored
(c) Uses a second layer to offer a speed increase
(d) Creates alternative sound tracks

55. A CPU has a 16-bit program counter. This means that the CPU can address
(a) 32K memory locations
(b) 16K memory locations
(c) 64K memory locations
(d) 256K memory locations

56. A JPG is...
(a) A Jumper Programmed Graphic
(b) A format for an image file
(c) A type of hard disk
(d) A unit of measure for memory

57. Windows Vista, the eventual replacement for Windows XP, will demand more from a computer. Which of the following statements is correct?
(a) You'll need at least 512 megabytes of RAM
(b) A separate graphics card, rather than onboard graphics, will be required
(c) A DVD drive is needed
(d) All the above

58. Changing computer language of 1's and 0's to characters that a person can understand is...
(a) Highlight
(b) Clip art
(c) Decode
(d) Execute

59. The smallest negative number that can be stored using 1 byte of storage and the two's complement number system is
(a) −127
(b) −256
(c) −255
(d) −128

60. An IBM compatiable PC386 SX system uses
(a) A 64-bit CPU
(b) A 32-bit CPU
(c) A 16-bit CPU
(d) A 386-bit CPU

61. A 3.5" double density floppy disk, which does not have any surface defects, can be formatted to store a maximum of
(a) 1.22 MB of data
(b) 1.2 MB of data
(c) 1.4 MB of data
(d) 1.44 MB of data

62. There are .... possible functions of 3 variables
(a) 64
(b) 8
(c) 3
(d) 256

63. Which one of the following is not a universal building block?
(a) 2-to-1 Multiplexer
(b) 3-input NAND gate
(c) 2-input NAND gate
(d) 2-input XOR gate

64. BASIC language is normally used along with a /an
(a) computer-aided software engineering (CASE) tool
(b) complier
(c) interpreter
(d) assembler

65. A diamond-shaped box in a flow chart refers to
(a) data input from a device
(b) printing of a file
(c) an if-then-else decision
(d) an assignment statement

66. A spooler allows printing
(a) of graphic files on a non-graphics printer
(b) the contents of the screen using Print Screen option
(c) a file in background while we do other tasks on the computer
(d) of different fonts on a laser jet printer

67. A linker is a program, which generates
    (a) the executable program from object programs
    (b) an assembly language program from a high-level language program
    (c) an object program from an assembly language program
    (d) the executable program from high level language program

68. A Pseudocode refers to a program, which
    (a) can be executed without compilation and linking
    (b) can be executed only using virtual memory
    (c) is written in a high-level language without following any syntax
    (d) is written in an assembly language for a non-existent architecture

69. Which one of the following violates the principles of structured programming?
    (a) The use of "do while" statements
    (b) The use of "go to" statements in a program
    (c) The use of global variables
    (d) The use of recursive procedures

70. A debugging tool is a program, which
    (a) removes viruses from the computer
    (b) removes bugs from a user program
    (c) helps the user find bugs in his program
    (d) displays the errors in a user's program

71. Which one of the following is not an output of an assembler?
    (a) Executable program
    (b) A symbol table
    (c) Source listing with line numbers and errors
    (d) Object program containing machine opcodes

72. Which one of the following is not an advantage of Dynamic RAMs?
    (a) Low cost
    (b) High density
    (c) High speed
    (d) No need for memory refresh

73. Hardware devices that are not part of the main computer system and are often added later to the system.
    (a) Peripheral   (b) Clip art
    (c) Highlight   (d) Execute

74. The main computer that stores the files that can be sent to computers that are networked together is...
    (a) Clip art   (b) Mother board
    (c) Peripheral   (d) File server

75. The computer architecture that follows the stored program concept is
    (a) Pascal   (b) Von-Neumann
    (c) Harvard   (d) None of these

76. A modulo-20 counter can be designed using
    (a) 4- flip-flops   (b) 5- flip-flops
    (c) 20- flip-flops   (d) None of these

77. The memory that requires refreshing of data is
    (a) Bubble memory   (b) EAROM
    (c) DRAM   (d) SRAM

78. A scheme, in which, the address specifies which memory word contains the address of the operand, is called
    (a) Based addressing
    (b) Indirect addressing
    (c) Direct addressing
    (d) Immediate addressing

79. A bootstrap is
    (a) Hardware of Computer used to check memory
    (b) A program to start up a computer
    (c) A memory device
    (d) An assembler

80. The process of accessing information from a CD-ROM is called
    (a) Sequential   (b) Random
    (c) Semi-random   (d) None of these

81. A program, embedded in semiconductor chips during their manufacture, is called
(a) Software (b) Firmware
(c) Hardware (d) Humanware

82. An array processor consists of a
(a) Single control unit and single ALU unit
(b) Single control unit and multiple ALU units
(c) Multiple control units and single ALU unit
(d) Multiple control units and multiple ALU units

83. A virtual memeory system allows the employment of an address space that is
(a) more than address space
(b) more than the hard disk space
(c) the full address space
(d) None of the above

84. In a J-K flip-flop, the fuction K = J is used to realise
(a) S-R flip-flop (b) T-flip-flop
(c) D- flip-flop (d) M / S JK-flip-flop

85. Serial-to-parallel data conversion is done using the
(a) ADC (b) Shift register
(c) Ring Counter (d) Counter

86. CACHE memory is implemented using
(a) Dynamic RAM (b) EAROM
(c) Static RAM (d) EPROM

87. To select text by shading as you drag the mouse arrow over the text is known as...
(a) Clip art (b) To highlight
(c) To fetch (d) To decode

88. A nano-control memory is implemented to
(a) reduce the complexity of hardware
(b) reduce the overall control memory size
(c) improve the speed of execution
(d) None of the above

89. The major objective, in choosing page replacement policy, is to
(a) reduce the size of the page
(b) maximise the hit ratio
(c) minimise the hit ratio
(d) None of the above

90. An error in software or hardware is called a bug. What is the alternative computer jargon for it?
(a) Leech (b) Squid
(c) Slug (d) Glitch

91. Complex entities can be constructed using the following operation
(a) Collection (b) Sum
(c) Aggregation (d) Union

92. The maximum height of a B+ tree of order n with k key values is
(a) $\log k / 2n$
(b) $\log nk$
(c) $\log n / 2(k / 2+1)$
(d) $(n+k) / 2$

93. The following entities / attributes in a relational database should not have null values :
(a) Keys (b) Variables
(c) Relations (d) All of these

94. The following relations need not be created each time the tables are used
(a) Intersections
(b) Persistent
(c) Functional dependent
(d) Loss-less decomposition

95. Insertion of data / record into a B-tree may cause leaf and internal nodes to
(a) split
(b) maintain the same order
(c) be deleted
(d) Any one of these

96. A view of a database that appears to an application program is known as a
(a) Structure (b) Report
(c) Subschema (d) Scheme

97. The universal quantifier in relational calculus can be implemented using the following SQL command

(a) SELECT
(b) NOT EXISTS
(c) SET RELATION TO
(d) None of these

98. Another word for the CPU is...
 (a) Execute (b) Microprocessor
 (c) Micro chip (d) Decode

99. Which of these is not a computer?
 (a) Aptiva (b) Macintosh
 (c) Acorn (d) Paseo

100. Which was an early mainframe computer?
 (a) ENIAC
 (b) UNIC
 (c) BRAINIA
 (d) FUNTRIA

ANSWERS

1	2	3	4	5	6	7	8	9	10
(a)	(a)	(d)	(c)	(c)	(d)	(b)	(d)	(c)	(b)
11	**12**	**13**	**14**	**15**	**16**	**17**	**18**	**19**	**20**
(a)	(c)	(d)	(c)	(c)	(b)	(d)	(c)	(c)	(b)
21	**22**	**23**	**24**	**25**	**26**	**27**	**28**	**29**	**30**
(c)	(d)	(d)	(a)	(b)	(b)	(b)	(d)	(d)	(b)
31	**32**	**33**	**34**	**35**	**36**	**37**	**38**	**39**	**40**
(d)	(b)	(c)	(a)	(d)	(c)	(b)	(d)	(c)	(d)
41	**42**	**43**	**44**	**45**	**46**	**47**	**48**	**49**	**50**
(b)	(d)	(b)	(d)	(b)	(a)	(d)	(a)	(d)	(b)
51	**52**	**53**	**54**	**55**	**56**	**57**	**58**	**59**	**60**
(d)	(c)	(c)	(a)	(c)	(b)	(d)	(c)	(a)	(b)
61	**62**	**63**	**64**	**65**	**66**	**67**	**68**	**69**	**70**
(d)	(d)	(d)	(c)	(c)	(c)	(a)	(c)	(b)	(c)
71	**72**	**73**	**74**	**75**	**76**	**77**	**78**	**79**	**80**
(a)	(c)	(a)	(d)	(b)	(b)	(c)	(b)	(b)	(c)
81	**82**	**83**	**84**	**85**	**86**	**87**	**88**	**89**	**90**
(b)	(b)	(a)	(c)	(b)	(a)	(d)	(b)	(b)	(d)
91	**92**	**93**	**94**	**95**	**96**	**97**	**98**	**99**	**100**
(c)	(c)	(a)	(b)	(a)	(c)	(b)	(b)	(d)	(a)

1. _____________ is a set of computer programs used on a computer to help perform tasks.
   (a) An instruction   (b) Software
   (c) Memory   (d) A processor

2. The two-phase commit protocol may introduce
   (a) Starving   (b) Deadlock
   (c) Blocking   (d) None of these

3. System software is the set of programs that enables your computer hardware devices and _____________ software to work together.
   (a) management   (b) processing
   (c) utility   (d) application

4. The PC (personal computer) and the Apple Macintosh are examples of two different:
   (a) platforms   (b) applications
   (c) programs   (d) storage devices

5. A multi-level indexing may lead to
   (a) Transaction failure
   (b) B-tree
   (c) Binary tree
   (d) Deadlock

6. The primary key indexing technique does not allow
   (a) Duplicate data in a field
   (b) Many-to-many relations
   (c) Sets of relations
   (d) Multiple attributes

7. Before a transaction is executed, the following is updated
   (a) Log
   (b) The query processor
   (c) Database manager
   (d) The database

8. All the objects created into a project are organised by the
   (a) Project manager
   (b) Sorting
   (c) Database administrator
   (d) Database manager

9. The data model in which, data is represented by collection of records and relations among data are represented by links, is called
   (a) Logical data model
   (b) Relational data model
   (c) Network data model
   (d) Hierarchical data model

10. It is a scheme representing the design of a network database
    (a) Network of records / fields
    (b) Data-Structure diagram
    (c) Wait-for graph
    (d) Entity-Relation diagram

11. A data structure diagram of a network model is analogous to
    (a) Entity-Relation diagram
    (b) B-tree representation
    (c) Relational-table
    (d) None of the above

12. Apple Macintoshes (Macs) and PCs use different _____________ to process data and different operating systems.
    (a) languages   (b) methods
    (c) CPUs   (d) storage devices

13. Smaller and less expensive PC-based servers are replacing ____________ in many businesses.
- (a) supercomputers
- (b) clients
- (c) laptops
- (d) Mainframes

14. What do you call the programs that are used to find out possible faults and their causes?
- (a) Operating system
- (b) Cookies
- (c) Diagnostic software
- (d) Boot diskettes

15. In order to find duplicate records in a network database, one can use the following DML command :
- (a) FIND DUPLICATE
- (b) AUTOMATIC
- (c) SELECTION
- (d) READ

16. Which of the following is not a type of Software
- (a) System Software
- (b) Application Software
- (c) Utility Software
- (d) Entertainment Software

17. Which of the following is not the classification of computers based on application?
- (a) Electronic Computers
- (b) Analog Computers
- (c) Digital Computers
- (d) Hybrid Computers

18. In Query-By-Example, the query is formed from the relations displayed by filling in the following
- (a) DDL statements
- (b) Templates
- (c) DML
- (d) SQL form

19. The data manipulation language of the DBTG model consists of a number of commands that are embedded in
- (a) DDL
- (b) Command language
- (c) SQL
- (d) Host language

20. Which one of the following is an example of a network database?
- (a) IDMS
- (b) DBMS
- (c) INGRESS
- (d) ORACLE

21. Which of the following registers is used to keep track of address of the memory location where the next instruction is located?
- (a) Memory address register
- (b) Memory data register
- (c) Instruction register
- (d) Program counter

22. In a hierarchical database, a hashing function is used to locate the
- (a) Collisions
- (b) Root
- (c) Primary key
- (d) Duplicate records

23. The scheme for a hierarchical database is a
- (a) tree-structure diagram
- (b) graph of links between records
- (c) E-R diagram
- (d) None of these

24. In a hierarchical database, if a relation includes a descriptive attribute, the transformation from an E-R diagram to a tree structure is more complicated because
- (a) this leads to an ambiguous situation
- (b) the link can not contain any data value
- (c) the description cannot be quantified
- (d) the hierarchical nature cannot be specified

25. Which characteristic of computer distinguishes it from electronic calculators?
- (a) Accuracy
- (b) Storage
- (c) Versatility
- (d) Automatic

26. Which one of the following is an example of a hierarchical database?
- (a) ORACLE
- (b) INGRESS
- (c) DBII
- (d) SYSTEM2000

27. Which of the following is the largest manufacturer of Hard Disk Drives?
- (a) IBM
- (b) Seagate
- (c) Microsoft
- (d) 3M

28. In most of the implementations of hierarchical databases, parent-to-child links are stored with the help of
(*a*) Pointers
(*b*) Reference variables
(*c*) Virtual records
(*d*) Preorder threads

29. In a hierarchical database, a virtual record
(*a*) contains preorder threads
(*b*) does not contain data but contains a logical pointer for a particular record
(*c*) contains currency pointers
(*d*) contains redundant data of a particular data (duplication of a particular record)

30. Indexed sequential file is created using the following storage device
(*a*) Direct access   (*b*) Random access
(*c*) Sequential access (*d*) Primary

31. An association amongst several entities is called
(*a*) Table   (*b*) Relationship
(*c*) Data   (*d*) None of these

32. The principle means of identifying entities within an entity set is called
(*a*) Record   (*b*) Primary key
(*c*) Tuple   (*d*) Pointer

33. A language that enables users to access or manipulate data is called
(*a*) Data Manipulation Language (DML)
(*b*) Database language
(*c*) SQL
(*d*) All of these

34. A language that is used to specify the database scheme through a set of definitions is called
(*a*) SQL
(*b*) Data Definition Language (DDL)
(*c*) E-R diagram
(*d*) Fourth Generation Language (4GL)

35. A program module in a DBMS, which provides an interface between low level data stored in the database and the application programs & queries submitted to the system is
(*a*) Query processor
(*b*) Database manager
(*c*) Database creator
(*d*) DBMS

36. A collection of conceptual tools for describing data, data relationships, data semantics and data constraints is called
(*a*) Data model   (*b*) Scheme
(*c*) E-R Diagram   (*d*) All of these

37. LSI, VLSI & ULSI chips were used in which generation?
(*a*) First   (*b*) Second
(*c*) Third   (*d*) Fourth

38. What is the name of the display feature that highlights are of the screen which requires operator attention?
(*a*) Pixel   (*b*) Reverse video
(*c*) Touch screen   (*d*) Cursor

39. IMB launched its first personal computer called IBM-PC in 1981. It had chips from Intel, disk drives from Tandon, operating system from Microsoft, the printer from Epson and the application software from everywhere. Can you name the country which contributed the video display?
(*a*) India   (*b*) China
(*c*) Germany   (*d*) Taiwan

40. SQL is relationally
(*a*) a complete language
(*b*) cannot handle certain relations
(*c*) an incompelete language
(*d*) a sound language

41. Video conferencing
(*a*) permits two or more persons to communicate with one another while they can see one another on the computer terminal
(*b*) is possible only when one uses video-disks

(c) refers to video used in conference for pre senting ideas

(d) involves sending pictures through high-speed networks and audio signals over telephone lines

42. Personal computers use a number of chips mounted on a main circuit board. What is the common name for such boards?
(a) Daughter board (b) Motherboard
(c) Father board (d) Breadboard

43. Interlacing
(a) refers to displaying alternate columns on the screen
(b) refers to mixing various shades on the graphics screen
(c) refers to displaying alternate rows on the screen
(d) is another term for refreshing the screen

44. Choose the correct one from the following statements related to Bezier curves
(a) A closed Bezier curve can be drawn by tak-ing the first and last control point to be the same
(b) Given a sequence of 4 control points, the Bezier curve can take two different shapes
(c) If first 3 control points are in a straight line, no curve can be drawn
(d) To draw a curve on the screen, all the control points must be located within the boundaries of the screen

45. What is meant by a dedicated computer?
(a) Which is used by one person only
(b) Which is assigned one and only one task
(c) Which uses one kind of software
(d) Which is meant for application software

46. A computer program that converts an entire program into machine language is called a/an
(a) Interpreter (b) Simulator
(c) Compiler (d) Commander

47. A computer program that translates one program instructions at a time into machine language is called a/an
(a) Interpreter (b) CPU
(c) Compiler (d) Simulator

48. Regarding a VDU, Which statement is more correct?
(a) It is an output device
(b) It is an input device
(c) It is a peripheral device
(d) It is hardware item

49. Sometimes these lines appear to be broken or they show staircase effect on the screen because
(a) there are numerical errors in calculation
(b) the line drawing algorithm allows only specific pixels to be put ON
(c) the algorithm is not efficient for slanting lines
(d) the screen is not really flat

50. A circle drawn on the screen appears to be eliptical as
(a) our eyes are not at the same level as that of the screen
(b) the CRT is not completely spherical
(c) it is due to respect ratio of the monitor
(d) the screen has a rectangular shape

51. What is the name of the computer terminal which gives paper printout?
(a) Display screen
(b) Soft copy terminal
(c) Hard copy terminal
(d) Plotter

52. A kind of serial dot-matrix printer that forms characters with magnetically-charged ink sprayed dots is called
(a) Laser printer (b) Ink-jet printer
(c) Drum printer (d) Chan printer

53. An output device that uses words or messages recorded on a magnetic medium to produce audio response is

(a) Voice band
(b) Magnetic tape
(c) Voice response unit
(d) Voice recognition unit

54. One of the following terms is not associated with the field of computer graphics
(a) fonts
(b) deadlock
(c) icon
(d) buttons

55. Which of the following will happen when data is entered into a memory location?
(a) It will add to the content of the location
(b) It will change the address of the memory location
(c) It will erase the previous content
(d) It will not be fruitful if there is already some data at the location

56. In 2D graphics [4 2 0] represents a point
(a) lying at infinity
(b) (4, 2) and also (2, 1)
(c) (4, 2)
(d) invalid representation

57. The Floating Horizon technique is used in computer graphics for
(a) zooming
(b) hidden surface removal
(c) polygon clipping
(d) area filling

58. In order for two Bezier curves to join smoothly
(a) at last one control point should be common.
(b) all control points of both curves must overlap.
(c) last two points of first curve must be same as first, two points of second curve.
(d) last two points of first curve must be collinear with first two points of second curve.

59. A storage area used to store data to a compensate for the difference in speed at which the different units can handle data is

(a) Memory
(b) Buffer
(c) Accumulator
(d) Address

60. A rectangle has been drawn on the screen. It is desired to carry out a zoom in process to double the size of the rectangle. This process would involve
(a) scaling and rotation
(b) scaling and translation
(c) only scaling
(d) translation, scaling and translation back

61. Which of the following is not a programming language?
(a) Basic
(b) Java
(c) Turing
(d) C#

62. One of the following pairs has similar functions. Tick the correct pair
(a) Mouse and light pen
(b) Digitizing tablet and the mouse
(c) Track ball and light pen
(d) Light pen and digitizing tablet

63. Which of the following is NOT a type of expansion slot or bus design used in Advanced-Technology class systems?
(a) PCMCIA
(b) ISA
(c) PROM
(d) EISA

64. Which company created the most used networking software in the 1980's
(a) Microsoft
(b) Sun
(c) IBM
(d) Novell

65. Tick the correct statement.
(a) Each one of the colour monitor screens is painted with 3 layers of red, green and blue phosphorescence material
(b) Usually, no bits are allocated to Blue colour in RGB monitors as it contributes very little to overall colours on the screen
(c) The refresh buffer or the display buffer holds the picture information which is displayed on the screen at regular intervals

(*d*) When the mouse is moved, the cursor moves on the screen. The same effect can be observed when the mouse is picked up and placed in a new location

66. Which Intel chip was the first to support a 32-bit bus architecture?
(*a*) 486SI
(*b*) Pentium
(*c*) 286
(*d*) 386DX

67. Which of the following word processors came first?
(*a*) WordPerfect
(*b*) Lotus Notes
(*c*) MS Word
(*d*) WordStar

68. A 14 inches monitor implies
(*a*) a circle of 14 inches diameter is available for display
(*b*) the screen is 14 inches high
(*c*) the screen is 14 inches wide
(*d*) the diagonal across the screen is 14 inches

69. The Central Processing Unit is an embeded chip that acts as the 'brains' of a computer. What Intel chip was used in the Altair (the first real personal computer)?
(*a*) 6502
(*b*) 8080
(*c*) 6400
(*d*) 8286

70. One of the following sampling rates for storing digital audio signals is not preferred for multimedia applications
(*a*) 11 KHz, stereo
(*b*) 22.05 KHz, stereo
(*c*) 44.1 KHz, mono
(*d*) 5.5 KHz, mono

71. The invention of the transistor, or semiconductor, was one of the most important developments leading to the personal computer revolution. What company invented the transistor in 1947?
(*a*) International Business Machines
(*b*) MITS
(*c*) Xerox
(*d*) Bell Laboratories

72. ___________ are specially designed computers that perform complex calculations extremely rapidly.
(*a*) Servers
(*b*) Supercomputers
(*c*) Laptops
(*d*) Mainframes

73. A prespective view is being generated by a viewer located at distance b from the origin on Z axis. If this distance were doubled, the distance of vanishing point from the origin, would
(*a*) be at twice the distance
(*b*) be at an infinite distance
(*c*) be half the original
(*d*) remain unchanged

74. The dot product of two vectors
(*a*) decreases as the angle between them decreases
(*b*) decreases as the angle between them increases
(*c*) remain constant irrespective of angle between the vectors
(*d*) increase as the angle between them increases

75. DSL is an example of a(n) _______ connection.
(*a*) network
(*b*) wireless
(*c*) slow
(*d*) broadband

76. In order to draw two smoothly joining cubic Bezier curves segments, one needs
(*a*) 9 control points
(*b*) 7 control points
(*c*) 8 control points
(*d*) 4 control points

77. ___________ is the science revolving around the use of nanostructures to build devices on an extremely small scale.
(*a*) Nanotechnology
(*b*) Micro-technology
(*c*) Computer forensics
(*d*) Artificial intelligence

78. Which of the following is the correct order of the four major functions of a computer?
(*a*) Process Ã Output Ã Input Ã Storage

(b) Input Ã Output Ã Process Ã Storage
(c) Process Ã Storage Ã Input Ã Output
(d) Input Ã Process Ã Output Ã Storage

79. _____________ controls the way in which the computer system functions and provides a means by which users can interact with the computer.
(a) The platform
(b) The operating system
(c) Application software
(d) The motherboard

80. One of the following DOES NOT represent the point lying on the Y axis at infinity
(a) [0 5 0 0] (b) [1 0 0 0]
(c) [0 1 0 0] (d) [0 10 0 0]

81. A line is parallel to one of the edges of a window and locked far from it. The algorithm that would fail to indicate this is
(a) Sutherland Cohen algorithm
(b) Midpoint subdivision algorithm
(c) Explicit line clipping algorithm
(d) there is no such algorithm

82. A point (x, y, z) is transformed to (x', y', z') using one of the following equations:

$$[x'\ y'\ z'\ 1] = [x\ y\ z\ 1]\begin{bmatrix} 1 & 0 & 0 & 0 \\ 0 & 0 & 1 & 0 \\ 0 & -1 & 0 & 0 \\ 0 & 0 & 0 & 1 \end{bmatrix}$$

OR

$$\begin{matrix} X' = \\ Y' = \\ Z' = \\ 1 = \end{matrix} \begin{bmatrix} 1 & 0 & 0 & 0 \\ 0 & 0 & -1 & 0 \\ 0 & 1 & 0 & 0 \\ 0 & 0 & 0 & 1 \end{bmatrix} \begin{bmatrix} x \\ y \\ z \\ 1 \end{bmatrix}$$

What does this transform correspond to?
(a) rotation by 90 degrees about Z-axis
(b) rotation by 90 degrees about X-axis
(c) rotation by 90 degrees about Y axis
(d) translation by unit distance

83. In order to store good-quality sound, the audio signal in a multimedia PC is sampled at the rate of

(a) 4.41 MHz (b) 4.41 KHz
(c) 44 KHz (d) 44.1 Hz

84. Pick out the correct statement for Bezier curves
(a) The control points should be so placed that values of x coordinate are in the increasing order
(b) A curve is proper only if the cubic polynomials for x and y are identical
(c) The control points may lie anywhere on the screen
(d) Best curves are drawn when starting and end slope of the curves are same

85. A cube of side 5 is placed at the origin such that its edges are parallel to the X, Y and Z axes. A viewer standing on the Z-axis is looking at the cube. The perspective view so generated would have a vanishing point. This would be the point where all edges
(a) on top of the cube appear to meet
(b) of the cube parallel to Y-axis appear to meet
(c) of the cube parallel to Z-axis appear to meet
(d) of the cube parallel to X-axis appear to meet

86. The use of lookup tables in a display monitor is to
(a) store the colour information of the picture
(b) increase the range of colour shades
(c) provide a variety of colour palettes but number of available colours remain same
(d) increase the resolution of the picture on the screen

87. The back-face removal algorithm is being applied to an object, one of whose sides is a quadrilateral. The vertices of the side, read clockwise are A, B, C, D, A. Pick out the correct statement from the choices given below

(a) Vectors DA and BC can be used to determine the inward normal

(b) Vectors AB and CD can be used to determine the inward normal

(c) Vectors BC and AB can be used to detemine the inward normal

(d) The method is not applicable because the side has to be rectangular or square

88. The cross product of two vectors

(a) has a larger magnitude than that of either   of the vectors

(b) has a smaller magnitude than either of the vectors

(c) lies in the same plane as the vectors

(d) is perpendicular to the plane containing the vectors

89. The format for storing digital audio signals in multimedia applications is

(a) BMP   (b) TIFF

(c) WAV   (d) JPEG

90. Pick out the INCORRECT statement related to authoring tools for multimedia

(a) Director has no built-in capabilities for electronic spreadsheet and charting

(b) Animations in Authorware are better than those in Director

(c) As compared to Director, Authorware lacks the ability to synchronise sound effectively

(d) Authorware is simple and icon-driven

91. ____________ are specially designed computer chips that reside inside other devices, such as your car or your electronic thermostat.

(a) Servers

(b) Embedded computers

(c) Robotic computers

(d) Mainframes

92. The two broad categories of software are:

(a) word processing and spreadsheet.

(b) transaction and application.

(c) Windows and Mac OS.

(d) system and application.

93. This virus activated every Friday the 13th, affects both .EXE and .COM files and deletes any programs run on that day. What is the name of that virus?

(a) Chernobyl   (b) Jerusalem

(c) Melissa   (d) I Love You

94. The quality of a picture produced by a laser printer would depend upon

(a) its resolution

(b) resolution of the monitor where it is displayed before it is sent for printing

(c) its internal memory

(d) size of picture file

95. AUTOCAD is

(a) used to provide shading effects in drawings

(b) a standard software for drawing machine parts and buildings

(c) a software to generate scenarios

(d) an abbreviation for automatic calculation and drawing

96. Hypermedia

(a) is another name for multimedia

(b) provides links between two media

(c) is a facility to permits two media to be played together

(d) is another medium like graphics, text etc

97. Pick out the correct statement from the ones given below

(a) Midpoint subdivision algorithm can be implemented in hardware

(b) Lines parallel to window edge cannot be clipped

(c) The clipping window must always be rectangular in shape

(d) Midpoint algorithm takes less time as compared to Sutherland-Cohen clipping algorithm.

98. In what year did the Symantec Corporation first release Norton Antivirus?
- (a) 1990
- (b) 1995
- (c) 1988
- (d) 1997

99. Cubic polynomials are mostly used for parametric curves because
- (a) it gives us the flexibility to draw arbitrary shaped curves
- (b) the cubic curve ensures control over two end points and slope at one end
- (c) it ensures control on two end points as well as slope at both ends
- (d) cubic functions are smooth and continuous

100. A computer virus that actively attacks an anti-virus program or programs in an effort to prevent detection is...
- (a) Worm
- (b) Retrovirus
- (c) Trojan
- (d) Ghost virus

ANSWERS

1	2	3	4	5	6	7	8	9	10
(b)	(c)	(d)	(a)	(b)	(a)	(a)	(a)	(c)	(b)
11	**12**	**13**	**14**	**15**	**16**	**17**	**18**	**19**	**20**
(a)	(c)	(d)	(c)	(a)	(d)	(c)	(b)	(a)	(a)
21	**22**	**23**	**24**	**25**	**26**	**27**	**28**	**29**	**30**
(d)	(b)	(a)	(b)	(b)	(d)	(b)	(d)	(b)	(a)
31	**32**	**33**	**34**	**35**	**36**	**37**	**38**	**39**	**40**
(b)	(b)	(a)	(b)	(b)	(a)	(c)	(b)	(d)	(a)
41	**42**	**43**	**44**	**45**	**46**	**47**	**48**	**49**	**50**
(a)	(b)	(c)	(a)	(b)	(c)	(a)	(c)	(b)	(c)
51	**52**	**53**	**54**	**55**	**56**	**57**	**58**	**59**	**60**
(c)	(b)	(c)	(b)	(c)	(a)	(b)	(d)	(b)	(d)
61	**62**	**63**	**64**	**65**	**66**	**67**	**68**	**69**	**70**
(c)	(b)	(c)	(d)	(c)	(d)	(d)	(d)	(b)	(d)
71	**72**	**73**	**74**	**75**	**76**	**77**	**78**	**79**	**80**
(d)	(b)	(a)	(b)	(d)	(b)	(a)	(d)	(b)	(b)
81	**82**	**83**	**84**	**85**	**86**	**87**	**88**	**89**	**90**
(d)	(b)	(c)	(c)	(c)	(c)	(c)	(d)	(c)	(b)
91	**92**	**93**	**94**	**95**	**96**	**97**	**98**	**99**	**100**
(b)	(d)	(b)	(a)	(b)	(b)	(a)	(a)	(c)	(b)

TEST PAPER 6

1. In 3D graphics, one of the following martices would carry out rotation about the Y axis by 45 degrees

   (a)
1	0	0	0
0	.707	.707	0
0	−.707	.707	0
0	0	0	1

   (b)
.707	0	−.707	0
0	1	0	0
.707	0	.707	0
0	0	0	1

   (c)
.707	−.707	0	0
−.707	.707	0	0
0	0	1	0
0	0	0	1

   (d)
1	0	−1	0
0	1	0	0
.707	0	.707	0
0	0	0	1

2. A program that neither replicates or copies itself, but does damage or compromises the security of the computer. Which 'Computer Virus' it is?
   (a) Joke Program (b) Worm
   (c) Trojan (d) Hoax

3. Pick out the WRONG statement regarding the Floating Horizon techniques
   (a) is used for hidden surface elimination
   (b) is used to plot 3D mathematical functions on the screen
   (c) is used to create out-door scenery on the screen
   (d) can be used only for Cuboid, Cones and Spheres etc

4. In 3D graphics, the homogeneous coordinates (0, 5, 0, 0)
   (a) represent a point on X-axis or Z-axis at infinity
   (b) represent a point X = 0, Y = 5, Z = 0
   (c) represent a point in Y axis at infinity
   (d) are not allowed

5. A clockwise rotation of 90 degrees about X axis would transfer the point
   (a) on Y-axis to X-axis
   (b) on Y-axis to Z-axis
   (c) on X-axis to Z-axis
   (d) on Z-axis to Y-axis

6. Anti-clockwise rotation of 90 degrees about Z axis would transfer a point
   (a) on X-axis to negative Y-axis
   (b) on Y-axis to X-axis
   (c) on X-axis to Y-axis
   (d) on X-axis to negative

7. Which of these is a documented hoax virus?
   (a) McDonalds screensaver
   (b) Alien.worm
   (c) Merry Xmas
   (d) Adolph

8. In 1983, which person was the first to offer a definition of the term 'computer virus'?
   (a) McAfee (b) Smith
   (c) Cohen (d) Norton

9. A multimedia PC gets booted through its
   (a) ROM (b) CD-ROM
   (c) Cache (d) RAM

10. What is RISC?
   (a) Remodeled Interface System Computer

(*b*) Remote Intranet Secured Connection
(*c*) Runtime Instruction Set Compiler
(*d*) Reduced Instruction Set Computer

11. One of the following is not related to multimedia
(*a*) FoxPro
(*b*) animatorpro
(*c*) director
(*d*) authorware

12. The perspective projection of the point (2, 3, 1) on the Z = 0 plane with the eye placed at (0, 0, −5) is
(*a*) (2 1/3, 3.5)
(*b*) (1 2/3, 2.5)
(*c*) (2/3, 1.5)
(*d*) None of these

13. The perspective projection of the point (1, 2, 2) on the Z = 0 plane with the eye being placed at (0, 0, −2) is
(*a*) (0.5, 1)
(*b*) (1.5, 2)
(*c*) (1, 1.5)
(*d*) None of these

14. What is a GPU?
(*a*) Grouped Processing Unit
(*b*) Graphics Processing Unit
(*c*) Graphical Performance Utility
(*d*) Graphical Portable Unit

15. Which one of the following transmits digital information to the computer?
(*a*) graphics tablet
(*b*) mouse
(*c*) joystick
(*d*) None of these

16. A B-spline curve is called a uniform B-spline when
(*a*) the spacing between the adjacent knot values is a constant
(*b*) the curve is infinite times differentiable
(*c*) the distance between the adjacent control points is a constant
(*d*) None of these

17. Reflection about the line $y = -x$ transformation is equal to
(*a*) the sequence of transformations:
(*i*) clockwise rotations by 45 degrees
(*ii*) reflection about the X-axis
(*iii*) counter clockwise rotation by 45 degrees
(*b*) the matrix transformation
0 1 0
1 0 0
0 0 1
in homogeneous coordinate system
(*c*) reflection about the X-axis followed by a counter clockwise rotation of 90 degrees
(*d*) None of the above

18. What does ECP stand for?
(*a*) Extended Capabilities Port
(*b*) Extra Compatible Part
(*c*) Extended Connection Port
(*d*) External Cordless Peripheral

19. Let p(.) and q(.) be two Bezier curves defined by the sets of control points $\{p_0, p_1, p_2, p_3\}$ and $\{q_0, q_1, q_2, q_3\}$ respectively. The two curves are joined with first order continuity at $p_{(1)} = q_{(0)}$ provided
(*a*) $p_3 = (p_2 + q_1)/2$
(*b*) $p_3 = (p_1 + q_2)/3$
(*c*) $p_3 = (p_1 + q_2)/2$
(*d*) $p_3 = (p_2 + q_1)/3$

20. Display resolution of a typical monitor would be around
(*a*) 300DPI
(*b*) 60DPI
(*c*) 200DPI
(*d*) 10DPI

21. One of the following techniques is used to provide variety of colour palettes on the graphics screen
(*a*) Increasing no. of resolution of screen
(*b*) Increasing no of bit planes for R, G and B
(*c*) Using a look-up table
(*d*) Using a multi-coloured electron gun

22. What is TTL?
(*a*) Technical Talk Language
(*b*) Transparent Transfer Layer
(*c*) Time To Live
(*d*) True Technology Lives

23. What is FMD?
(*a*) FastEthernet Measuring Device

(b) Flashing Media Diode
(c) Fluorescent Multi-Layer Disc
(d) Flash Media Driver

24. What does DOCSIS stand for?
(a) Data Over Cable Service Interface Specification
(b) Data Over Cable Security Internet Std
(c) Data Over Cable Secure International Stds
(d) Data Over Cable Service Internet Standard

25. What is VCM?
(a) Virtual Connection Manager
(b) Virtual Channel Memory
(c) Voice Controlled Modem
(d) Voice Communications Module

26. What is NAT?
(a) Network Address Translation
(b) Network Administration Tool
(c) Novell Address Transfer
(d) Newly Added Technology

27. What is a NIC?
(a) Netware Intranet Controller
(b) No Internet Connection
(c) Network Interface Card
(d) Network Interference Control

28. What are the end point codes of the line between $P_1(4,-7)$ and $P_2(-2,10)$, if the window coordinates $x_{min}=-3$, $x_{max}=2$, $y_{min}=1$ and $y_{max}=6$
(a) (1001), (1000) (b) (0101), (0100)
(c) (0000), (0010) (d) (1010), (1001)

29. What is a MAC?
(a) A Computer made by Apple
(b) Memory Address Corruption
(c) Mediocre Apple Computer
(d) Media Access Control

30. Seed fill algorithm, using a stack, uses the principle of
(a) First in First Out (b) Last in First Out
(c) First in Last Out (d) None of these

31. The result of midpoint subdivision algorithm is to perform
(a) logarithmic search
(b) depth first search
(c) breadth first search
(d) best first search for the intersection point of the line with the window edge

32. For generation of a circle by the Bresenham's algorithm, it is easier to generate
(a) one octant first and other by successive translations
(b) one octant first and others by successive reflections
(c) one octant first and others octants by successive rotations
(d) all octants at one go

33. What does PPTP stand for?
(a) Point to Point Transmission Protocol
(b) Point to Point Transfer Protocol
(c) Point to Point Tunneling Protocol
(d) Point to Point Traffic Protocol

34. B-spline curves allow
(a) First derivative at one end and the second derivative at the other end of the curve
(b) Only the second derivative to be continuous at the end points of curve
(c) Both first and second derivative to be continuous at the end points
(d) Only the first order derivative to be continuous at the end points of curve

35. What is LCP?
(a) Local Connection Protocol
(b) Lost Connection Problem
(c) Link Control Protocol
(d) Laggy Connection Problem

36. What does SSL stand for?
(a) Secure Socket Layer
(b) System Socket Layer
(c) Superuser System Login
(d) Secure System Login

37. What does ICMP stand for?
 (a) Internet Connection Modem Protocol
 (b) Intranet Control Message Program
 (c) Internal Conflict Management Program
 (d) Internet Control Message Protocol

38. Programs designed to perform specific tasks is known as
 (a) system software
 (b) application software
 (c) utility programs
 (d) operating system

39. Perforated paper used as input of output media is known as
 (a) paper tapes
 (b) magnetic tape
 (c) punched papers tape
 (d) card punch

40. If vector = 1 (unit vector along X-axis) and vector = J (Unit vector along Y-axis), the cross product of these vectors would be along
 (a) I − J
 (b) I + J
 (c) K
 (d) I

41. Pick out the correct statement from the following, in the context of the nature of multimedia
 (a) it is same as a video, as both deal with selection of audio and video material
 (b) it is same as a television program, as both involves sound and moving pictures
 (c) it is the same as word processing, as it also handles text
 (d) None of these statements is true

42. In ink jet printers, colour printing is possible through generation of colour by
 (a) four colour cartridges
 (b) a device, which mixes different colours insidethe printer to produce the desired shade
 (c) spraying electrons of different colours and shades on the paper
 (d) seven colour cartridges

43. A computer which CPU speed around 100 million instruction per second and with the word length of around 64 bits is known as
 (a) Super computer (b) Mini computer
 (c) Micro computer (d) Macro computer

44. A graphics screen needs to be refreshed periodically by the processor because
 (a) the electron beams can light up only one pixel at a time on the screen
 (b) interlacing is never perfect
 (c) it permits the monitor to be under the direct control of the processor
 (d) the memory to hold the information on screen it not sufficient

45. For carrying out animations, you would
 (a) prefer to draw the object at current position in background colour and then, redraw it at the new position
 (b) prefer to draw the object at a new position and then, delete the old one
 (c) blank out the screen before making the next changes in objects position
 (d) adjust the rate of refreshing

46. An approach that permits the computer to work on several programs instead of one is
 (a) On-line thesaurus
 (b) Multiprogramming
 (c) Over lapped processing
 (d) Outline processor

47. On a 300 × 200, screen, it is desired to locate the origin at the centre of screen. A point x, y would correspond to following screen coordinates
 (a) $-x + 300, y + 200$
 (b) $x - 300, y + 200$
 (c) $x + 300, y + 200$
 (d) $x + 300, y + 200$

48. Which one of the following attributes is important for presenting text in a multimedia document?
 (a) Colour

(b) Character format

(c) Font

(d) All the three mentioned above

49. Which of the following processors use RISC technology?

(a) 486dx (b) Power PC

(c) 486sx (d) 6340

50. The following matrix carries out translation

$$\begin{matrix} 1 & 0 & 0 \\ 0 & 1 & 0 \\ -2 & 4 & 1 \end{matrix}$$

Pick out the inverse of this matrix

(a) $\begin{matrix} -2 & 0 & 1 \\ 4 & 1 & 0 \\ 1 & 0 & 0 \end{matrix}$

(b) $\begin{matrix} 1 & 0 & 0 \\ 0 & 1 & 0 \\ 1/2 & 1/4 & 1 \end{matrix}$

(c) $\begin{matrix} 1 & 0 & 0 \\ 0 & 1 & 0 \\ 2 & -4 & 1 \end{matrix}$

(d) $\begin{matrix} 0 & 1 & 0 \\ 1 & 0 & 0 \\ 4 & 2 & -1 \end{matrix}$

51. Current SIMMs have either … or … connectors (pins)

(a) 9 or 32 (b) 30 or 70

(c) 28 or 72 (d) 30 or 72

52. A cube placed at the origin is rotated about the X-axis in clockwise direction. A viewer located on Z-axis at distance 10 from origin at any point in time will be able to see

(a) the maximum of 3 sides of the cube

(b) always two sides of the cube

(c) the maximum of two sides of the cube

(d) just one side of the cube

53. A scanner is specified by

(a) vertical and horizontal resolution

(b) dots per inch it can scan

(c) length of paper it can scan

(d) rate of scanning

54. The storage subsystem in a microcomputer consists mainly of … or … media with varying capacities

(a) Memory or video

(b) Magnetic or optical

(c) Optical or memory

(d) Video or magnetic

55. Which of the following is not an input device?

(a) OCR

(b) Optical scanners

(c) Voice recognition device

(d) COM (Computer Output to Microfilm)

56. The co-ordinate of a point(−30, 70) reflected about X-axis will be

(a) 30, −70 (b) −30, −70

(c) 70, −30 (d) 30, 70

57. The central processing unit (CPU) consists of

(a) Input, output and processing

(b) Control unit, primary storage, and secondary storage

(c) Control unit, arithmetic-logic unit and primary storage

(d) Control unit, processing, and primary storage

58. Which one of the following attributes is important for presenting text in a multimedia document?

(a) Colour

(b) Character format

(c) Font

(d) All the three mentioned above

59. The first successful packet broadcast network is

(a) BITNET (b) ALOHA

(c) ARPANET (d) TYMNET

60. RABMN network belongs to

(a) the American business community

(b) the European bank

(c) the DOE (India)

(d) the American defense

61. A medium-sized network is termed as
   (*a*) VAN   (*b*) LAN
   (*c*) MAN   (*d*) WAN

62. Which one of the following standards is followed in India?
   (*a*) ANSI   (*b*) CCITT
   (*c*) ISO   (*d*) IFIP

63. Which of the following is not a goal of a computer network?
   (*a*) Load sharing
   (*b*) Low reliability
   (*c*) Resources sharing
   (*d*) To avoid physical movement

64. Computers in a computer network are connected via
   (*a*) Coxial cable only
   (*b*) Satellite channel only
   (*c*) Either telephone line or satellite channel or both
   (*d*) Telephone line only

65. E-mail stands for
   (*a*) Electronic mail   (*b*) Express mail
   (*c*) Education mail   (*d*) Excess mail

66. Modem refers to
   (*a*) Modern modes of communication
   (*b*) Modulator
   (*c*) Modulator and Demodulator
   (*d*) Modulation

67. The latest modulation techinque used by data modems is
   (*a*) ASK   (*b*) FSK
   (*c*) DPSK   (*d*) QPSK

68. DTE is popularly known as
   (*a*) Data Terminal Equipment
   (*b*) Dual Time Equipment
   (*c*) Discrete Time Equipment
   (*d*) Digital Type Equipment

69. EBCDIC can code up to how many different characters?
   (*a*) 256   (*b*) 16
   (*c*) 32   (*d*) 64

70. Messages are transferred in a computer network through
   (*a*) Multiplexing   (*b*) Message switching
   (*c*) Packet switching (*d*) Circuit switching

71. Which one of the following is not a guided transmission line?
   (*a*) Fibre optic channel
   (*b*) Wave guides
   (*c*) Laser beam
   (*d*) Pair of wires

72. Signals that involves human communication are generally
   (*a*) analog
   (*b*) digital
   (*c*) either digital or analog
   (*d*) none of these

73. A digital channel implies that the channel
   (*a*) is without a carrier
   (*b*) is carrying digital data
   (*c*) adopts a digital modulation techniques
   (*d*) is digitized

74. Frequency range of the human voice is usually
   (*a*) 100 - 4000 Hz   (*b*) 400 - 800 Hz
   (*c*) 199 - 200 Hz   (*d*) 200 - 600 Hz

75. In twisted-pair cables, the mode of communication is
   (*a*) TDMA   (*b*) CDMA
   (*c*) TDM   (*d*) FDM

76. Which is considered a direct entry input device?
   (*a*) Optical scanner
   (*b*) Mouse and digitizer
   (*c*) Light pen
   (*d*) All of the above

77. The computer code for the interchange of information between terminals is
   (*a*) ASCII   (*b*) BCD
   (*c*) EBCDIC   (*d*) All of above

78. A hybrid computer
   (*a*) Resembles digital computer
   (*b*) Resembles analog computer

(c) Resembles both a digital and analog computer

(d) None of the above

79. Which one of the following input device is user-programmable?
(a) Dumb terminal
(b) Smart terminal
(c) VDT
(d) Intelligent terminal

80. Computer instructions written with the use of English words instead of binary machine code is called
(a) Mnemonics
(b) Symbolic code
(c) Gray codes
(d) Opcode

81. Telephone networks usually use
(a) Full-duplex transmission
(b) Half-duplex transmission
(c) Simplex transmission
(d) None of these

82. Data networks usually use
(a) Duplex transmission
(b) Half-duplex transmission
(c) Full-duplex transmission
(d) Simplex transmission

83. For long-distance data transmissions, the preferable mode of communication is
(a) Parallel transmission
(b) Serial transmission
(c) either (a) or (b)
(d) Both (a) and (b)

84. The transmission of a digital signal at its original frequency without modulation is called
(a) Digital signalling
(b) Base band signalling
(c) Broad band signalling
(d) Pass band signalling

85. During transmission, the distortion of the signal depends upon
(a) the frequency of the signal
(b) the length of transmission
(c) Both (a) and (b)
(d) None of these

86. Signal rate of a communication channel depends upon
(a) frequency and time responses of the channel
(b) time of responses of the channel only
(c) frequency responses of the channel only
(d) None of these

87. A computer programmer
(a) Dies all the thinking for a compute
(b) Can enter input data quickly
(c) Can operate all types of computer equipment
(d) Can draw only flowchart

88. A name or number used to identify a storage location is called
(a) A byte
(b) A record
(c) An address
(d) All of above

89. In a coxial cable, the signal power decreases
(a) but does not depend on the propagation distance
(b) inversely with the propagation distance
(c) exponentially with the propagation distance
(d) linearly with the propagation distance

90. A twisted-pair wire can accommodate a maximum data rate of
(a) 19200 bps
(b) 4800 bps
(c) 9600 bps
(d) 2400 bps

91. Coaxial cables are widely used in
(a) cable TV networks
(b) telephone networks
(c) both in telephone and cable TV networks
(d) computer networks

92. The Width of a processor's data path is measured in bits. Which of the following are common data paths?
(a) 8 bits
(b) 12 bits
(c) 16 bits
(d) 32 bits

93. In satellite communication, uplink frequency differs from the downlink frequency in order to

(a) follow the convention
(b) permit full duplex operation
(c) avoid interference
(d) None of these

94. What type of memory is not directly address-able by the CPU and requires special software called EMS (expanded memory specification)?
(a) Extended   (b) Expanded
(c) Base   (d) Conventional

95. ASK is rarely used in modems because it
(a) takes care of the amplitude only
(b) shifts only between 'on' and 'off' state
(c) is highly susceptible to noise
(d) None of these

96. The original ASCII code used...bits of each byte, reserving that last bit for error checking
(a) 5   (b) 6
(c) 7   (d) 8

97. Channel coding is used to
(a) protect against unnecessary tapping of a signal from the channel
(b) minimise interference in the channel
(c) protect the information against channel noise
(d) secure the channel

98. Which company is the biggest player in the microprocessor industry?
(a) Motorola   (b) IBM
(c) Intel   (d) AMD

99. What is required when more than one person uses a central computer at the same time?
(a) Light pen   (b) Mouse
(c) Digitizer   (d) Terminal

100. A hard copy would be prepared on a
(a) Line printer
(b) Dot matrix Printer
(c) Typewriter terminal
(d) All of the above

ANSWERS

1	2	3	4	5	6	7	8	9	10
(b)	(c)	(d)	(c)	(d)	(c)	(a)	(c)	(a)	(d)
11	**12**	**13**	**14**	**15**	**16**	**17**	**18**	**19**	**20**
(a)	(b)	(a)	(b)	(d)	(a)	(d)	(a)	(a)	(b)
21	**22**	**23**	**24**	**25**	**26**	**27**	**28**	**29**	**30**
(c)	(c)	(c)	(a)	(b)	(a)	(c)	(a)	(d)	(c)
31	**32**	**33**	**34**	**35**	**36**	**37**	**38**	**39**	**40**
(c)	(b)	(c)	(c)	(c)	(a)	(d)	(b)	(a)	(c)
41	**42**	**43**	**44**	**45**	**46**	**47**	**48**	**49**	**50**
(d)	(a)	(a)	(a)	(d)	(c)	(c)	(d)	(b)	(c)
51	**52**	**53**	**54**	**55**	**56**	**57**	**58**	**59**	**60**
(d)	(c)	(a)	(b)	(d)	(b)	(c)	(b)	(b)	(c)
61	**62**	**63**	**64**	**65**	**66**	**67**	**68**	**69**	**70**
(c)	(b)	(b)	(c)	(a)	(c)	(c)	(a)	(a)	(c)
71	**72**	**73**	**74**	**75**	**76**	**77**	**78**	**79**	**80**
(c)	(a)	(b)	(a)	(c)	(d)	(a)	(c)	(d)	(b)
81	**82**	**83**	**84**	**85**	**86**	**87**	**88**	**89**	**90**
(b)	(c)	(b)	(b)	(c)	(a)	(a)	(c)	(c)	(c)
91	**92**	**93**	**94**	**95**	**96**	**97**	**98**	**99**	**100**
(c)	(a)	(d)	(b)	(c)	(c)	(c)	(c)	(d)	(d)

TEST PAPER 7

1. IEEE 802.5 employs
   (a) Differential Manchester coding
   (b) Manchester-II coding
   (c) 50% differential Manchester coding
   (d) Manchester coding

2. Radio broadcasting is a common example of
   (a) TDM   (b) FDM
   (c) both of these   (d) None of these

3. In network terminology, SAP refers to
   (a) simple access protocol
   (b) service access points
   (c) secured application
   (d) service access protocol

4. Which one of the following is the correct structure for ARPANET ?
   (a) 6-layer structure (b) 7-layer structure
   (c) 4-layer structure (d) 3-layer structure

5. Double bit errors can be detected through
   (a) LRC   (b) CRC
   (c) VRC   (d) None of these

6. Most commonly used protocol in DLC (Data Link Control) procedures is
   (a) sliding window with selective repeat
   (b) stop and wait sliding window protocol
   (c) sliding window protocol with go back-N
   (d) sliding window protocol (in general)

7. ATM breaks all traffic into 53-Byte cells because
   (a) 53-Byte cells are the ideal size for the voice communication
   (b) 53-Byte cells are the ideal size for data communication
   (c) 53-Byte cells are the ideal size for circuit switching
   (d) 53-Byte cells are the compromised size for both voice and data communication

8. "Bit Stuffing" is a common technique available in
   (a) Sliding window with go back-N
   (b) Bit oriented protocol
   (c) Sliding window protocol with selective repeat
   (d) Character oriented protocol

9. What gives ATM network the ability to operate at different data rates and why?
   (a) Its short,fixed length cells:Allows the prediction of the size of buffers to be used.
   (b) Its short,fixed length cells:Enables the cells to be transported via different routes.
   (c) Its short,fixed length cells:Short delays for voice traffic.
   (d) it's short,5-Byte header:Less delay for routing the cells.

10. A token ring uses
    (a) Manchester encoding
    (b) Analog modulation encoding
    (c) Differential Manchester encoding
    (d) None of the above

11. Which one of the following types of signal requires the highest bandwidth for transmission?
    (a) Music   (b) Video
    (c) Speech   (d) Facsimile

12. An example of base band data communication may be found in
(a) TV   (b) broadcast radio
(c) telephone   (d) satellite links

13. The advantage of an optical fiber is
(a) low interference   (b) high bandwidth
(c) low attenuation   (d) all of the above

14. Why is ATM the goal for future networking?
(a) It is efficient for data transfer.
(b) It's the only technology suitable for transmission of digital television.
(c) It allows the integration of voice, data and video into one network.
(d) It creates an error free network.

15. Why is Frame Relay's throughput lower than that of ATM?
(a) Frame Relaying have error control(ARQ) functionality but not ATM.
(b) ATM does not need to have CRC checking/generation or bit stuffings functionality in the packets as in Frame Relay.
(c) Frame Relaying needs to do multiplexing of logical channels but not ATM.
(d) Although both Frame relay and ATM have frame boundary recognition (flags), ATM dosen't have bit stuffing as in Frame Relaying.

16. A twisted wire cable cannot be used for the transmission of
(a) digitized voice   (b) analog voice
(c) analog video   (d) None of these

17. Which of the following is done in the physical layer of the ATM network?
(a) Cell multiplexing and demultiplexing
(b) Generic flow control
(c) Transmission frame generation/recovery
(d) Monitoring of the user information field for bit errors and possible corrective actions

18. The following transmission link supports the lowest transmission bandwidth
(a) Wireless links   (b) Coaxial cable
(c) Twisted wire pair (d) Optical fibres

19. ATM is said to be a connection oriented technology. What does this mean and why is it necessary?
(a) Cells travels through the same path to the receiver. By This, cell do not have to be rearranged.
(b) Cells travels through different paths. Therefore cells can reach the receiver faster.
(c) A path is reserved exclusively for one user. Arrangement of cells is not necessary.
(d) Cells are transmitted using fibre optic cables. Cells would be less susceptible to errors.

20. An FSK signal can be demodulated using a / an
(a) low-pass filter
(b) envelope detector
(c) frequency discriminator
(d) All of the above

21. Which of the following is not the function of the AAL?
(a) Cell header generation.
(b) Handling of lost and misinserted cell.
(c) Handling of cell delay variation.
(d) Segmentation and reassembly of user information.

22. The following modulation can be detected by a non-coherent receiver
(a) QPSK   (b) PSK
(c) FSK   (d) None of these

23. Which of the following is not the benefit of an ATM LAN ?
(a) Better performance concerning with delays.
(b) Very high aggregate throughput

   (c) Interconnecting existing LANs
   (d) Simpler control and network management.

24. What advantage does ATM have over STM ?
   (a) Unlike ATM, time slots provided by STM for a particular user cannot be grabbed by another user.
   (b) It is cheaper to implement.
   (c) ATM is suitable for real time traffic but not ATM
   (d) Time slots for STM occurs at regular intervals.

25. Which of the following is not true about the difference of B-ISDN as compared to ISDN?
   (a) B-ISDN provides for communication services with very high bit rate requirements such as digital television
   (b) B-ISDN uses optical fibre cable whereas ISDN makes use of the existing infrastructure.
   (c) B-ISDN uses only packet switching whereas ISDN does not perform packet switching.
   (d) The bit rate for ISDN is prespecified unlike B-ISDN

26. The _______ is the physical path over which a message travels.
   (a) Protocol   (b) Medium
   (c) Signal   (d) All the above

27. When an analog signal, which is band limited to 5 kHz, is to be transmitted using an 8-bit PCM encoder, the minimum data rate required is
   (a) 8 kbits / sec   (b) 16 kbits / sec
   (c) 8 kbits / sec   (d) 64 kbits / sec

28. Information to be communicated in a data communications system is the _______.
   (a) Medium   (b) Protocol
   (c) Message   (d) Transmission

29. An example of full duplex transmission is a
   (a) telephone channel

   (b) satellite channel
   (c) graphics channel
   (d) None of these

30. An example of half duplex transmission is a
   (a) broadcast radio
   (b) satellite channel
   (c) telephone channel
   (d) None of these

31. Frequency of failure and network recovery time after a failure are measures of the _______ of a network.
   (a) Performance   (b) Reliability
   (c) Security   (d) Feasibility

32. An unauthorized user is a network _______ issue.
   (a) Performance   (b) Reliability
   (c) Security   (d) All the above

33. Which topology requires a central controller or hub?
   (a) Mesh   (b) Star
   (c) Bus   (d) Ring

34. The lowest optical signal attenuation, in a fibre made of para silica, is obtained at
   (a) 1300 nm   (b) 1100 nm
   (c) 800 nm   (d) 1500 nm

35. Single mode fibers have the following advantage over multimode fibers
   (a) lower cost
   (b) lower dispersion
   (c) lower attenuation
   (d) easier to manufacture

36. A graded index fibre has the following advantage over a step index fibre
   (a) lower cost
   (b) lower dispersion
   (c) lower attenuation
   (d) easier to manufacture

37. A laser diode has the following advantage over the LED as a fiber optic source
   (a) high directivity

(b) coherent optical output
(c) high power
(d) All of these

38. The intrinsic layer in a PIN photodiode is used for
(a) reducing noise at the receiver
(b) increasing light absorption
(c) increasing bandwidth of the receiver
(d) None of these

39. Which topology requires a multipoint connection?
(a) Mesh   (b) Star
(c) Bus   (d) Ring

40. The following can support highest rates of data transmission
(a) A coaxial cable
(b) A graded-index multi-mode fiber
(c) A step-index multi-mode fiber
(d) A single mode fiber

41. Communication between a computer and a keyboard involves __________ transmission.
(a) simplex   (b) half-duplex
(c) full-duplex   (d) automatic

42. A television broadcast is an example of _______ transmission.
(a) simplex   (b) half-duplex
(c) full-duplex   (d) automatic

43. A _______ connection provides a dedicated link between two devices.
(a) point-to-point   (b) multipoint
(c) primary   (d) secondary

44. Dispersion-shifted fibres are made by the use of specific reference index profiles to change the following properties of a fibre
(a) material dispersion
(b) waveguide dispersion
(c) intermodel dispersion
(d) attenuation

45. The cladding layer in an optical fibre is used for

(a) providing protection to the fibre
(b) providing better dispersion properties
(c) confining the optical signal within the core
(d) providing better attenuation properties

46. The numerical aperture of an optical fibre gives a measure of its
(a) thickness
(b) core refractive index
(c) cladding refractive index
(d) light gathering capability of the fibre

47. A laser diode source is used with a non-zero extinction ratio for
(a) higher lifetime of the laser
(b) simpler driving circuit
(c) lower noise figure at the receiver
(d) higher speed of operation

48. Carrier recovery is usually difficult in a satellite communication system because of
(a) high frequency of transmission
(b) signal fading
(c) large distance
(d) lower power in the satellite

49. In a telephone network, an echo may be introduced at the
(a) switch
(b) multiplexer
(c) transmission cable
(d) hybrid

50. In a _______ connection, more than two devices can share a single link.
(a) point-to-point   (b) multipoint
(c) primary   (d) secondary

51. In _______ transmission, the channel capacity is shared by both communicating devices at all times.
(a) simplex   (b) half-duplex
(c) full-duplex   (d) half-simplex

52. The following is not a part of a FAX transmitter

(a) PCM encoder
(b) scanning
(c) data compaction
(d) digital modulation

53. In time division multiplexing of n channels, each having a data rate of R kb / sec, the multiplexed signal will have a nett bit rate of
(a) nR kb / sec
(b) slightly more than nR kb / sec
(c) 2nR kb / sec
(d) slightly more than 2nR kb / sec

54. The overhead in a time division multiplexed signal is required for
(a) synchronisation   (b) error control
(c) clock recovery   (d) None of these

55. If sufficient channel separation is used in a frequency division multiplexing system, the effect is
(a) intersymbol interference
(b) intermodulation
(c) echo
(d) cross-talk

56. A satellite must be equipped with a
(a) tunable receiver
(b) baseband receiver
(c) narrow band receiver
(d) wideband receiver

57. In the original ARPANET, ________ were directly connected together.
(a) IMPs   (b) hostcomputers
(c) networks   (d) routers

58. Satellite-to-ground communication takes place through the
(a) short wave   (b) medium wave
(c) microwave   (d) optical signals

59. Sampling a bandlimited signals, at less than twice its maximum frequency causes
(a) aliasing
(b) intermodulation
(c) time jitter
(d) redundancy in the samples

60. The objective of a time-sharing operating system is to
(a) maximise processor utilisation
(b) minimise the net execution time
(c) minimise the user response time
(d) None of the above

61. The objective of a multiprogramming operating system is to
(a) minimise the user response time
(b) maximise processor utilisation
(c) minimise the net execution time
(d) None of the above

62. UNIX is an example of
(a) real time sharing system
(b) time sharing operating system
(c) batch processing operating system
(d) None of these

63. In UNIX terminology, a process is a
(a) program in execution
(b) subprogram, which can be called from other programs
(c) sequence of commands, which are to be given in order to run a program
(d) None of these

64. An operating system is a software, which
(a) helps the operators who are maintaining a computer system
(b) helps other programs run
(c) helps in resources management
(d) is run to recover lost data when power failure occurs

65. The functions of the fork system call is to
(a) change the standard output to a specified device
(b) create a another copy of the process, which are then, executed concurrently
(c) split a process into several parts
(d) None of the above

66. ________ are special-interest groups that quickly test, evaluate, and standardize new technologies.

(a) Forums
(b) Regulatory agencies
(c) Standards organizations
(d) All of the above

67. _______ is the protocol suite for the current Internet.
(a) TCP/IP
(b) NCP
(c) UNIX
(d) ACM

68. The binary equivalent of 63 is
(a) 0110   0011
(b) 0111   1110
(c) 0111   0001
(d) None of these

69. The maximum and minimum numbers (unsigned) that can be stored in one 8-bit word is
(a) −128 and 127
(b) 0 and 255
(c) 0 and 99
(d) 0 and 127

70. _______ refers to the structure or format of the data, meaning the order in which they are presented.
(a) Semantics
(b) Syntax
(c) Timing
(d) All of the above

71. Almost all computers store characters strings
(a) as sequences of ASCII coded binary strings
(b) as sequences of integers indicating the position of the characters in the alphabetical sequence
(c) in a BCD code
(d) None of the above

72. _______ defines how a particular pattern to be interpreted, and what action is to be taken based on that interpretation.
(a) Semantics
(b) Syntax
(c) Timing
(d) None of the above

73. _______ refers to two characteristics: when data should be sent and how fast it can be sent.
(a) Semantics
(b) Syntax
(c) Timing
(d) none of the above

74. In UNIX the command to redirect the output of a program (say, sort) to a file called sort.out is
(a) sort sort.out
(b) sort -> sort.out
(c) sort > sort.out
(d) None of these

75. The instruction of a program, which is currently being executed is sorted in
(a) Read-only memory
(b) Main memory
(c) Secondary memory
(d) None of these

76. The programming language FORTRAN is mainly used for
(a) data processing applications
(b) scientific applications
(c) real-time applications
(d) None of the above

77. In the programming language C
(a) variable names are case-sensitive
(b) blanks can be given within a variable name
(c) there are no reserved words, which are not allowed as variable names
(d) None of the above

78. The functions of the UNIX system calls are to
(a) request for service(s) offered by the operating system kernel
(b) a signal generated by the operating system for signalling an error
(c) a mechanism through which, one program can call another
(d) None of the above

79. The UNIX command "ls | more" displays a list of
(a) all the files in the current directory and then, waits for the next command
(b) files In the current directory one screen at a time
(c) files in the current directory one line at a time
(d) None of the above

80. The UNIX command "cat *xyz* | grep computer"
(*a*) counts number of times the string computer appears in file *xyz*
(*b*) displays all lines in file *xyz* containing the string computer
(*c*) adds the string computer to the end of the file *xyz*
(*d*) None of the above

81. The UNIX command "a.out \ &" runs the program a.out
(*a*) only when no other process is running on the system
(*b*) with highest priority
(*c*) in the background
(*d*) None of the above

82. In a typical operating system, shell is a program, which
(*a*) reads a command line from the standard input and interprets it according to a fixed set of rules
(*b*) helps in the efficient running of a program
(*c*) is a framework into which, functions or utilities can be added when required
(*d*) None of the above

83. __________ refers to the physical or logical arrangement of a network.
(*a*) Data flow
(*b*) Mode of operation
(*c*) Topology
(*d*) None of the above

84. Suppose that the current directory is /home / user / *xyz* / prog. A possible command to change to a directory / home / user / *abc* / letters is
(*a*) cd ../ ../ abc / letters
(*b*) cd . / home / user / *abc* / letters
(*c*) cd . / . / *abc* /letters
(*d*) None of the above

85. Devices may be arranged in a ______ topology.

(*a*) mesh
(*b*) ring
(*c*) bus
(*d*) all of the above

86. __________ is an idea or concept that is a precursor to an Internet standard.
(*a*) RCF
(*b*) RFC
(*c*) ID
(*d*) none of the above

87. Which of the following printers are you sure will not to use if your objective is to print on multi carbon forms?
(*a*) Daisy wheel
(*b*) Dot matrix
(*c*) Laser
(*d*) Thimble

88. The personal computer industry was started by
(*a*) IBM
(*b*) Apple
(*c*) Compaq
(*d*) HCL

89. The include directive in C is used to
(*a*) specify a list of files from where data will be read at the time of execution
(*b*) include header files in a program
(*c*) link other object modules to the current program at the time of compilation
(*d*) None of the above

90. In C, the statement out = fopen("test.dat", r)
(*a*) opens an existing file called test.dat in read mode, and assigns the file pointer to out
(*b*) creates a new file called test.dat into which, data will be read in, and assigns the file pointer to out
(*c*) reads the contents of the file test.dat and stores it in out
(*d*) None of the above

91. The "chmod" command in UNIX
(*a*) changes the current execution status from user mode to kernel mode
(*b*) makes a file hidden so that it cannot be seen using the ls command
(*c*) changes the access permissions of a file or directory
(*d*) None of the above

92. If in a computer, 16 bits are used to specify address in a RAM, the number of addresses will be
(a) 216
(b) 65,536
(c) 64K
(d) Any of the above

93. Which was the most popular first generation computer?
(a) IBM 1650   (b) IBM 360
(c) IBM 1130   (d) IBM 2700

94. In UNIX, mounting a file system means
(a) loading a file system from backup medium like tape
(b) moving all the files from one file system to another
(c) copying all the files from one file system to another
(d) providing a link to the file system to be mounted so that it appears as a local subdirectory

95. The correct order of the storage devices main memory, tape and disk in an increasing order of access time is
(a) disk, tape, main, memory
(b) disk, main, memory, tape
(c) main, memory, tape, disk
(d) main memory, disk, tape

96. Which of the following memories allows simultaneous read and write operations?
(a) ROM   (b) RAM
(c) EPROM   (d) None of above

97. A 32 bit microprocessor has the word length equal to
(a) 2 byte   (b) 32 byte
(c) 4 byte   (d) 8 byte

98. In terms of print quality a / an
(a) laser printer is better than an ink-jet printer, which is better than a dot-matrix printer
(b) laser printer is better than a dot-matrix printer, which is better than an ink-jet printer
(c) ink-jet printer is better than a laser printer, which is better than a dot-matrix printer
(d) None of these

99. A set of information that defines the status of resources allocated to a process is
(a) Process control   (b) ALU
(c) Register Unit   (d) Process description

100. The MSDOS operating system is a
(a) distributed operating system
(b) single user operating system
(c) time sharing operating system
(d) None of the above

ANSWERS

1	2	3	4	5	6	7	8	9	10
(c)	(b)	(b)	(c)	(b)	(c)	(d)	(b)	(a)	(c)
11	**12**	**13**	**14**	**15**	**16**	**17**	**18**	**19**	**20**
(b)	(c)	(d)	(c)	(b)	(c)	(c)	(c)	(a)	(c)
21	**22**	**23**	**24**	**25**	**26**	**27**	**28**	**29**	**30**
(a)	(c)	(a)	(a)	(c)	(b)	(d)	(c)	(a)	(b)
31	**32**	**33**	**34**	**35**	**36**	**37**	**38**	**39**	**40**
(b)	(c)	(c)	(d)	(b)	(b)	(d)	(b)	(c)	(d)
41	**42**	**43**	**44**	**45**	**46**	**47**	**48**	**49**	**50**
(a)	(a)	(a)	(b)	(c)	(d)	(d)	(b)	(d)	(b)

51	52	53	54	55	56	57	58	59	60
(c)	(a)	(b)	(a)	(d)	(d)	(a)	(c)	(a)	(c)
61	62	63	64	65	66	67	68	69	70
(b)	(b)	(a)	(b)	(b)	(a)	(a)	(d)	(b)	(b)
71	72	73	74	75	76	77	78	79	80
(a)	(a)	(c)	(c)	(b)	(b)	(a)	(a)	(b)	(b)
81	82	83	84	85	86	87	88	89	90
(c)	(a)	(c)	(a)	(d)	(b)	(c)	(a)	(b)	(a)
91	92	93	94	95	96	97	98	99	100
(c)	(b)	(a)	(d)	(d)	(b)	(c)	(a)	(d)	(b)

____

1. An error in the program logic can be detected
   (a) by the operating system
   (b) by the compiler
   (c) during execution of the program
   (d) None of the above

2. The shut down procedure must be run in a UNIX system before switching off the power because
   (a) otherwise, the file system may become inconsistent
   (b) all users must informed that the system is being switched off
   (c) the power to the disk and display units must be shut off first
   (d) None of the above

3. What command would you use to change your password in a UNIX system ?
   (a) pass
   (b) passwd
   (c) chpass
   (d) set pass

4. The memory address of the first element of an array is called
   (a) floor address
   (b) foundation address
   (c) first address
   (d) base address

5. The memory address of fifth element of an array can be calculated by the formula
   (a) LOC(Array[5] = Base (Array) + w(5-lower bound), where w is the number of words per memory cell for the array
   (b) LOC(Array[5]) = Base (Array[5]) + (5-lower bound), where w is the number of words per memory cell for the array
   (c) LOC(Array[5]) = Base (Array[4]) + (5-Upper bound), where w is the number of words per memory cell for the array
   (d) None of above

6. What are the three types of files in the UNIX system?
   (a) Regular files, directories, device files
   (b) Regular disk files, special files, device files
   (c) Tape files, directories, special files
   (d) None of the above

7. Which UNIX command provides the type of information contained in a particular file?
   (a) more filename
   (b) type filename
   (c) file filename
   (d) None of these

8. In UNIX, full pathname originates from
   (a) your home directory
   (b) the root directory
   (c) your working directory
   (d) None of these

9. Which of the following data structures are indexed structures?
   (a) linear arrays
   (b) linked lists
   (c) both of above
   (d) none of above

10. Which one of the following is not a basic data type in C?
    (a) Integer
    (b) Complex
    (c) Character
    (d) None of these

11. Which ones of the following statements are true in the context of symbolic links?
    (a) can be made to a directory
    (b) The file can be accessed through the symbolic link even after the original file has been deleted

(c) The creation of each symbolic link causes the link count to be incremented

(d) None of the above

12. Which one of the following commands will you use to copy files from a remote UNIX system to your local UNIX system?
(a) cp
(b) finger
(c) telnet
(d) rcp

13. Which of the following is not the required condition for binary search algorithm?
(a) The list must be sorted
(b) there should be the direct access to the middle element in any sublist
(c) There must be mechanism to delete and/ or insert elements in list
(d) none of the above

14. Which of the following is not a limitation of binary search algorithm?
(a) must use a sorted array
(b) requirement of sorted array is expensive when a lot of insertion and deletions are needed
(c) there must be a mechanism to access middle element directly
(d) binary search algorithm is not efficient when the data elements are more than 1000.

15. A variable P is called pointer if
(a) P contains the address of an element in DATA.
(b) P points to the address of first element in DATA
(c) P can store only memory addresses
(d) P contain the DATA and the address of DATA

16. The file / usr / lib crontab is a handy place to put files that are to be run
(a) at the highest execution priority
(b) each time a user logs out of the system
(c) each time a user logs into the system
(d) periodically by the system at a specific time and date

17. The file / etc / motd contains a message, which is to be displayed on the screen
(a) whenever the number of user logged on exceeds a certain threshold
(b) each time a user logs out of the system
(c) each time a user logs into the system
(d) periodically by the system at a specific time and date

18. The primary purpose of the pr command is to
(a) print files to the default printer
(b) format print pages for standard output
(c) provide a list of print requests in the printer queue
(d) None of the above

19. Which command is used to remove a print job from the printer queue?
(a) lprm
(b) lpq
(c) lpstat
(d) None of these

20. The command to take a backup of files and directories on a magnetic tape is
(a) tar -xv
(b) tar -tv
(c) tar -cv
(d) None of these

21. Which of the following data structure can't store the non-homogeneous data elements?
(a) Arrays
(b) Records
(c) Pointers
(d) None of these

22. The command to list files and directories stored in a magnetic tape is
(a) tar - xv
(b) tar - tv
(c) rat - cv
(d) None of these

23. Each data item in a record may be a group item composed of sub-items; those items which are indecomposable are called
(a) elementary items
(b) atoms
(c) scalars
(d) all of the above

24. The hidden files in UNIX
(a) have a special status bit associated with the file descriptor
(b) have names starting with a dot

(c) can be accessed only by the operating system kernel

(d) None of the above

25. The grep command in UNIX is used to
(a) sort the records of a given file
(b) search a file for the presence of a given string
(c) globally replace a string by another
(d) None of the above

26. The following is not a UNIX shell
(a) Bourne shell   (b) C shell
(c) Kron shell   (d) Perl shell

27. Two main measures for the efficiency of an algorithm are
(a) Processor and memory
(b) Complexity and capacity
(c) Time and space
(d) Data and space

28. The priority of a process can be increased through the
(a) pr command   (b) renice command
(c) proc command   (d) None of these

29. The priority of a process can be increased only by
(a) the user who has started the process
(b) any user presently logged into the system
(c) the superuser
(d) None of the above

30. The default shell, which is to be used when a user logs in, is defined in the
(a) / etc / passwd file
(b) / etc / shell file
(c) startup file in the user home directory
(d) None of these

31. A write permission to a directory allows a user to
(a) execute any file located in the directory
(b) edit any file located in the directory
(c) search a directory for the presence of a file
(d) None of these

32. The execute permission to a directory allows a user to
(a) execute any file located in the directory
(b) edit any file located in the directory
(c) search a directory for the presence of a file
(d) None of the above

33. Information about a file is stored in
(a) a system-wide file table
(b) the inode associated with the file
(c) a file allocation table within the kernel
(d) None of the above

34. The time factor when determining the efficiency of algorithm is measured by
(a) Counting microseconds
(b) Counting the number of key operations
(c) Counting the number of statements
(d) Counting the kilobytes of algorithm

35. The space factor when determining the efficiency of algorithm is measured by
(a) Counting the maximum memory needed by the algorithm
(b) Counting the minimum memory needed by the algorithm
(c) Counting the average memory needed by the algorithm
(d) Counting the maximum disk space needed by the algorithm

36. The UNIX system calls are used to
(a) informs the system administrator about an abnormal situation
(b) obtain some service from the kernel
(c) execute a Unix command from a shell script
(d) None of the above

37. The Worst case occur in linear search algorithm when
(a) Item is somewhere in the middle of the array
(b) Item is not in the array at all
(c) Item is the last element in the array

(*d*) Item is the last element in the array or is not there at all

38. The command used to copy a file from remote machine to a local machine, in ftp is
(*a*) get
(*b*) copy
(*c*) rep
(*d*) bring

39. In UNIX, the free data blocks are arranged
(*a*) as a linked list
(*b*) as an array
(*c*) sequentially
(*d*) None of these

40. The comm -12 f1 f2 prints lines
(*a*) in file f1 only
(*b*) common in both files
(*c*) in file f2 only
(*d*) not common in files

41. The excessive movement of page back and forth between memory and disk is called
(*a*) fragmentation
(*b*) page fault
(*c*) thrashing
(*d*) flashing

42. The Average case occur in linear search algorithm
(*a*) When Item is somewhere in the middle of the array
(*b*) When Item is not in the array at all
(*c*) When Item is the last element in the array
(*d*) When Item is the last element in the array or is not there at all

43. Protected data members can be accessed
(*a*) only from the base class itself
(*b*) both from the base class and its derived classes
(*c*) from the class, which is a friend of the base class
(*d*) none of the above is correct

44. Public data member can be accessed
(*a*) only from the base class itself
(*b*) both from the base class and its derived classes
(*c*) from the class, which is a friend of the base class
(*d*) none of the above are correct

45. The complexity of the average case of an algorithm is
(*a*) Much more complicated to analyze than that of worst case
(*b*) Much more simpler to analyze than that of worst case
(*c*) Sometimes more complicated and some other times simpler than that of worst case
(*d*) None of the above

46. The complexity of linear search algorithm is
(*a*) $O(n)$
(*b*) $O(\log n)$
(*c*) $O(n^2)$
(*d*) $O(n \log n)$

47. The complexity of Binary search algorithm is
(*a*) $O(n)$
(*b*) $O(\log)$
(*c*) $O(n^2)$
(*d*) $O(n \log n)$

48. The complexity of Bubble sort algorithm is
(*a*) $O(n)$
(*b*) $O(\log n)$
(*c*) $O(n^2)$
(*d*) $O(n \log n)$

49. A command which informs the user automatically about arrival of new mail, is
(*a*) mailcheck
(*b*) notify
(*c*) rmail
(*d*) mailx

50. The difference between linear array and a record is
(*a*) An array is suitable for homogeneous data but the data items in a record may have different data type
(*b*) In a record, there may not be a natural ordering in opposed to linear array.
(*c*) A record form a hierarchical structure but a lienear array does not
(*d*) All of the above

51. The prime factor of numbers can be obtained by using the command
(*a*) prime
(*b*) prmfact
(*c*) factor
(*d*) factorise

52. Which of the following statement is false?
(*a*) Arrays are dense lists and static data structure

(b) data elements in linked list need not be stored in adjacent space in memory

(c) pointers store the next data element of a list

(d) linked lists are collection of the nodes that contain information part and next pointer

53. When new data are to be inserted into a data structure, but there is no available space; this situation is usually called
(a) underflow
(b) overflow
(c) housefull
(d) saturated

54. A big file can be broken into smaller files using
(a) break
(b) split
(c) divide
(d) bifrcate

55. In order to store the current terminal session in a file, we use the command
(a) screen
(b) termstor
(c) session
(d) script

56. The command to be used to remove inconsistencies in a file system is
(a) fsclean
(b) fsck
(c) clearfs
(d) mkfs

57. The default sh in UNIX OS is
(a) jsh
(b) csh
(c) bourne shell
(d) ksh

58. The command, which takes inputs from the user, interprets it and takes necessary actions is
(a) kernel
(b) system calls
(c) sh
(d) scheduler

59. The situation when in a linked list START = NULL is
(a) underflow
(b) overflow
(c) housefull
(d) saturated

60. Upon changing the permissions of a file, the following field is modified
(a) File modify time
(b) Inode modification time
(c) File access time
(d) None of the above

61. Its main job is to allocate CPU to processes
(a) login
(b) shell
(c) getty
(d) scheduler

62. In C++, a function contained within a class is called a/an
(a) member function
(b) operator
(c) class function
(d) method

63. Which one of the following are good reasons to use an object oriented language?
(a) You can define your own data types
(b) Program statements are simpler than they are in procedural languages
(c) An OO program can be taught to correct its own errors
(d) It's easier to conceptualise an OO program

64. When a language has the capacity to produce a new data type, it is said to be
(a) reprehensible
(b) encapsulated
(c) overloaded
(d) extensible

65. A normal C++ operator that acts in a special way on newly defined data types is said to be
(a) glorified
(b) encapsulated
(c) classified
(d) overloaded

66. main() returns a value of type
(a) real
(b) character
(c) int
(d) null

67. Sharing of common information is achieved by the concept of
(a) virtual copying
(b) inheritance
(c) encapsulation
(d) None of these

68. Memorising the new terms used in C++ is
(a) critically important
(b) something you can do later
(c) vital for making good programs
(d) completely irrelevant

69. An expression
  (a) usually evaluates to a numerical value
  (b) indicates the emotional state of the program
  (c) always occurs outside a function
  (d) may be a part of a statement

70. In a loop with a multi-statement loop body, semicolons should appear following
  (a) the for statement itself
  (b) the closing brace in a multi-statement loop body
  (c) each statement within the loop body
  (d) the test expression

71. A variable defined within a block is visible
  (a) from the point of definition onwards in the program
  (b) from the point of definition onwards in the function
  (c) from the point of definition onwards in the block
  (d) throughout the function

72. The library function exit() causes an exit from
  (a) the loop in which, it occurs
  (b) the block in which, it occurs
  (c) the function in which, it occurs
  (d) the program in which, it occurs

73. The getch() library
  (a) returns a character when any key is pressed
  (b) returns a charactr when ENTER is pressed
  (c) displays a character on the screen when a key is pressed
  (d) does not display a character on the screen

74. Which of the following name does not relate to stacks?
  (a) FIFO lists
  (b) LIFO list
  (c) Piles
  (d) Push-down lists

75. When inorder traversing a tree resulted E A C K F H D B G; the preorder traversal would return
  (a) FAEKCDBHG
  (b) FAEKCDHGB
  (c) EAFKHDCBG
  (d) FEAKDCHBG

76. The && and | | operators
  (a) compare two numeric values
  (b) combine two numeric values
  (c) compare two Boolean values
  (d) combine two Boolean values

77. The break statement causes an exit
  (a) only from the innermost loop
  (b) only from the innermost switch
  (c) from all the loops and switches
  (d) from the innermost loop or switch

78. The goto statement causes control to go to
  (a) an operator
  (b) a label
  (c) a variable
  (d) a function

79. The complexity of merge sort algorithm is
  (a) $O(n)$
  (b) $O(\log n)$
  (c) $O(n^2)$
  (d) $O(n \log n)$

80. Which of the following data structure is linear data structure?
  (a) Trees
  (b) Graphs
  (c) Arrays
  (d) None of these

81. The operation of processing each element in the list is known as
  (a) Sorting
  (b) Merging
  (c) Inserting
  (d) Traversal

82. A function argument is
  (a) a variable in the function that receives a value from the calling program
  (b) a way that functions resist accepting the calling program's values
  (c) a value sent to the function by the calling program
  (d) a value returned by the function to the calling program

83. : : is known as
  (a) scope resolution operator
  (b) global operator
  (c) both (a) & (b)
  (d) none of these

84. Arrays are best data structures
   (a) for relatively permanent collections of data
   (b) for the size of the structure and the data in the structure are constantly changing
   (c) for both of above situation
   (d) for none of above situation

85. When an argument is passed by reference
   (a) a variable is created in the function to hold the argument's value
   (b) the function cannot access the argument's value
   (c) a temporary variable is created in the calling program to hold the argument's value
   (d) the function acceses the argument's original value in the calling program

86. Linked lists are best suited
   (a) for relatively permanent collections of data
   (b) for the size of the structure and the data in the structure are constantly changing
   (c) for both of above situation
   (d) for none of above situation

87. Overload functions
   (a) are a group of functions with the same name
   (b) all have the same number and types of arguments
   (c) make life simpler for programmer
   (d) may fail unexpectedly due to stress

88. The default argument has a value that
   (a) may be supplied by the calling program
   (b) may be supplied by the function
   (c) must have a constant value
   (d) must have a variable value

89. A static automatic variable is used to
   (a) make a variable visible to several function
   (b) make a variable visible to only one function
   (c) converse memory when a function is not executing

   (d) retain a value when a function is not executing

90. In a class specifier, data or function designed private are accessible
   (a) to any function in the program
   (b) only if you know the password
   (c) to member functions of that class
   (d) only to public members of the class

91. Each array declaration need not give, implicitly or explicitly, the information about
   (a) the name of array
   (b) the data type of array
   (c) the first data from the set to be stored
   (d) the index set of the array

92. A member function can always access the data
   (a) in the object of which, it is a member
   (b) in the class of which, it is a member
   (c) in any object of the class of which, it is a member
   (d) in the public part of its class

93. Classes are useful because they
   (a) are removed from memory when not in use
   (b) permits data to be hidden from other classes
   (c) bring together all aspects of an entity in one place
   (d) can closely model objects in the real world

94. Element double Array[7] is which element of the array?
   (a) The sixth one   (b) The seventh one
   (c) The eight one   (d) Impossible to tell

95. The elements of an array are stored successively in memory cells because
   (a) by this way computer can keep track only the address of the first element and the addresses of other elements can be calculated
   (b) the architecture of computer memory does not allow arrays to store other than serially

(c) both the above

(d) none of the above

96. When an array name is passed to a function, the function

(a) accesses exactly the same array as the calling program

(b) accesses a copy of the array passes by the program

(c) refers to the array using the same name as was used by the calling program

(d) refers to the array using a different name from that was used by the calling program

97. In a stack, data items placed on the stack first are

(a) not given an index number

(b) given the index number 0

(c) the first data items to be removed

(d) the last data items to be removed

98. Registers, which are partially visible to users and used to hold conditional, are known as

(a) PC

(b) Memory address registers

(c) General purpose register

(d) Flags

99. Operator overloading is

(a) making C++ operators work with objects

(b) giving C++ operators more than they can handle

(c) giving new meaning to existing C++ operators

(d) making new C++ operators

100. Private data members can be accessed

(a) only from the base class itself

(b) both from the base class and from its derived classes

(c) from the class, which is a friend of the base class

(d) None of these is correct

ANSWERS

1	2	3	4	5	6	7	8	9	10
(c)	(b)	(b)	(d)	(a)	(d)	(c)	(c)	(a)	(d)
11	12	13	14	15	16	17	18	19	20
(b)	(c)	(c)	(d)	(a)	(a)	(d)	(c)	(b)	(a)
21	22	23	24	25	26	27	28	29	30
(a)	(a)	(d)	(d)	(b)	(d)	(c)	(c)	(b)	(c)
31	32	33	34	35	36	37	38	39	40
(a)	(a)	(b)	(b)	(c)	(b)	(d)	(a)	(a)	(b)
41	42	43	44	45	46	47	48	49	50
(c)	(a)	(b)	(c)	(a)	(a)	(b)	(c)	(b)	(d)
51	52	53	54	55	56	57	58	59	60
(c)	(c)	(b)	(b)	(d)	(b)	(c)	(c)	(a)	(b)
61	62	63	64	65	66	67	68	69	70
(d)	(a)	(a)	(d)	(d)	(d)	(b)	(c)	(d)	(c)
71	72	73	74	75	76	77	78	79	80
(c)	(d)	(a)	(a)	(b)	(c)	(a)	(b)	(d)	(c)
81	82	83	84	85	86	87	88	89	90
(d)	(c)	(c)	(a)	(a)	(b)	(a)	(c)	(c)	(c)
91	92	93	94	95	96	97	98	99	100
(c)	(b)	(b)	(c)	(a)	(b)	(d)	(c)	(c)	(b)

1. The worst case efficiency of this search is n
   (a) Sequential search (b) Indexed search
   (c) Binary search   (d) None of these

2. Which one is not a hashing technique?
   (a) Mid square
   (b) Folding
   (c) Division remainder method
   (d) All are hashing techniques

3. Every time attribute A appears, it is matched with the same value of attribute B, but not the same value of attribute C. Therefore, it is true that:
   (a) $A \rightarrow B$ (b) $A \rightarrow C$
   (c) $A \rightarrow B, C$ (d) $B, C \rightarrow C$

4. Extra space in each record is kept for this collision processing method
   (a) Quadratic collision processing
   (b) Linked collision processing
   (c) Linear collision processing
   (d) None of these

5. The different classes of relations created by the technique for preventing modification anomalies are called:
   (a) normal forms.
   (b) referential integrity constraints.
   (c) functional dependencies.
   (d) None of the above is correct.

6. A relation is in this form if it is in BCNF and has no multivalued dependencies:
   (a) second normal form.
   (b) third normal form.
   (c) fourth normal form.
   (d) domain/key normal form.

7. In which case, adjacency list representation of a graph is not useful ?
   (a) In breadth first traversal
   (b) When the number of vertices is changing due to insertion and / or deletion
   (c) When the number of edges is small
   (d) It is useful in all these cases

8. Which method of traversal uses queue to hold nodes that are waiting to be processed?
   (a) Breadth first   (b) D-search
   (c) Depth first   (d) None of these

9. Which method of traversal does not use a stack to hold nodes that are waiting to be processed?
   (a) Breadth first   (b) D-search
   (c) Depth first   (d) None of these

10. Pattern matching refers to
   (a) finding the position where a string pattern P first appears in a given string Q
   (b) checking whether a pattern P occurs in a given string Q
   (c) checking whether two strings are identical
   (d) None of these

11. Row is synonymous with the term:
   (a) record   (b) relation
   (c) column   (d) field

12. The primary key is selected from the:
   (a) composite keys
   (b) determinants
   (c) candidate keys
   (d) foreign keys

13. A suitable structure for Breadth First and Depth First traversal of graphs is
   (a) Edge listing   (b) Adjacency matrix
   (c) Adjacency list   (d) None of these

14. In this type of search, keys must be ordered
   (a) Hashing   (b) Sequential search
   (c) Binary search   (d) None of these

15. This search method requires that all keys reside in internal memory
   (a) Binary search   (b) Hashing
   (c) Sequential search   (d) None of these

16. In this sorting method, a file is divided into subfiles which are to be independently sorted and then, merged
   (a) Bubble sort   (b) Heap sort
   (c) Quick sort   (d) None of these

17. With this method of string representation, the problem of garbage collection arises
   (a) Linked list method
   (b) Index table method
   (c) Fixed length method
   (d) None of these

18. Back tracking is another name for this method of traversal
   (a) Depth first   (b) D-search
   (c) Breadth first   (d) None of these

19. What is not true for the adjacency matrix of a graph?
   (a) It is a symmetric matrix
   (b) The diagonal has all zeros
   (c) It is a bit matrix
   (d) All are true statements

20. Which of the following is a group of one or more attributes that uniquely identifies a row?
   (a) Key   (b) Determinant
   (c) Tuple   (d) Relation

21. When the values in one or more attributes being used as a foreign key must exist in another set of one or more attributes in another table, we have created a(n):
   (a) transitive dependency
   (b) insertion anomaly
   (c) referential integrity constraint
   (d) normal form

22. A relation is considered a:
   (a) Column
   (b) one-dimensional table
   (c) two-dimensional table
   (d) three-dimensional table

23. Which one of the following is an example of a linear data structure?
   (a) linked list   (b) graph
   (c) binary tree   (d) trees

24. Dynamic storage allocations cannot be used in C without
   (a) files
   (b) unions
   (c) pointers
   (d) enumerated data types

25. Average case time complexity of the quicksort algorithm is more than
   (a) $O(Nlog_2N)$ (b) $O(N^2)$
   (c) $O(NlnN)$ (d) $O(N^3)$

26. Worst case time complexity of the heap-sort algorithm is
   (a) $O(Nlog_2N)$ (b) $O(N^3)$
   (c) $O(N^2)$ (d) $O(NlnN)$

27. A sparse matrix is better represented using a /an
   (a) stack   (b) binary tree
   (c) multi-linked list (d) array

28. Which of the following is not a restriction for a table to be a relation?
   (a) The cells of the table must contain a single value.
   (b) All of the entries in any column must be of the same kind.
   (c) The columns must be ordered.
   (d) No two rows in a table may be identical.

29. A binary tree, with the property that the key stored at each node is greater than those stored in its children, is a
(a) binary search tree
(b) heap
(c) AVL tree
(d) None of these

30. Row major ordering of a rectangular array means that
(a) greatest element of each row is stored first in memory
(b) rows are stored in a sequence starting from the first element
(c) columns are stored before rows
(d) none of the above

31. For some relations, changing the data can have undesirable consequences called:
(a) referential integrity constraints
(b) modification anomalies
(c) normal forms
(d) transitive dependencies

32. The technique of linear probing for collision resolution can lead to
(a) clustering
(b) efficient storage utilisation
(c) radix sort
(d) overflow

33. In C, it is best to implement chained hash table as an array of
(a) structures
(b) string
(c) pointers
(d) None of these

34. For sorting a contiguous list of records, quicksort may be preferred over mergesort because
(a) some programming languages do not support recursion
(b) it does not require extra space for an auxilliary storage
(c) it requires more programming effort
(d) it always requires less time

35. In Quicksort, a desirable choice for the partitioning element will be
(a) first element of the list
(b) a randomly chosen element of the list
(c) median of the list
(d) last element of the list

36. Recursion provides an attractive mechanism for designing efficient program for
(a) computing square root of a number
(b) generating n!
(c) searching with backtrack
(d) generating the nth fibonacci number

37. For implementation of recursive and re-entrant programs, we need to use computer memory as a/an
(a) heap
(b) queue
(c) array
(d) stack

38. A key:
(a) must always be composed of two or more columns.
(b) can only be one column.
(c) identifies a row.
(d) identifies a column.

39. In order traversal of the binary search tree implies visiting records in
(a) the order of increasing magnitude of their key
(b) an arbitrary order
(c) the order of decreasing magnitude of their key
(d) None of the above

40. Knuth-Morris-Pratt string matching algorithm, for finding an instance of a string of length p, in another string of length m runs, in an amount of time at worst proportional to
(a) m
(b) $m*p$
(c) p
(d) $m+p$

41. In C, strings are stored in a/an
(a) linked list of unsigned characters
(b) linked list of characters

(c) array of characters
(d) array of integers

42. A relation in this form is free of all modification anomalies.
(a) First normal form
(b) Second normal form
(c) Third normal form
(d) Domain/key normal form

43. A threaded binary tree has the following problem
(a) non-sequential memory allocation
(b) more time consuming tree traversal
(c) additional storage requirement
(d) None of these

44. Representation of list structures, with items that are either sublists or individual items, by a singly linked list is
(a) possible with an additional tag field (storing information or address of the sublist in the information field of the node)
(b) not possible without additional link fields
(c) possible without additonal tag field
(d) not possible

45. Compaction is
(a) conversion of a link-list to an array
(b) moving all memory locations currently in use into a single contiguous region of the memory
(c) compression of information fields of a list
(d) None of the above

46. If attributes A and B determine attribute C, then it is also true that:
(a) $A \rightarrow C$
(b) $B \rightarrow C$
(c) (A, B) is a composite determinant.
(d) C is a determinant.

47. Stability of a sorting algorithm is important for
(a) sorting records on the basis of multiple keys
(b) sorting alphanumeric keys because they are likely to be the same
(c) worst case performance for the sorting algorithm
(d) None of the above

48. Sparse matrices are represented using
(a) doubly linked
(b) circularly linked list for each row and column with each node corresponding to non-zero element
(c) a binary tree
(d) singly linked list where each node contains non-zero elements of the matrix list

49. In which collision processing method, detection of a given list position is not needed (whether it is occupied or not)?
(a) rehashing
(b) linked
(c) quadratic
(d) None of these

50. When a new element is inserted in the middle of a linked list
(a) the elements before and after the new element need to be moved
(b) only the elements that appear before the new element need to be moved
(c) only the elements that appear after the new element need to be moved
(d) None of the above

51. When we concatenate two strings $s1$ and $s2$ of size m and n, size of the resultant string is always
(a) of size $m + m$
(b) of size $max(m,n)$
(c) of size $m * n$
(d) of size less than $m + n$

52. The following data structure can suffer from an overflow problem
(a) stack implemented using array
(b) circularly linked list
(c) linked-list
(d) None of the above

53. One solution to the multivalued dependency constraint problem is to:
   (a) split the relation into two relations, each with a single theme
   (b) change the theme
   (c) create a new theme
   (d) add a composite key

54. The tree traversal technique in which, the root is traversed before its children, is known as
   (a) in-order traversal
   (b) pre-order traversal
   (c) post-order traversal
   (d) None of the above

55. A data structure, in which, insertion and deletion can take place at both the ends is called
   (a) dequeue   (b) circular queue
   (c) stack   (d) None of these

56. The maximum number of nodes in a binary tree, of depth 5 is
   (a) 31   (b) 32
   (c) 16   (d) 15

57. ODL supports which of the following types of association relationships?
   (a) Unary
   (b) Unary and Binary
   (c) Unary and Binary and Ternary
   (d) Unary and Binary and Ternary and higher

58. An extent is which of the following?
   (a) A keyword that indicates that the subclass inherits from a superclass
   (b) A keyword that indicates that the superclass inherits from a subclass
   (c) The set of all instances of a class within a database
   (d) Only one instance of a class within a database

59. A binary tree of depth d is alomost complete binary tree, if
   (a) For any node n in the tree with a right

descedent at level d, all the left descendants of n that are leaves are also at level d
   (b) Each leaf in the tree is either at level d or at level $d - 1$
   (c) Both (a) and (b) are true
   (d) None of these

60. The object definition language (ODL) is which of the following?
   (a) Used to develop logical schemas
   (b) A data definition language for OODB
   (c) A method to implement a logical schema
   (d) All of the above

61. Adjacency matrix of a digraph is a/an
   (a) symmetric matrix
   (b) identity matrix
   (c) asymmetric matrix
   (d) None of these

62. Let p be a pointer to a structure. A member mem of that structure is referenced by
   (a) $^*(p.m)$ (b) $^*p$.mem
   (c) $(^*p)$.mem   (d) None of these

63. Using arrays, the most efficient implementation of a queue is
   (a) Priority queue   (b) Linear queue
   (c) Circular queue   (d) None of these

64. The best fit policy for selection of a memory block for satisfying a memory request involves
   (a) finding the largest block that meets the requirement
   (b) finding the smallest block that meets the requirement
   (c) finding the first block that meets the requirement
   (d) None of the above

65. A n-ary tree can be represented using
   (a) input restricted dequeue
   (b) priority queue
   (c) binary tree
   (d) None of the above

66. A complete *k*-ary tree can be efficiently represented using a/an
(*a*) graph
(*b*) array
(*c*) binary tree
(*d*) None of these

67. We can efficiently reverse a string using a
(*a*) circular queue
(*b*) linear queue
(*c*) stack
(*d*) doubly linked list

68. We can convert an infix expression to a postfix expression using a
(*a*) stack
(*b*) dequeue
(*c*) queue
(*d*) None of these

69. The simplest way to organise the information about available memory blocks in a system is
(*a*) File
(*b*) Doubly linked circular list
(*c*) Stack
(*d*) AVL tree

70. Select the one right answer
A method is
(*a*) a category of objects
(*b*) an attribute defining the property of a particular abstraction
(*c*) an implementation of an abstraction
(*d*) an operation defining the behaviour for a particular abstraction

71. Select the one right answer
An object is
(*a*) a reference to an attribute
(*b*) an instance of a class
(*c*) a blueprint for creating concrete realisation of abstractions
(*d*) what classes are instantiated from

72. Which line contains a constructor in this class definition?

```
public class Counter {
                    // (1)
    int current, step;
    public Counter(int startValue, int stepValue) {
                    // (2)
        set(startValue);
    setSetValue(stepValue);
}
public int get() { return current; }
                    // (3)
public void set(int value) { current = value; }
                    // (4)
public void setStepValue(int stepValue) { step = stepValue; }        // (5)
}
```

Select the one right answer
(*a*) The code marked (3) is a constructor
(*b*) The code marked (2) is a constructor
(*c*) The code marked (1) is a constructor
(*d*) The code marked (4) is a constructor

73. Given that Thing is a class, how many objects and reference variables are created by the following code ?

```
Thing item, stuff;
item = new object();
Thing entity = new object();
```

Select all valid answers
(*a*) One reference variable is created
(*b*) Two objects are creats
(*c*) Three objects are created
(*d*) One object is created

74. Select the one right answer
An instance member
(*a*) is always a variable
(*b*) is also called a static member
(*c*) is never a method
(*d*) belongs to a single instance, not to the class as a whole

75. How do objects pass messages in Java?
Select the one right answer
(*a*) They pass messages by calling static member methods of one another's classes
(*b*) They pass messages by modifying the static member variables of one another's classes
(*c*) They pass messages by calling one another's instance member methods

(*d*) They pass messages by modifying one another's member variables

76. Given the following code, which statements are true ?

```
class A {
    int value1;
}
    class B extends A {
        int value2;
}
```

Select all valid answers
(*a*) Class A inherits from class B
(*b*) Class B is the superclass of class A
(*c*) Class A extends class B
(*d*) Class B is a subclass of class A

77. Which of the following is true concerning an ODBMS?
(*a*) They have the ability to store complex data types on the Web.
(*b*) They are overtaking RDBMS for all applications.
(*c*) They are most useful for traditional, two-dimensional database table applications.
(*d*) All of the above.

78. Which of the following is true concerning the following statement: class Manager extends Employee
(*a*) Manager is a concrete class and a superclass.
(*b*) Manager is a concrete class and a subclass.
(*c*) Manager is an abstract class and a superclass.
(*d*) Manager is an abstract class and a subclass.

79. Given the following class, which statements can be inserted at position 1 without causing the code to fail during its compilation ?

```
public class Q6db8 {
    int a;
    int b = 0;
    static int c;
    public void m() {
        int d;
        int e = 0;
                // position 1
    }
}
```

Select all the valid answers
(*a*) *a*++;   (*b*) *c*+1;
(*c*) *b*+1;   (*d*) *d*++;

80. Which statements are true in the context of the effect of the >> and >>> operators ?
Select all the valid answers
(*a*) For non-negative values of the left operator   and the >> and >>> operators will have the same effect
(*b*) The result of (-1 >>> 1) is -1
(*c*) The result of (-1 >> 1) is 0
(*d*) None of the above

81. What is wrong with the following code?

```
class MyException extends Exception {}
    public class Qb4ab {
    public void foo() {
try {
bar();
} finally {
baz();
    } catch (MyException e) {}
}
public void bar () throws MyException {
throw new RuntimeException();
}
}
```

Select all valid answers
(*a*) A try block cannot be followed by both a catch and a finally block.
(*b*) Since the method foo() does not catch the exception generated by the method baz(), it must declare the Runtime Exception in the throws clause.
(*c*) An empty catch block is not allowed.
(*d*) A catch block cannot follow a finally block.

82. What will be written to the standard output when the following program is run?

```
public class Qd803 {
    public static void main(String args [ ]) {
    String word = "restructure";
    System.out.println(word.substring(2, 3));
}
}
```

Select the only right answer

(a) str (b) es

(c) est (d) s

83. Given that a static method doIt() in a class Work represents work to be done, which block of code will succeed in starting a new thread that will do the work?

Select all the valid answers

```
(a) Runnable r = new Runnable() {
                    public void run() {
                        work.doIt();
                    }
        };
        Thread t = new Thread(r);
                    t.start();
(b) Thread t = new Thread() {
        public void start() {
                        Work.doIt();
                    }
        };
        t.start();
(c) Thread t = new Thread(new Work());
        t.start();
(d) Runnable r = new Runnable() {
                public void run() {
                Work.doIt();
                }
        };
        r.start();
```

84. What will be the result of attempting to compile and run the following code?

```
public class Q275d {
static int a;
    int b;
public Q275d() {
int c;
c = a;
    a++;
    b += c;
}
public static void main(String args [ ]) {
new Q275d( );
}
}
```

Select the only right answer

(a) The code will fail to compile, since the constructor is trying to use member variable *b* before it has been intialized

(b) The code will fail to compile, since the constructor is trying to use static member variable *a* before it has been initialised

(c) The code will fail to compile since the constructor is trying to access static members.

(d) The code will compile and run without any problem

85. Using OQL, you may do which of the following?

(a) Return an entire collection of elements including duplicates.

(b) Return a collection of elements without duplicates.

(c) Return a specific subset of elements using a given criteria.

(d) All of the above.

86. Which of the following statements are true in the context of the default layout manager for containers in the java.awt package?

Select all the valid answers

(a) Objects instantiated from Window have the same default layout manager as instances of Applet.

(b) Objects instantiated from panel do not have FlowLayout as defalut layout manager.

(c) Objects instantiated from Applet have Border Layout as default layout manager.

    (*d*) Objects instantiated from panel do not have a default layout manager.

87. Which declaration will allow a class to be started as a standalone program?
Select all the valid answers
    (*a*) public static main(String[ ] argv)
    (*b*) public void static main(String args[ ])
    (*c*) public void main(String args[ ])
    (*d*) final public static void main(String[ ] array)

88. The Object Query Language is which of the following"?
    (*a*) Similar to SQL and uses a select-from-where structure
    (*b*) Similar to SQL and uses a select-where structure
    (*c*) Similar to SQL and uses a from-where structure
    (*d*) Not similar to SQL

89. When creating a class that associates a set of keys with a set of values, which one of these interfaces is most applicable?
Select the only right answer
    (*a*) SortedSet
    (*b*) Set
    (*c*) Collection
    (*d*) Map

90. Data scrubbing is which of the following?
    (*a*) A process to reject data from the data warehouse and to create the necessary indexes
    (*b*) A process to load the data in the data warehouse and to create the necessary indexes
    (*c*) A process to upgrade the quality of data after it is moved into a data warehouse
    (*d*) A process to upgrade the quality of data before it is moved into a data warehouse

91. What will be written to the standard output when the following program is run?

```java
class Base {
    int i;
    Base() {
        add(1);
    }
    void add(int v) {
        i += v;
    }
    void print() {
        System.out.println(i);
    }
}
class Extension extends Base {
    Extension() {
        add(2);
    }
    void add(int v); {
        i += v*2;
    }
}
public class Qd073 {
    public static void main(String args[ ]) {
        bogo(new Extension());
    }
    static void bogo(Base b) {
        b.add(B);
        b.print();
    }
}
```

Select the only right answer
    (*a*) 20
    (*b*) 18
    (*c*) 9
    (*d*) 22

92. An operational system is which of the following?
    (*a*) A system that is used to run the business in real time and is based on historical data.
    (*b*) A system that is used to run the business in real time and is based on current data.
    (*c*) A system that is used to support decision making and is based on current data.

(d) A system that is used to support decision making and is based on historical data.

93. How does the wighty property of the GridBagConstraints objects used in grid bag layout affect the layout of the components?

Select the only right answer
(a) It affects the alignment of each component
(b) It affects how the extra vertical space is distributed
(c) It affects which grid cell components end up in
(d) It affects the whether the components completely fill their allotted display area vertically

94. Which statements can be inserted at the indicated position in the following code to make the program write 1 on the standard output when run?

```java
public class Q4a39 {
    int a = 1;
    int b = 1;
    int c = 1;
            class Inner {
                    int a = 2;
                    int get() {
                    int c = 3;
            // insert statement here
            return c;
        }
    }
    Q4a39() {
        Inner 1 = new Inner();
        System.out.println(i.get());
    }
    public static void main(String args[]) {
    new Q4a39();
    }
}
```

Select all the valid answers
(a) c = b;   (b) c = this.b;
(c) c = this.a;   (d) c = c;

95. Which one of the earliest lines in the following code after which the object created on the line marked (0) will be a candidate for being garbage collected, assuming no compiler optimisations are done?

```java
public class Q76a9 {
static String f() {
String a = "hello";
String b = "bye";
                              // (0)
String c = b + "!";   // (1)
String d = b;
b = a;                        // (2)
d = a;                        // (3)
return c;                     // (4)
}
public static void main(String args[ ]) {
String msg = f();
System.out.println(msg);
                              // (5)
}
}
```

Select the only right answer
(a) The line marked (4)
(b) The line marked (2)
(c) The line marked (3)
(d) The line marked (1)

96. Which methods from the String and StringBuffer classes modify the object on which, they are called?
Select all the valid answers
(a) The replace() method of the String class
(b) The toUpperCase() mehod of the String class
(c) The charAt() method of the String class
(d) The reverse() method of the StringBuffer class

97. Which statements, when inserted at the indicated position in the following code, will cause a runtime exception when attempting to run the program?

```java
class A {}
```

```
class B extends A {}
class C extends A {}
    public class Q3ae4 {
    public static void main(String args[]) {
A x = new A();
B y = new B();
C z = new C();
    // insert statement here
}
}
```

Select all the valid answers

(a) z = (C) y;   (b) z = x;
(c) y = (B) x;   (d) x = y;

98. Which ones of these are keywords in Java ?
Select all the valid answers

(a) default   (b) except
(c) String   (d) NULL

99. It is desirable that a certain method within a certain class can only be accessed by classes that are defined within the same package as the class of the method. How can such restrictions be enforced?
Select the only right answer

(a) Mark the method with the keyword private

(b) Mark the method with the keyword protected

(c) Mark the method with the keyword public

(d) Do not mark the method with any accessibility modifiers

100. Which code fragments will succeed in intialising a two dimensional array named tab with a size that will cause the expression tab [3] [2] to access a valid element?
Select all the valid answers

(a) int [ ] [ ] tab = {
```
                { 0, 0, 0 },
                { 0, 0, 0 }
                };
```

(b) int tab [ ] [ ] = new int [4] [ ];
```
                    for   (int   i=0;
    i<tab.length; i++) tab[i] = new
    int[3];
```

(c) int tab[3] [2];

(d) int tab [ ] [ ] = {
```
        0, 0, 0, 0,
        0, 0, 0, 0,
        0, 0, 0, 0,
        0, 0, 0, 0
    };
```

ANSWERS

1	2	3	4	5	6	7	8	9	10
(a)	(d)	(a)	(b)	(a)	(c)	(d)	(a)	(a)	(a)
11	**12**	**13**	**14**	**15**	**16**	**17**	**18**	**19**	**20**
(a)	(c)	(c)	(c)	(a)	(d)	(b)	(a)	(a)	(a)
21	**22**	**23**	**24**	**25**	**26**	**27**	**28**	**29**	**30**
(c)	(c)	(a)	(c)	(a)	(a)	(c)	(c)	(b)	(b)
31	**32**	**33**	**34**	**35**	**36**	**37**	**38**	**39**	**40**
(b)	(a)	(c)	(b)	(c)	(c)	(d)	(c)	(a)	(a)
41	**42**	**43**	**44**	**45**	**46**	**47**	**48**	**49**	**50**
(c)	(d)	(c)	(a)	(b)	(c)	(a)	(b)	(d)	(d)
51	**52**	**53**	**54**	**55**	**56**	**57**	**58**	**59**	**60**
(a)	(a)	(a)	(b)	(a)	(a)	(b)	(c)	(a)	(d)

61	62	63	64	65	66	67	68	69	70
(c)	(c)	(c)	(b)	(c)	(b)	(c)	(a)	(b)	(d)
71	72	73	74	75	76	77	78	79	80
(b)	(b)	(b)	(d)	(c)	(d)	(a)	(b)	(a)	(a)
81	82	83	84	85	86	87	88	89	90
(d)	(d)	(a)	(d)	(d)	(d)	(d)	(a)	(d)	(d)
91	92	93	94	95	96	97	98	99	100
(d)	(b)	(b)	(a)	(c)	(d)	(c)	(a)	(d)	(b)

---

1. What will be the result of attempting to run the following program?

```
public class Qaa75 {
public static void main(String args [ ]) {
String [ ] [ ] [ ] arr = {
{ {}, null },
{ { "1", "2" }, { "1", null, "3" } },
{},
{ { "1", null } }
};
System.out.println(arr.length + arr[1]
[2].length);
}
}
```

   Select the only right answer

   (*a*) The program will terminate with an Array Index Out Of Bounds Exception

   (*b*) 6 will be written to standard output

   (*c*) 4 will be written to standard output

   (*d*) The program will terminate with a Null Pointer Exception

2. Which expression will evaluate to true, if preceded by the following code?

```
String a = "hello";
String b = new String(a);
String c = a;
char [ ] d = { 'h', 'e', 'l', 'l', 'o' };
```

   Select all valid answers.

   (*a*) *a*.equals(*d*) (*b*) (*a* = = *b*)

   (*c*) (*a* – – *c*) (*d*) (*a* = = "Hello")

3. Which statement in the context of the following code are true?

```
class A {
public A() {}
```

```
public A(int i) { this(); }
}
class B extends A {
public boolean B(String msg) {return false; }
}
  class C extends B {
private C () { super(); }
public C(String msg) {this(); }
public C(int i) {}
}
```

   Select all the valid answers

   (*a*) At most one of the constructors of each is called as a result of constructing an object of class C

   (*b*) The constructor in A that takes an int as an argument will never be called as a result of constructing an object of class B or C

   (*c*) Objects of class B cannot be constructed

   (*d*) The code will fail to compile

4. Given two collection objects referenced by col1 and col2, which of these statements are true?

   Select all the valid answers

   (*a*) The operation col1.addAll(col2) will return a new collection object, containing elements from both col1 and col2

   (*b*) The operation col1.removeAll(col2) will not modify the col2 object

   (*c*) The operation col1.retainAll(col2) will not modify the col1 object

   (*d*) None of the above

5. Which statements concerning the relationships between the following classes are true?

```
class Foo {
    int num;
    Baz comp = new Baz();
}
class Bar {
    boolean flag;
}
class Baz extends Foo {
    Bar thing = new Bar();
    double limit;
}
```

Select all the valid answers

(*a*) A Foo has a Bar (*b*) A Bar is a Baz
(*c*) A Baz is a Foo   (*d*) A Foo is a Baz

6. Which statements concerning the value of a member variable are true, when no explicit assignments have been made?

Select all the valid answers

(*a*) The value of a String variable is " " (empty string)

(*b*) The value of all numeric types is zero

(*c*) The compiler may issue an error if the variable is used before it is initialised

(*d*) The value of an int is undetermined

7. Which statements describe guaranteed behaviour of the garbage collection and finalisation mechanisms ?

Select all the valid answers

(*a*) The finalise() method will eventually be called on every object.

(*b*) Objects are deleted when they can do longer be accessed through any reference

(*c*) The finalize() method will never be called more than once on an object

(*d*) The garbage collector will use a mark and sweep algorithm

8. Which code fragments will succeed in printing the last argument given on the command line to the standard output and exit gracefully with no output if no arguments are given?

Select all the valid answers

(*a*) public static void main(String args [])
```
    {
    if (args.length ! = 0)
    System.out.println(agrs[args.length - 1]
    );
    }
```

(*b*) public static void main(String args [])
```
    {
    try{ System.out.println(args[args.length]);
    }catch
    (ArrayIndexOutOfBoundsException e) {}
    }
```

(*c*) public static void main(String args[])
```
    {
                      int ix = args.length-1;
                        if (ix > 0)
    System.out.println(args[ix]);
    }
```

(*d*) public static void main(String args[])
```
    {
              int ix = args.length;
              String last = args[ix];
    }
              if (ix > 0) System.out.println(last);
```

9. Which ones of the following statements concerning the collection interfaces are true?

Select all the valid answers

(*a*) Set extends Collections

(*b*) All methods defined in List are also defined in Collection

(*c*) Map extends Collection

(*d*) None of the above

10. Which is the legal range of values for a short?

Select the only right answer

(*a*) -2^{16} to $2^{16} -1$ (*b*) -2^8 to 2^8
(*c*) -2^{15} to $2^{15} -1$ (*d*) -2^7 to $2^7 -1$

11. Given the following class definitions, which expression identifies whether the object referred to by obj was created by instantiating class B rather than class A, C and D ?

```
class A {}
class B extends A {}
```

```
class C extends B {}
class D extends A {}
```
Select all the valid answers

(a) ! (obj instanceof C | | obj instanceof D)
(b) obj instanceof A && ! (obj instanceof C)
(c) obj instanceof B && ! (obj instanceof C)
(d) obj instanceof B.

12. What will be written to the standard output when the following program is run?

```
public class Q8499 {
public static void main(String args[ ]) {
double d = -2, 9;
int i = (int) d;
i *= (int) Math.ceil(d);
i *=(int) Math.abs(d);
System.out.println(i);
}
}
```

Select the only right answer

(a) 18   (b) −12
(c) 8   (d) 12

13. What will be written to the standard output when the following program is run?

```
public class Qcb90 {
    int a;
    int b;
    public void f() {
        a = 0;
        b = 0;
        int [ ] c = { 0 };
        g(b, c);
System.out.println(a + " " + b + " " + c[0] +
" ");
}
public void g(int b, int [ ] c) {
    a = 1;
    b = 1;
    c[0] = 1;
}
public static void main(String args[ ]) {
Qcb90 obj = new Qcb90();
obj.f();
```

```
}
}
```
Select the only right answer

(a) 0 1 0   (b) 0 0 1
(c) 0 0 0   (d) 1 0 1

14. Which statements in the context of the effect of the statement *gfx*.drawRect(5, 5, 10, 10) are true, given that *gfx* is a reference to a valid Graphics object?

Select all the valid answers

(a) The drawn rectangle will have a total width of 10 pixels.
(b) The drawn rectangle will have a total height of 6 pixels.
(c) The drawn rectangle will have a total width of 5 pixels.
(d) The drawn rectangle will have a total height of 11 pixels.

15. Given the following code, which fragments, when inserted at the indicated location, will succeed in making the program display a button spanning the whole window area?

```
import java.awt.*;
public class Q1e65 {
public static void main(String args[ ]) {
Window win = new Frame();
Button but = new Button("button");
// insert code fragment here
win.setSize(200, 200);
win.setVisible(true);
}
}
```

Select all the valid answers

(a) win.setLayout(new BorderLayout());
    win.add(but);
(b) win.setLayout(new BorderLayout(1, 2));
    win.add(but, BorderLayout.CENTER);
(c) win.setLayout(new GridLayout(12, 1));
    win.add(but);
(d) win.setLayout(new FlowLayout());
    win.add(but);

16. Which method implements will write the given string to a file named "file", using UTF8 encoding?

Select all the valid answers

(*a*) public void write(String *msg*) throws IOException {

```
FileWriter fw = new FileWriter(new File("file"));
fw.setEncoding("UTF8");
fw.write(msg);
fw.close();
}
```

(*b*) public void write(String *msg*) throws IOException {

```
OutputStreamWriter osw = new OutputStreamWriter(new fileOutputStream("file"), "UFT8");
osw.write(msg);
osw.close();
}
```

(*c*) public void write(String *msg*) throws IOException {

```
FileWriter fw = new FileWriter(new File("file"));
fw.write(msg);
fw.close();
}
```

(*d*) public void write(String *msg*) throws IOException {

```
FilterWriter fw = FilterWriter(new FilterWriter("file"), "UTF8");
fw.write(msg);
fw.close();
}
```

17. What will be output if you will compile and execute the following c code?

```c
void main(){
    int i=320;
    char *ptr=(char *)&i;
    printf("%d",*ptr);
}
```

(*a*) 320   (*b*) 1

(*c*) 64   (*d*) Compiler error

18. What will be the result of attempting to compile and run the following program?

```java
public class Q28fd {
    public static void main(String args[]) {
        int counter = 0;
        l2;
        for (int i=10; i<0; i--) {
            12:
            int j = 0;
            while (j < 10) {
                if (j > i) break 12;
                if (i = = j) {
                    counter++;
                    continue l1;
                }
            }
        }
        counter - -;
    }
System.out.println(counter);
}
}
```

Select the only right answer

(*a*) The program will fail to compile

(*b*) The program will write 10 to the standard output

(*c*) The program will not terminate normally

(*d*) The program will write 0 to the standard output

19. Given the following definition, which definitions are valid?

```java
interface I {
    void setValue(int val);
    int getValue();
}
```

Select all the valid answers

(*a*) abstract class C implements I {
int getValue() { return 0; }
abstract void increment();
}

(*b*) interface B extends I {
void increment();
}

(c) class A extends I {
    int value;
    void setValue(int val) { value = val; }
    int getValue() { return value; }
    }
(d) interface D implements I {
    void increment();
    }

20. Which statements concerning the methods notify() and notifyAll() are true?
Select all the valid answers
(a) Instances of class Thread have a method called notify()
(b) The method notifyAll() is defined in class Thread
(c) The method notify() is synchronised
(d) A call to the method notify() will wake the thread that currently owns the monitor of the object

21. What will be output if you will compile and execute the following c code?

```c
void main(){
    float a = 5.2;
 if(a==5.2)
    printf("Equal");
  else if(a<5.2)
    printf("Less than");
  else
    printf("Greater than");
}
```

(a) Equal   (b) Less than
(c) Greater than   (d) Compiler error

22. What will be the result of attempting to compile and run the following code?

```java
public class Q6b0c {
    public static void main(String args[]) {
        int i = 4;
        float f = 4.3;
        double d = 1.8;
        int c = 0;
        if ( i = = f) c++;
        if ((int) (f + d)) = = ((int) f + (int) d)) c +=
```

2;
        System.out.println(c);
    }
}

Select the only right answer
(a) The code will fail to compile
(b) 2 will be written to the standard output
(c) 1 will be written to the standard output
(d) 0 will be written to the standard output

23. Which operators will always evaluate all the operands?
Select all the valid answers
(a) &&   (b) +
(c) || (d) ? :

24. Which statements concerning the switch construct are true?
Select all the valid answers
(a) No case label may follow a default label within a single switch statement
(b) The keyword continue can never occur within the body of a switch statement
(c) There must be exactly one label for each code segment in a switch statement
(d) A character literal can be used as a value for a case label

25. Which modifiers and return types will be valid in the declaration of a working main() method for a java standalone application?
Select all the valid answers
(a) int   (b) final
(c) private   (d) abstract

26. What will be the appearance of an applet with the following init() method?

```java
public void init() {
    add(new Button("hello"));
}
```

Select the only right answer
(a) A button will appear in the top left corner of the applet
(b) A button will cover the whole area of the applet

(c) Nothing appears in the applet

(d) A button will appear, centered in the top region of the applet

27. Which of the following is the correct usage of conditional operators used in C?

(a) a>b ? c=30 : c=40;

(b) a>b ? c=30;

(c) max = a>b ? a>c?a:c:b>c?b:c

(d) return (a>b)?(a:b)

28. Which statements are true, given the code new FileOutputStream("data", true) for creating an object of class FileOutputStream? Select all the valid answers

(a) If a file named "data" exists, its contents will be reset and overwritten

(b) An IOException will be thrown if a file named "data" does not already exists

(c) An IOException will be thrown if a file named "data" already exists

(d) If a file named "data" exists, output will be appended to its current contents

29. Which of the following are unary operators in C?

1. !   2. sizeof
3. ~   4. &&

(a) 1, 2   (b) 1, 3
(c) 2, 4   (d) 1, 2, 3

30. What will be written to the standard output when the following program is run?

```
public class Q03e4 {
public static void main(String args[ ]) {
String space = " ";
String composite = space + "hello" + space + space;
composite.concat("world");
String trimmed = composite.trim();
System.out.println(trimmed.length());
}
}
```

Select the only right answer

(a) 5   (b) 13
(c) 12   (d) 7

31. Given the following code, which statements in the context of the objects referenced through the member variables i,j and k are true, given that any thread may call the method a,b and c at any time?

```
class Counter {
int v = 0;
synchronized void inc() { v++; }
synchronized void dec() { v--; }
}
public class Q7ed5 {
Counter i;
Counter j;
Counter k;
public synchronized void a() {
i.inc();
System.out.println("a");
i.dec();
}
public synchronized void b() {
i.inc(); j.inc(); k.inc();
System.out.println("b");
i.dec(); j.dec(); k.dec();
}
public void c() {
    k.inc();
    System.out.println("c");
    k.dec();
}
}
```

Select all the valid answers

(a) i.v is guaranteed always to be 0 or 1

(b) k.v will always be greater than or equal to j.v at any give time

(c) j.v will always be greater than or equal to k.v at any give time

(d) k.v is guaranteed always to be 0 or 1

32. What is error in following declaration?

```
struct outer{
int a;
struct inner{
char c;
};
```

```
};
```
(a) Nesting of structure is not allowed in c.
(b) It is necessary to initialize the member variable.
(c) Inner structure must have name.
(d) Outer structure must have name.

33. Given the following code, which method declarations, when inserted at the indicated position, will not cause the program to fail compilation?

```
public class Qdd1f {
public long sum( long a, long b) { return a +
b;          }
// insert new method declaration here
}
```

Selected all the valid answers   .
(a) public int sum(int a, int b) { return a + b;
    }
(b) private long sum(long a, long b) { return
    a + b; }
(c) abstract int sum();
(d) public int sum(int a, int b) {return 0; }

34. What will be output if you will compile and execute the following c code?

```
void main(){
int array[]={10,20,30,40};
printf("%d",-2[array]);
}
```
(a) −60   (b) −30
(c) 60   (d) Garbage value

35.
```
main()
{
    int counter = 40;
    for(;counter;)
    counter - -;
    printf("%d\n", counter);
}
```
In the above program, the output is
(a) − 40   (b) 40
(c) 0   (d) None of these

36.
```
#define max (a,b) (a b ? a : b)
main()
```
```
{
    int m;
    m = max (123, 456);
    /* more program lines*/
}
```
The above program
(a) Assigns 456 to m
(b) Assigns the string "(a,b)" to m
(c) Assigns 123 to m
(d) None of the above

37.
```
main()
{
    int i, j, r ;
    i = 100 ; j = 5 ; r = 20 ;
    printf("Value of i+j-r is %o\n", i+j-r) ;
}
```
When the above program segment is run, it prints
(a) 85   (b) 55
(c) 125   (d) None of these

38. Consider the following program
```
char oadd ( char c )
{
    return &c ;
}
void ost ( char *cad, char val)
{
    *cad = val ;
}
main()
{
    char a = 'A', b = 'B' ;
    ost (oadd (a), b) ;
    printf("Value of a = %c \n", a);
}
```
Which of the following is true for the above program?
(a) Program prints "Value of a = B"
(b) Program prints "Value of a = A"
(c) This program contains a syntax error
(d) None of these

39. What does the following program segment print?

```c
main()
{
    int i;
    int iarray[4] = {1, 2, 3, 4 };
    #define SIZE (sizeof(iarray) / sizeof(int))
    for (i=0; i<SIZE; ++i)
    iarray[i] +=2;
    printf("Value is %d\n", iarray[3]);

}
```

(a) Compilation error because of #define within main module

(b) 6

(c) 3

(d) None of the above

40. Find out the error in the following program:

```c
main()
{
    int mark;
    char grade;
switch (mark)
    {
case 5: grade = 'A'; break;
case 4; grade = 'B'; break;
case 4; grade = 'B'; break;
default; grade = 'c'; break;
}/*switch*/
}
```

(a) **case** labels cannot be numbers

(b) **switch** statement cannot have more than three labels

(c) No two labels may be identical

(d) None of these

41.
```c
main()
{
    int buf[5];
    int *btr = *buf[2];
    btr[-1] = 20;
    btr[-2] = 10;
    btr[-3] = 0;
    printf("buf[1] = %d\n", buf[1]);

}
```

The above program prints

(a) buf[1] = 20   (b) buf[1] = 0

(c) but[1] = 10   (d) None of these

42. What is output of the following program?

```c
#define ROWS 3
#define COLUMNS 4
int z[ROWS][COLUMNS] = {1, 2, 3, 4, 5, 6, 7,
8, 9, 10, 11, 12}
main()
{
    int a, b, c = 999;
    for(a=0; a<ROWS; ++a)
    for(b=0; b<COLUMNS; ++b)
    if (z[a][b] < c)
    c = z[a][b];
    printf("%d", c);

}
```

(a) 1   (b) 12

(c) 999   (d) None of these

43. Consider the following program segment:

```c
main()
{
    int fa;
    fa = fac (5);
    /* more program lines */
}
    fac ( num )
    int num;
{
    if (num = = 1)
    return 1;
    return ( num *fac (num - 1));
}
```

The above program segment

(a) Assigns 1 to **fa**   (b) Assigns 120 to **fa**

(c) Assigns 5 to **fa**   (d) None of these

44. Consider the following program segment:

```c
main()
{
    printf ( "Hello\n");
    main();
}
```

Which of the following is true for the above program segment?
(a) Compilation error because of main within main module
(b) Infinite loop
(c) Prints only once
(d) None of these

45. Consider the program segment:
```
#define SQUARE(x)=(x*x)
#define cs(m,n) (SQUARE(m) > SQUARE(n) ?
n : m)
main()
{
    int s;
    s = csi(2, –3);
    printf("%d\n",a);
    /*more program lines*/
}
```
In the above program segment, the output is
(a) -3   (b) 2
(c) 4   (d) None of these

46. Consider the following program segment
```
main()
{
    char c_arry[ ] = {'A', 'B', 'C', 'D'}, *ptr ;
    *ptr = c_arry;
    *++ptr = *(c_arry + 2);
    printf("c = %c", *ptr +1);
}
```
The output of the above program segment is
(a) C   (b) D
(c) A   (d) None of these

47. Consider the following program segment
```
main()
{
    int n = 2, *ptr;
    ptr = &n;
    n*=3;
    printf("%d\n", *ptr**ptr );
}
```

The above program segments prints
(a) 6   (b) 36
(c) 4   (d) None of these

48. Consider the following program segment:
```
main()
{
    int i, j = 1;
    for (i = j - 2; i < 5; i++)
            j += j;
printf ( "The value of j is :%d\n", j);
}
```
The output of the above program segment is
(a) 12   (b) 13
(c) 5   (d) None of these

49. What is the output of the following program segment?
```
main()
{
    int val, x;
    val = 5;
    call_func1 (val) ;
printf("The Output is : %d\n", val);
}
call_func1 (val)
int val ;
{
return ( call_func2 (val*2));
}
    call_func2 (val)
    int val;
{
    val = 2;
return (val);
}
```
(a) 5   (b) 20
(c) 10   (d) None of these

50. Consider the following program segment:
```
func (a, b)
int a, b;
{
    return (a = (a = = b));
```

```
}
    main()
{
    int process(), func();
printf("The value of the process:%d\n",
process (func, 3, 4));
}
    process ( pf, val1, val2)
    int (*pf)();
    int val1, val2;
    {
    return ((*pf)(val1, val2));
}
```

The above program segment prints

(a) 4   (b) 3
(c) 0   (d) None of these

51. What will be output if you will compile and execute the following c code?

```
void main(){
int i=10;
static int x=i;
if(x==i)
printf("Equal");
else if(x>i)
printf("Greater than");
else
printf("Less than");
}
```

(a) Equal   (b) Greater than
(c) Less than   (d) Compiler error

52. In which order do the following gets evaluated

1. Relational   2. Arithmetic
3. Logical   4. Assignment
(a) 2134   (b) 1234
(c) 4321   (d) 3214

53. Specify the 2 library functions to dynamically allocate memory?
(a) malloc() and memalloc()
(b) alloc() and memalloc()
(c) malloc() and calloc()
(d) memalloc() and faralloc()

54. An association of several entities in an Entity-Relation model is called
(a) Field   (b) Record
(c) Relationship   (d) Tuple

55. The overall logical structure of a database can be expressed graphically by
(a) Directed graph
(b) Flow Chart
(c) Data Flow Chart
(d) Entity-Relationship diagram

56. In an object oriented model, one object can access data of another object by passing a/an
(a) Function   (b) Variable
(c) Message   (d) Instance variable

57. The collection of information stored in a database at a particular moment is called
(a) Scheme   (b) Instance
(c) View   (d) None of these

58. The overall design of a database is called
(a) Scheme of the database
(b) View of the database
(c) Structure of the database
(d) Screen of database

59. To update an SQL view, the DBMS must be able to associate the column(s) to be updated with:
(a) a particular column in a particular underlying table.
(b) a particular column in a particular row.
(c) a particular row in a particular underlying table.
(d) None of the above is correct.

60. A _________ is a program that performs some common action on database data and that is stored in the database.
(a) trigger
(b) stored procedure
(c) pseudofile
(d) None of the above is correct

61. The statement requesting the retrieval of information is usually in the form of a
(a) Data entry screen
(b) Query
(c) Report
(d) Record

62. The part of Data Manipulation Language (DML) that involves information retrieval is called
(a) Query language
(b) Data definition language
(c) Report generation
(d) Meta language

63. This is NOT one of the functions of a database administrator
(a) Storage structure and access method definition
(b) Scheme definition
(c) Interaction with the file manager
(d) Granting of authorisation for data access

64. Data about data is normally termed as
(a) Meta data   (b) Data base
(c) Data dictionary   (d) None of these

65. What is an SQL virtual table that is constructed from other tables?
(a) Just another table
(b) A view
(c) A relation
(d) Query results

66. When using the SQL INSERT statement:
(a) rows can be modified according to criteria only.
(b) rows cannot be copied in mass from one table to another only.
(c) rows can be inserted into a table only one at a time only.
(d) rows can either be inserted into a table one at a time or in groups.

67. The number of entities to which, another entity can be associated via a relationship set is expressed as

(a) Attributes   (b) Cardinality
(c) Scheme   (d) Entity

68. The mapping cardinally for a binary relationship between entity sets A and B can be
(a) Many-to-one only
(b) One-to-many only
(c) One-to-one only
(d) one-to-one, one-to-many, Many-to-one or Many-to-many

69. What SQL structure is used to limit column values of a table?
(a) The LIMIT constraint
(b) The CHECK constraint
(c) The VALUE constraint
(d) None of the above is correct.

70. One limitation of the Entity-Relation model is that it cannot
(a) use one single primary key
(b) express relationships among relationships
(c) use generalisation
(d) None of the above

71. Every weak entity set can be converted into a strong entity set by
(a) Simply adding appropriate attributes
(b) Repeating the entity set several times
(c) Using aggregation
(d) Using generalisation

72. What is an advantage of placing computations in SQL views?
(a) To save users from having to write an expression.
(b) To ensure that the results are consistent.
(c) To accomplish both of the above.
(d) None of the above is correct - computations cannot be placed in a view.

73. Views constructed from SQL SELECT statements that conform to the SQL-92 standard may not contain:
(a) GROUP BY   (b) WHERE
(c) ORDER BY   (d) FROM

74. A database which conforms to an Entity-Relationship diagram can be represented by
  (a) a collection of tables
  (b) relations
  (c) a tuple
  (d) None of the above

75. If E1 and E2 are relational algebra expressions, then which of the following is NOT a relational algebra expression
  (a) E1 - E2
  (b) E1 / E2
  (c) E1 U E2
  (d) E1 ´ E2

76. Which of the following is NOT a type of SQL constraint?
  (a) PRIMARY KEY
  (b) FOREIGN KEY
  (c) ALTERNATE KEY
  (d) UNIQUE

77. One of the main feature that distinguish microprocessors from micro-computers is
  (a) Words are usually larger in microprocessors
  (b) Words are shorter in microprocessors
  (c) Microprocessor does not contain I/O devices
  (d) Exactly the same as the machine cycle time

78. Which one of the following is an aggregate function in SQL?
  (a) avg
  (b) ordered by
  (c) select
  (d) None of these

79. Quel is a query language for the following database :
  (a) ORACLE
  (b) DBASEIV
  (c) INGRESS
  (d) DBII

80. Every Boyce-Codd Normal Form (BCNF) is in
  (a) Second Normal Form (2NF)
  (b) First Normal Form (1NF)
  (c) Third Normal Form (3NF)
  (d) None of these

81. The least significant bit of the binary number, which is equivalent to any odd decimal number, is:
  (a) 0
  (b) 1
  (c) 1 or 0
  (d) 3

82. What type of control pins are needed in a microprocessor to regulate traffic on the bus, in order to prevent two devices from trying to use it at the same time?
  (a) Bus control
  (b) Interrupts
  (c) Bus arbitration
  (d) Status

83. Which normal form is most desirable?
  (a) Domain-key Normal Form (DKNF)
  (b) Forth Normal Form (4NF)
  (c) Third Normal Form (3NF)
  (d) Boyce-Codd Normal Form (BCNF)

84. The main disadvantage of Indexed Sequential File is
  (a) Accessing is very difficult
  (b) Performance degrades with the increase in file size
  (c) It consumes lot of space
  (d) None of the above

85. The redundant storage of search key values in B+ trees is eliminated in
  (a) B-Trees
  (b) Binary trees
  (c) AVL Trees
  (d) Indexed sequential file

86. The strategy for processing a query is improved by
  (a) Decomposition
  (b) Query optimisation
  (c) Query evaluation
  (d) None of these

87. The first microprocessor built by the Intel Corporation was called
  (a) 8008
  (b) 8080
  (c) 4004
  (d) 8800

88. The syntax of the user's query is verified by the
  (a) Parser
  (b) Query optimisation
  (c) Database manager
  (d) Database administrator

89. Most important advantage of an IC is its
    (*a*) Easy replacement in case of circuit failure
    (*b*) Extremely high reliability
    (*c*) Reduced cost
    (*d*) Low powers consumption

90. Roll-back of transactions is normally used to
    (*a*) recover from transaction failure
    (*b*) retrieve old records
    (*c*) update the transaction
    (*d*) restore the record

91. Cascading Roll-backs can be avoided by using
    (*a*) Validation protocol
    (*b*) Transaction processing
    (*c*) Time stamped-based protocol
    (*d*) None of the above

92. If there exists a set of transactions such that every transaction in the set is waiting for another transaction in the set, then the system is called
    (*a*) Transaction processing
    (*b*) Transaction failure
    (*c*) Dead-lock
    (*d*) Two-phase lock

93. In order to ensure that the system will never enter a deadlock, we can use
    (*a*) Deadlock prevention protocol
    (*b*) Time-stamped transaction
    (*c*) Boyce-Codd Normal Form
    (*d*) Validation protocol

94. Locking the data before the beginning of transaction execution in order to prevent deadlock may lead to
    (*a*) Delay
    (*b*) Starvation
    (*c*) Program abortion
    (*d*) Poor performance

95. A deadlock prevention scheme, which avoid starvation, is
    (*a*) Deadlock detection and prevention scheme
    (*b*) A deadlock prevention scheme using time stamps
    (*c*) Locking of data by transactions before execution
    (*d*) All of these

96. A directed graph, which represents the deadlock is called
    (*a*) Deadlock detection graph
    (*b*) Deadlock graph
    (*c*) Wait-for graph
    (*d*) Cyclic graph

97. A deadlock exists in the system if and only if the wait for the graph
    (*a*) contains a cycle
    (*b*) contains a non-reachable node from the first node
    (*c*) there is no path from fisrt node to last node
    (*d*) there is a path from first node to last node

98. In order to reduce the overhead imposed on transaction processing by the O.S, one can use a
    (*a*) Transaction monitor
    (*b*) High-performance transactions
    (*c*) Concurrency in transactions
    (*d*) Parallel processing

99. When the detection algorithm detects a deadlock, the recovery is normally accomplished by
    (*a*) Roll-back of transactions
    (*b*) Calling back the same transaction
    (*c*) Locking of data
    (*d*) Consistency checking

100. In the third Generation of computers
    (*a*) Distributed data processing first became popular
    (*b*) An operating system was first developed
    (*c*) High level procedural language were first used
    (*d*) Online real time systems first become popular

ANSWERS

1	2	3	4	5	6	7	8	9	10
(a)	(c)	(b)	(b)	(c)	(b)	(c)	(a)	(a)	(c)
11	12	13	14	15	16	17	18	19	20
(c)	(c)	(d)	(d)	(a)	(b)	(c)	(a)	(b)	(a)
21	22	23	24	25	26	27	28	29	30
(b)	(a)	(b)	(d)	(b)	(d)	(c)	(d)	(d)	(a)
31	32	33	34	35	36	37	38	39	40
(a)	(c)	(a)	(b)	(c)	(a)	(c)	(b)	(b)	(c)
41	42	43	44	45	46	47	48	49	50
(a)	(d)	(b)	(b)	(d)	(b)	(b)	(d)	(a)	(c)
51	52	53	54	55	56	57	58	59	60
(d)	(a)	(d)	(c)	(d)	(c)	(b)	(a)	(c)	(b)
61	62	63	64	65	66	67	68	69	70
(b)	(a)	(c)	(a)	(b)	(d)	(b)	(d)	(b)	(b)
71	72	73	74	75	76	77	78	79	80
(a)	(c)	(c)	(a)	(b)	(c)	(c)	(a)	(c)	(c)
81	82	83	84	85	86	87	88	89	90
(a)	(c)	(a)	(b)	(a)	(b)	(c)	(a)	(b)	(a)
91	92	93	94	95	96	97	98	99	100
(a)	(c)	(a)	(b)	(b)	(c)	(a)	(a)	(a)	(d)

1. Which of the following is not a basic element within the microprocessor?
   (a) Microcontroller
   (b) Arithmetic logic unit (ALU)
   (c) Register array
   (d) Control unit

2. Boot algorithm gives the procedure for multiplying binary integers in
   (a) unsigned representation
   (b) signed magnitude representation
   (c) 2's complement representation
   (d) None of the above

3. If K = J, in a J-K flip-flop, this results in
   (a) T-flip-flop   (b) S-R flip-flop
   (c) D-flip-flop   (d) Not defined

4. The racing condition, in J-K flip-flop, is eliminated by
   (a) connecting J and K together
   (b) using Master-Slave JK flip-flop
   (c) cascading a D-flip flop to the Q output of JK-flip flop
   (d) None of the above

5. Which of the following is not an enhancement to the Pentium that was unavailable in the 8086/8088?
   (a) "Pipelined" architecture
   (b) Expansion of cache memory
   (c) Inclusion of an internal math coprocessor
   (d) Data/address line multiplexing

6. Which one of the following algorithms is not related to the removal in demand-paged memory management?
   (a) LRU   (b) FIFO

7. Floating point multiplication requires
   (a) Fixed-point multiplication of the mantissa and fixed point addition of exponents
   (b) Fixed-point addition of mantissa and fixed point addition of exponents
   (c) Fixed-point addition of mantissa and fixed point multiplication of exponents
   (d) None of the above

8. In a compiler, the recognition of basic elements and creation of uniform symbols is carried out during
   (a) Lexical Analysis   (b) Interpretation
   (c) Syntax analysis   (d) Code generation

9. Which bus is bidirectional?
   (a) Address bus   (b) Control bus
   (c) Data bus   (d) None of these

10. DMA is particularly suited for data transfer between the _________.
    (a) disk drive and CPU
    (b) disk drive and RAM
    (c) disk drive and ROM
    (d) disk drive and I/O

11. In an 8088 microprocessor
    (a) internal and external data bus sizes are equal
    (b) internal data bus is 8-bit wide and external data bus is 16-bit wide
    (c) internal data bus is 16-bit wide and external data bus is 8-bit wide
    (d) None of these

12. What is occurring when two or more sources of data attempt to use the same bus?

(c) Round robin   (d) All of the above — [for Q6]

COM.Sc.-13

(a) Bus contention
(b) Direct memory access
(c) Bus interruption
(d) PPI

13. With interrupt-driven I/O, if two or more devices request service at the same time, _________.

(a) the device closest to the CPU gets priority
(b) the device that is fastest gets priority
(c) the device assigned the highest priority is serviced first
(d) the system is likely to crash

14. The difference between a PLA and a PAL is:

(a) The PLA has a programmable OR plane and a programmable AND plane, while the PAL only has a programmable AND plane.
(b) The PAL has a programmable OR plane and a programmable AND plane, while the PLA only has a programmable AND plane.
(c) The PAL has more possible product terms than the PLA.
(d) PALs and PLAs are the same thing.

15. Assembler directives

(a) allocate storage for constants and program variables
(b) are converted into machine instructions to be included into an object code
(c) are instructions to the assembler to tell how assembly of source program is to be performed
(d) None of the above

16. In order to transfer the contents of a register R1 to register R2, enable the

(a) input of register R1 and input of register R2
(b) input of register R1 and output of register R2

(c) output of register R1 and input of register R2
(d) None of these

17. Each programmable array logic (PAL) gate product is applied to an OR gate and, if combinational logic is desired, the product is ORed and then:

(a) the polarity fuse is restored
(b) sent to an inverter for output
(c) sent immediately to an output pin
(d) passed to the AND function for output

18. _________ are used at the inputs of PAL/GAL devices in order to prevent input loading from a large number of AND gates.

(a) Simplified AND gates
(b) Fuses
(c) Buffers
(d) Latches

19. ASIC stands for:

(a) advanced speed integrated circuit.
(b) advanced standard integrated circuit.
(c) application specific integrated circuit.
(d) application speedy integrated circuit.

20. Stack based architecture supports

(a) two-address instructions
(b) three-address address instructions
(c) zero-address instructions
(d) None of these

21. The read / write head of a hard disk drive

(a) does not make physical contact with magnetic media while reading / writing
(b) makes physical contact with magnetic media while reading / writing
(c) makes physical contact while writing only
(d) None of these

22. Which four options describe the correct default values for array elements of the types indicated?

1. int -> 0
2. String -> "null"
3. Dog -> null

4. char -> '\u0000'
5. float -> 0.0f
6. boolean -> true

(a) 1, 2, 3, 4   (b) 1, 3, 4, 5
(c) 2, 4, 5, 6   (d) 3, 4, 5, 6

23. Which one of these lists contains only Java programming language keywords?
(a) class, if, void, long, Int, continue
(b) goto, instanceof, native, finally, default, throws
(c) try, virtual, throw, final, volatile, transient
(d) strictfp, constant, super, implements, do

24. Which one of the following statements is true after execution of the program

```
int a[10], i, *p;
a[0] = 1;
a[1] = 2;
p = a;
(*p)++;
```

(a) a[0] = 2   (b) a[1] = 3
(c) a[1] = 2   (d) all

25. It is necessary to declare the type of a function in the calling prorgam if
(a) the function returns an integer
(b) the function returns a non-integer value
(c) the function is not defined in the same file
(d) None of the above

26. Which will legally declare, construct, and initialize an array?
(a) int [] myList = {"1", "2", "3"};
(b) int [] myList = (5, 8, 2) ;
(c) int myList [] [] = {4,9,7,0};
(d) int myList [] = {4, 3, 7};

27. Recursive functions are executed in a
(a) last in first out order
(b) first in first out order
(c) parallel fashion
(d) Any one of these

28. When a function is recursively called, all automatic variables

(a) are initialised during each execution of the function
(b) are retained from the last execution
(c) are maintained in a stack
(d) None of the above

29. A static variable is one
(a) which cannot be initialised
(b) which is initialised once at the commencement of execution and cannot be changed at run-time
(c) retains its value throughout the life of the program
(d) which is the same as an automatic variable but is placed at the head of a program

30. An external variable is one
(a) which is globally accessible by all the functions
(b) has a declaration 'extern' associated with it when declared within a function
(c) will be initialised to 0 if not initialized
(d) All of the above

31. Consider the following program fragment:

```
main()
{
    int a, b, c;
    b = 2;
    a = 2*(b++);
c = 2*(++b);
}
```

Which one of the given answer is correct?
(a) a = 4, c = 6   (b) a = 3, c = 8
(c) b = 3, c = 6   (d) a = 4, c = 8

32. Given the following program fragment, which one of the alternatives is correct?

```
main()
{
    char status;
    int balance;
    balance = 1000;
    status = (balance >= 1000) ? 'C': 'O';
}
```

(a) status = 'O' (b) status = 'C'
(c) status = O; (d) status = NIL

33. What will be value of count after the following program is executed?

```c
main()
{
    int count, digit = 0;
    count = 1;
    while (digit <= 9) {
    printf ("%d\n,++count);
            ++digit:}
}
```

(a) 10 (b) 9
(c) 12 (d) 11

34. What will be the value of the sum after the following program is executed?

```c
main()
{
    int sum, index,
    sum = 1;
    index = 9;
            do {
            index = index -1;
            sum = 2* sum;
            } while (index > 9);
```

(a) 1 (b) 2
(c) 9 (d) 0.5

35. How many times will the print statement be executed?

```c
main()
{
    int n;
    n = 10;
    while (n < 10) {
    printf ("hello!");
            - - n;
}   }
```

(a) never (b) once
(c) 10 (d) 9

36. If the following loop is implemented

```c
{int num;
num = 0;
```

```c
do { - - num;
    printf ("%d", num);
    num++;
    } while (num > = 0)
}
```

(a) the loop will run infinitely many times
(b) the program will not enter the loop
(c) there will be a compilation error reported
(d) a run time error will be reported

37. What is the final value of digit?

```c
main()
{
int  digit;
for (digit = 0; digit <= 9; ++digit)
printf ("%d\n", digit);
digit = 2*digit;
- - digit;
}
```

(a) 19 (b) −1
(c) 17 (d) 16

38. What is the final value of sum?

```c
main()
{
    int sum = 1;
    for (;sum <= 9;)
    printf("%d\n", ++sum);
}
```

(a) 10 (b) 9
(c) 11 (d) None of these

39. What is the value of 'average' after the following program is executed?

```c
main()
{
    int sum, index;
    index = 0;
    sum = 0;
    for(;;){
    sum = sum + index;
    ++index;
    if(sum >= 100) break;
}
    average = sum / index;
}
```

(a) 91 / 14 (b) 91 / 13
(c) 105 / 15 (d) 105 / 14

40. What is the output of the following program?

```
main()
{
    int x, y, z;
    x = 2;
    y = 1;
    z = 1;
            if(x > y + z)
            printf("Hello!\n");
            else if (x < y + z)
            printf ("Hi!\n");
    else
            printf("Hey!\n");
}
```

(a) Hi! (b) Hello!
(c) Hey! (d) None of these

41. What is the value of variable POLYGON?

```
main ()
{
    int POLYGON, L, B;
    L = B = 2;
    POLYGON = (L = = B) ? 1:0;
}
```

(a) 0 (b) 1
(c) 2 (d) None of these

42. Which three are legal array declarations?
1. int [] myScores [];
2. char [] myChars;
3. int [6] myScores;
4. Dog myDogs [];
5. Dog myDogs [7];

(a) 1, 2, 4 (b) 2, 4, 5
(c) 2, 3, 4 (d) All are correct

43. Which one of the following will declare an array and initialize it with five numbers?
(a) Array a = new Array(5) ;
(b) int [] a = {23,22,21,20,19};
(c) int a [] = new int[5];
(d) int [5] array;

44.
```
# define two(x) 2*x
# define ddouble(x) x+x
main()
{
    int num, sum, product;
    num = 1;
    sum = - -two(num); - -sum;
    product = - -ddouble(num);
    printf("%d%d\n", sum, product);
}
```
The output of the above program is
(a) 0 0 (b) 0 1
(c) 1 1 (d) 1 0

45. The following program fragment
```
{
    int sum, index;
    index = 50;
    while(index >= 0) {
    sum = sum / index;
    - index;
}
}
```
(a) will give a run time error
(b) will give a compilation error
(c) will give a linking error
(d) none of the above

46. What is the output of the following program?
```
main()
{
    int B, X, Y, Z;
    X = 1;
    Y = 2;
    Z = 3;
            if ((X > 1) (Y > 1))
            if (Z > 1)
            printf("O.K.\n");
    else break;
            if ((X > 1) && (Z > 3))
            printf("Bye\n");
            printf("Hello!");
}
```
(a) O.K. Bye (b) Bye
(c) O.K. (d) Hello !

47.
```
main()
{
    float balance, loan;
    balance = 1000.0;
    loan = balance / 10;
    if((balance > 500) (loan < 500))
    printf("good account\n");
    if(balance < 500) (loan < 500)
printf("caution !\n");
}
```
What is the output of the above program?
(a) good account
(b) caution
(c) good account caution
(d) none of the above

48. The following lines, if included in a program, will cause one of the following errors. Indicate the correct one
```
{double c;
    scanf("%c", c);
}
```
(a) Run time error   (b) Compilation error
(c) Type def error   (d) No error

49. Which three are valid declarations of a char?
1. char c1 = 064770;
2. char c2 = 'face';
3. char c3 = 0xbeef;
4. char c4 = \u0022;
5. char c5 = '\iface';
6. char c6 = '\uface';
(a) 1, 2, 4   (b) 1, 3, 6
(c) 3, 5   (d) 5 only

50. What type of memory is not directly addressable by the CPU and requires special software called EMS (expanded memory specification)   ?
(a) Extended   (b) Expanded
(c) Base   (d) Conventional

51. What is the following program doing?
```
main()
{
    int digit = 0;
    do
    printf("%d\n", digit++);
    while (digit <=9);
```
(a) Adding 9 integer
(b) Adding integers from 1 to 9
(c) Displaying any 9 integers
(d) Displaying integers from 1 to 9

52. Consider the program fragment
```
switch (choice) {
case 'R' : printf("RED");
case 'W' : printf("WHITE");
case 'B' : printf("BLUE");
default : printf("ERROR");
break;
}
```
What would be the output if choice = 'R'?
(a) RED
(b) RED ERROR
(c) RED WHITE BLUE ERROR
(d) RED WHITE BLUE

53. If c is a variable initialised to 1, how many times will be following loop be executed?
```
while((c > 0) && (c < 60)) {
loop body
c ++;
}
```
(a) 61   (b) 59
(c) 60   (d) 1

54. One of a class of storage device devices that can access storage locations in any order is
(a) DTE   (b) DASD
(c) DDE   (d) none of these

55. A term used to describe interconnected computer configuration is
(a) Multiprogramming
(b) Modulation
(c) Multiprocessing
(d) Micro program sequence

56. The for statement, which can precede a loop to be executed 50 times or till a Boolean variable 'found' becomes false, is given by

(a) for (i = 0; i < 50 found = = true; i++)
(b) for (i = 0; i <= 50 found = = false; i++)
(c) for (i = 1; i <= 50 && found = = true; i++)
(d) None of the above

57. The declarations:
typedef float height [100];
height men, women;
  (a) define men and women as 100 element floating point arrays
  (b) define height, men and women as floating point variables
  (c) define men and women as floating point variables
  (d) are illegal

58. Consider the following declarations:
typedef struct {
char name [20];
char middlename [5];
char surname [20];
    }NAME
    NAME class [20];
  (a) class is a new type
  (b) class is an array of 20 names where each name consists of a name, middlename and surname
  (c) class is an array of 20 characters only
  (d) None of these

59. What will be the values assigned to a, b, c if the statement scanf("%d %d %d", &a,&b,&c) is extended with input data item 123456?
  (a) a and b are not assigned anything, c = 23456
  (b) a = 1, b = 2, c = 3
  (c) a = 123456 and nothing is assigned to b and c
  (d) a = 12, b = 34, c = 56

60. What will be the values assigned to a, b and c if the statement scanf("%3d,%3d,%3d", &a, &b, &c) is executed with input data as 1234b5678b9(b denotes blank)?
  (a) a = 123, b = 4, c = 567

(b) a = 123, b = 456, c = 789
(c) a = 123, b = 567, c = 9
(d) a = 1234, b = 5678, c = 9

61. What will be the values of i, x and c if scanf ("%3d,%5f,%c", &i,&x&c) is executed with input data 10b256.875bT?
  (a) i = 010, b = 256.87, c = '5'
  (b) i = 100, b = 256.87, c = T
  (c) i = 10, b = 56.875, c = T
  (d) i = 10, b = 256.8, c = '7'

62. What will be the assignments if
char s[100]; int d; float f;
scanf ("%s, %*d, %f", s, &d, &f) is executed with input data
fastener b12345b5
  (a) s = "fastener", d = 123*45, f = 0.05
  (b) s = "fastener", d = 12345, f = 0.05
  (c) s = "fastener", f = 0.05
  (d) s = "fastener", d = 0.05

63. What will be the output of the following program fragment?
```
{
    int i = 12345
    float x = 145.678;
    printf("%3d,%5d,%8d", i, i, i);
}
```
  (a) 1 2 3
  (b) 12345 12345 12345
  (c) 12345
  (d) 123 123 123

64. Which of the following is an acronym for electronic delay storage automatic calculator?
  (a) UNIVAC   (b) EDSAC
  (c) EDVAC   (d) Abacus

65. A method of implementing a memory management system Is
  (a) Buddy system
  (b) Bridgeware
  (c) Broadband coaxial system
  (d) All of the above

66. Consider the following definitions:
```
struct circle {
float radius;
struct point center;
} circle1;
    struct point {
int x;
int y;
}
```
One can define a circle by the following assignment statement
(a) circle1.radius = 10; circle1.center.x = 0; center.y = 0;
(b) circle1.circle.radius=10; circle1.circle.centre.point.x = 0; circle1.circle.centre.point.y = 0;
(c) circle1.radius = 10, circle1.x = circle1.y = 0;
(d) radius = 10; x = 0; y = 0;

67. Consider the following declaration
```
struct list {
    int x;
    struct list *next;
}*head;
```
The statement head.x = 100
(a) creates a head of the list
(b) creates a node to type list and assigns a value to x
(c) assigns 100 to one element of the structure list
(d) is an erroneous statement

68. How many times, will the following loop be executed?
```
c1 = 'a';
while (c1 >= 'a' && c1 <= 'z')
{
    c1 ++;
}
```
(a) 0   (b) 26
(c) 25   (d) 1

69. What is the following function computing?
```
test (n)
```

```
int n;
{
int i;
long int prod = 1;
if (n > 1)
for (i = 2; i <= n; i++)
prod * = i;
return(prod);
}
```
(a) It checks whether n is a non-negative integer
(b) It calculates the value of factorial n
(c) It calculates the product to any n positive integers
(d) None of these

70. What is the following function doing?
```
test (a,b)
int a, b;
{
    int z = (abs(a) >= abs(b)) ? a:b;
    return(z);
}
```
(a) It returns the minimum of a and b
(b) It finds the maximum of a and b
(c) It returns the member whose absolute value is largest
(d) None of these

71.
```
void summation(n)
int n;
{
int i; sum = 0;
i = 1;
    for (i = 1; i <= n; i++)
    sum += i;
}
```
The above program returns
(a) sum of 1, 2,........, n
(b) the nth number
(c) the sum of n numbers
(d) None of these

72.
```
void Test(void)
{
```

```
char c;
if ((c = getchar())! = EOLN) Test ();
putchar(c);
return;
}
```

The above function
(a) reads a line character by character
(b) reads a line and prints it one character at a time
(c) prints a line as it is read from the standard input, character by character
(d) reads line character by character, reverses it and prints it

73. What will be the output of the following program?

```
{
    int i = 1234; j = 0177, k =0xa08c;
    printf("%8dx\n",i,j,k);
}
```

(a) 1234 1777 a08c
(b) 0000 1234 01aa ax
(c) 1234 1abc a08c
(d) 1234 0777 ao8o

74. What is the following function doing?

```
main()
{
    char line [80];
    gets (line);
    puts (line);
}
```

(a) It reads in a line of 80 characters
(b) It prints 80 vertical lines on the screen
(c) It prints horizontal straight lines on the screen
(d) It reads and prints lines composed of characters

75. User programmable terminals that combine VDT hardware with built-in microprocessor is
(a) Kips
(b) PC
(c) Mainframe
(d) Intelligent terminals

76. Which three are methods of the Object class?
1. notify()   ;
2. notifyAll()   ;
3. isInterrupted()   ;
4. synchronized()   ;
5. interrupt()   ;
6. wait(long msecs) ;
7. sleep(long msecs) ;
8. yield()   ;

(a) 1, 2, 4   (b) 2, 4, 5
(c) 1, 2, 6   (d) 2, 3, 4

77. How many bytes are occupied by near, far and huge pointers (DOS) ?
(a) near=2 far=4 huge=4
(b) near=4 far=8 huge=8
(c) near=2 far=4 huge=8
(d) near=4 far=4 huge=8

78. What would be the equivalent pointer expression for referring the array element a [i][j][k][l]
(a) ((((a+i)+j)+k)+l)
(b) *(*(*(*(a+i)+j)+k)+l)
(c) (((a+i)+j)+k+l)
(d) ((a+i)+j+k+l)

79. Which header file should be included to use functions like malloc() and calloc() ?
(a) memory.h   (b) stdlib.h
(c) string.h   (d) dos.h

80. What would be the value of c?

```
{
    int c;
    float a, b;
    a = 245.05;
    b = 40.02;
    c = a + b;
}
```

(a) 285.0   (b) 285.07
(c) 2850   (d) 285

81. What would be the value of *i* and *k*?
```
{
        int i, j, k;
        j = 5;
        i= 2*j/2;
        k= 2*(j/2);
}
```
(a) *i* = 4, *k* = 5   (b) *i* = 4, *k* = 4
(c) *i* = 5, *k* = 4   (d) *i* = 5, *k* = 5

82. In which order do the following gets evaluated
1. Relational
2. Arithmetic
3. Logical
4. Assignment

(a) 2134   (b) 1234
(c) 4321   (d) 3214

83. How many times will the following loop be executed?
```
{
        x = 5;
        if (x = 1) {
        :
        x ++;
}
```
(a) Once
(b) Never
(c) Five times
(d) Infinitely many times

84. If an integer occupies 4 bytes and a character occupies 1 byte of memory, each element of the following structure will occupy how many bytes?
```
struct name {
int age;
char name [20];
}
```
(a) 21   (b) 24
(c) 5   (d) 22

85. A short integer occupies 2 bytes, an ordinary integer 4 bytes and a long integer occupies 8 bytes of memory. A structure is defined as follows:
```
struct TAB {
short a;
int b;
long c;
}TABLE [10];
```
Then, the total memory requirement for TABLE is
(a) 40   (b) 140
(c) 14   (d) 24

86. The maximum combined length of the command-line arguments including the spaces between adjacent arguments is

(a) 128 characters
(b) 256 characters
(c) 67 characters
(d) It may vary from one operating system to another

87. Consider a part of a loop as shown below:
```
for(i = 0; i<= 10000; i++)
{:
:
        if(error < 0.005) break;
        }
```
The above loop will
(a) will never run for 10,000 times
(b) always run for 10,000 times
(c) may or may not run for 10000 times
(d) None of the above

88.
```
if (i > 1) c = 2;
else c = 3;
switch(c) {
        case 2 : printf("CAUTION");
        break;
        case 3 : printf("GOOD BYE");
        break;
        default : printf("ERROR");
        }
```
What is the output if *i* = 3?
(a) CAUTION   (b) ERROR
(c) GOOD BYE   (d) default

89. How many times, will the following loop be executed ?

```
x = 500;
while (x <= 500)
{
    x = x - 600;
    if (x < 0) break;
}
```

(a) 100   (b) 1
(c) 500   (d) 0

90. Consider the following program fragment:

```
for (count = 1, sum = 0; count <= 10; count ++) {
    scanf ("%d", &x);
    if (x < 0) continue;
    sum + = x;
}
```

What will be the value of sum with the following input values ?

1, −1, 2, −2, 3, −3, 4, −4, 5, −5.

(a) 10
(b) 30
(c) 0
(d) 15

91. Consider the following program fragment

```
sum = 0;
    do {
            scanf("%d", &x);
            if (x > 0) printf ("%d", x);
        else
        if (x = = 0) break;
        sum += x;
        } while (sum < 10);
```

What will be the output if input is 5, 2, 0, 3, 0 ?

(a) 5 2   (b) 5 2 0 3
(c) 5 2 0   (d) 5 2 3

92. If nstart = 10, n = 0 and nstop = 100, what will be the output of the following program fragment?

```
for(i = 0; n <= nstop; i++)
    {
        n = nstart + i* nstart;
        printf("%d", n);
```

(a) 10 11 12 100
(b) 10
(c) 10 20 30 40 110
(d) 100

93. What will be the output of the following program?

```
sum = 0;
for (i = 1; i <= 10; i++)
    if (i%2 = = 0) sum += i;
    printf("%d", sum);
```

(a) 0   (b) 45
(c) 40   (d) 30

94. What do the 'c' and 'v' in argv stands for?
(a) 'c' means argument control 'v' means argument vector
(b) 'c' means argument count 'v' means argument vertex
(c) 'c' means argument count 'v' means argument vector
(d) 'c' means argument configuration 'v' means argument visibility

95. What will be the output of the following program ?

```
sum = 0;
for (i = -100; i < 0; i++)
sum += abs(i);
printf("%d", sum);
```

(a) -5050   (b) 5050
(c) 100   (d) -100

96. What is the value of u1 and u2?

```
int u1, u2;
int v = 3;
int *pv;
    u1 - 2*(v + 5);
    pv = &v;
    u2 = 2*(*pv + 5);
```

(a) u1 = 16, u2 = 16   (b) u1 = 16, u2 = 3
(c) u1 = 8, u2 = 16   (d) u1 = 8, u2 = 3

97. What will be the output of the following program?

```
for (row = 1; row <= 100; row ++) {
    for (col = 0; col < 5; ++col)
    printf ("%d", row);
    printf ("\n");
}
```

(a) 1 2 3 4 5 100

(b) 1 2 3 4 5 }
    1 2 3 4 5 } 100 times
    1 2 3 4 5 }

(c) 1 2 3 4 5
    6 7 8 9 10

   . . . . . .

(d) 1 6 .... 9 6
    2 7 .... 9 7
    3 8 .... 9 8
    4 9 .... 9 9
    5 10 100

98. Consider the following program fragment:

```
if (marks > 80) grade = 'A';
else if ((marks > 70) && (attendance > 75))
grade = 'B';
else if (attendance < 75) grade = 'R'
if ((marks < 60) && (attendance < 500))
grade = 'F'
else grade = 'E';
```

What is the value of grade if marks = 55 and attendance = 80?

(a) F   (b) B

(c) A   (d) E

99. How will you free the allocated memory ?

(a) remove(var-name);   (b) free(var-name);

(c) delete(var-name); (d) dalloc(var-name);

100. What is the similarity between a structure, union and enumeration?

(a) All of them let you define new values

(b) All of them let you define new data types

(c) All of them let you define new pointers

(d) All of them let you define new structures

ANSWERS

1	2	3	4	5	6	7	8	9	10
(a)	(c)	(a)	(b)	(d)	(c)	(a)	(a)	(c)	(b)
11	12	13	14	15	16	17	18	19	20
(c)	(a)	(c)	(a)	(a)	(c)	(b)	(c)	(c)	(c)
21	22	23	24	25	26	27	28	29	30
(a)	(b)	(b)	(b)	(b)	(d)	(a)	(a)	(c)	(d)
31	32	33	34	35	36	37	38	39	40
(d)	(b)	(d)	(b)	(a)	(a)	(a)	(a)	(c)	(c)
41	42	43	44	45	46	47	48	49	50
(b)	(a)	(b)	(d)	(a)	(c)	(c)	(a)	(b)	(b)
51	52	53	54	55	56	57	58	59	60
(d)	(c)	(b)	(b)	(a)	(c)	(a)	(b)	(c)	(a)
61	62	63	64	65	66	67	68	69	70
(d)	(c)	(b)	(b)	(a)	(a)	(d)	(b)	(b)	(c)
71	72	73	74	75	76	77	78	79	80
(d)	(d)	(a)	(d)	(d)	(c)	(a)	(b)	(b)	(d)
81	82	83	84	85	86	87	88	89	90
(c)	(a)	(d)	(b)	(b)	(d)	(c)	(a)	(b)	(d)
91	92	93	94	95	96	97	98	99	100
(a)	(c)	(d)	(c)	(b)	(a)	(c)	(d)	(b)	(b)

1. Which of the following statements should be used to obtain a remainder after dividing 3.14 by 2.1 ?
   (a) rem = 3.14 % 2.1;
   (b) rem = modf(3.14, 2.1);
   (c) rem = fmod(3.14, 2.1);
   (d) Remainder cannot be obtain in floating point division.

2. What would be the output of the following program if input to the program is 'e'?
   ```
   main ()
   {
       int lower, upper;
       upper = getchar ();
       upper = toupper(lower);
       putchar(upper);
   }
   ```
   (a) e   (b) 53
   (c) E   (d) nothing

3. Is there any difference between following declarations?
   ```
   1 : extern int fun();
   2 : int fun();
   ```
   (a) Both are identical
   (b) No difference, except extern int fun(); is probably in another file
   (c) int fun(); is overrided with extern int fun();
   (d) None of these

4. If S is an array of 80 characters, then the value assigned to S through the statement scanf("%s", S) with input 12345, will be
   (a) "12345"
   (b) S is an illegal name for a string
   (c) nothing since 12345 is an integer
   (d) %s cannot be used for reading in values of S.

5. 1 : typedef long a; extern int a c;
   2 : typedef long a; extern a int c;
   3 : typedef long a; extern a c;
   (a) 1 correct   (b) 2 correct
   (c) 3 correct   (d) 1, 2, 3 are correct

6. The part of machine level instruction, which tells the central processor what has to be done, is
   (a) Operation code   (b) Address
   (c) Locator   (d) Flip-Flop

7. Which of the following refers to the associative memory?
   (a) the address of the data is generated by the CPU
   (b) the address of the data is supplied by the users
   (c) there is no need for an address i.e. the data is used as an address
   (d) the data are accessed sequentially

8. To avoid the race condition, the number of processes that may be simultaneously inside their critical section is
   (a) 8   (b) 1
   (c) 16   (d) 0

9. A system program that combines the separately compiled modules of a program into a form suitable for execution
   (a) assembler   (b) linking loader
   (c) cross compiler   (d) load and go

10. The maximum combined length of the command-line arguments including the spaces between adjacent arguments is
(a) 128 characters
(b) 256 characters
(c) 67 characters
(d) It may vary from one operating system to another

11. What do the 'c' and 'v' in argv stands for?
(a) 'c' means argument control 'v' means argument vector
(b) 'c' means argument count 'v' means argument vertex
(c) 'c' means argument count 'v' means argument vector
(d) 'c' means argument configuration 'v' means argument visibility

12. The declaration:
union id {
char color [12];
int size; } shirt, pant;
denotes shirt and pant are variables of type id and
(a) shirt and pant are the same as struct variables
(b) each can represent either a 12-character color or a integer size at a time
(c) each can have a value of colour and size
(d) variables shirt and pant cannot be used simultaneously in a statement

13. Identify the most appropriate sentence to describe unions
(a) Unions are used for set operations
(b) Unions contain members of different data types which share the same storage area in memory
(c) Unions are less frequently used in programs
(d) Unions are like structures

14. Consider the following declarations:
union id {
char color;

int size;
}
struct {
char country;
int date;
union id;
} flag;
To assign a color to a flag, the correct statement will be
(a) flag.color = 'White';
(b) flag.id.color = 'W';
(c) flag.color = 'W';
(d) flage.id.color = 'White';

15. Consider the following declaration
enum colors {black, blue, green};
This represents
(a) black = 0, blue = 1, green = 2
(b) color = 'black' or color = 'blue' or color = 'green'
(c) color[1] = 'black', color[2] = 'blue', color[3] = 'green'
(d) None of the above

16. With the following declaration
enum color {black = -1 blue, green}
(a) black = -1, blue = -2, green = -3
(b) black = -1, blue = 2, green = 3
(c) black = -1, blue = 0, green = 1
(d) this is an illegal declaration

17. What is the output of the following program?

```
main ()
{
    int u = 1, v = 3;
    printf ("%d %d", u,v);
    funct1 (&u, &v);
    printf ("%d %d\n", u,v);
}
void funct1 (int *pu, int *pv)
{
    *pu = 0;
    *pv = 0;
    return;
}
```

(a) $u = 3$ $v = 1$ $u = 3$ $v = 1$
(b) $u = 1$ $v = 3$ $u = 1$ $v = 1$
(c) $u = 1$ $v = 3$ $u = 0$ $v = 0$
(d) $u = 1$ $v = 3$ $u = 1$ $v = 3$

18. What is the output of the following program?

```
main()
{
    int i = 0;
    while (i < 5) {
    sum(i);
            i++;
    }
}
void sum(i)
    int i;
{
static k;
printf("%d", k +1);
    k ++;
}
```

(a) 012345   (b) 01234
(c) 13579   (d) 02468

19. What are the output of the following program?

```
main ()
{
    int u = 1;
    int v = 3;
void funct1 (int u, int v);
void funct2 (int *pu, int *pv);
printf ("u = %d", v = %d", u,  v);
funct1(u, v);
printf ("u = %d", v = %d", u,  v);
funct2 (&u, &v);
printf ("u = %d, v = %d", u, v);
}
funct1 (int u, int v)
{
u = u + V;
v = u - v;
u = u - v;
}
```

```
funct2 (int *pu, int *pv)
{
    *pu = *pu + *pv;
    *pv = *pu - pv;
    *pu = *pu - pv;
```

(a) $u = 1$ $v = 3$ $u = 3$ $v = 1$ $u = 1$ $v = 3$
(b) $u = 1$ $v = 3$ $u = 3$ $v = 1$ $u = 3$ $v = 1$
(c) $u = 1$ $v = 3$ $u = 1$ $v = 3$ $u = 1$ $v = 3$
(d) $u = 1$ $v = 3$ $u = 1$ $v = 3$ $u = 3$ $v = 1$

20. Consider the following fragment

```
main ()
{
    void f1 (int a);
    int i;
    for (i = 0; i<=5; i++)
    f1(i);
}
void f1 (int a)
{
    static int k;
int prod = 1;
while (k < 4) {
    prod *=a; k ++; }
    printf ("%d", prod);
}
```

The output of the program will be
(a) 0 1 2 3   (b) 0 1 2 3 4 5
(c) 0 1   (d) 0 1 4 9 16 25

21. If a = Oxaa and $b = a \ll 1$, then
(a) $a = 2b$ (b) $b = 2a$
(c) $b = a$ (d) $b = a-1$

22. When a new element is inserted in the middle of a linked list, which one of the following is true?
(a) The element that appears before and after the new element need to be moved
(b) Only the elements that appear before the new elements need to be moved
(c) Only the elements that appear after the new elements need to be moved
(d) None of these

23. Addressing structure
    (a) defines the fundamental method of determining effective operand addresses
    (b) are variations in the use of fundamental addressing structures, or some associated actions which are related to addressing.
    (c) performs indicated operations on two fast registers of the machine and leave the result in one of the registers.
    (d) all of the above

24. The Memory Buffer Register (MBR)
    (a) is a hardware memory device which denotes the location of the current instruction being executed.
    (b) is a group of electrical circuits (hardware), that performs the intent of instructions fetched from memory.
    (c) contains the address of the memory location that is to be read from or stored into.
    (d) contains a copy of the designated memory location specified by the MAR after a "read" or the new contents of the memory prior to a "write".

25. Which of the following 'C' type is not a primitive data structure?
    (a) float   (b) int
    (c) char   (d) none of the above

26. The strategy of allowing processes that are logically runnable to be temporarily suspended is called
    (a) preemptive scheduling
    (b) non preemptive scheduling
    (c) shortest job first
    (d) first come first served

27. If the address of the eighth element in a linked list of integers is 1022, then the address of 9th element is
    (a) 1026   (b) 1024
    (c) 1023   (d) None of these

28. What will be the value returned by the following functions, when it is called with 11?

```
recur (int num)
{
if ( (num /2) != 0) return (recur (num /2)
*10+num%2);
else return 1;
}
```
    (a) 11
    (b) The function does not return any value, because it goes into an infinite loop
    (c) 1011
    (d) None of these

29. Consider the following set of statements:

```
float x, y;
x = 7;
y = 10;
x* = y* = y + 28.5;
```
After the execution of the above set of statements, the value of x will be
    (a) 1995   (b) 2695
    (c) 70   (d) None of these

30. The Storage-to-Storage instructions
    (a) have both their operands in the main store.
    (b) which perform an operation on a register operand and an operand which is located in the main store, generally leaving the result in the register, expect in the case of store operation when it is also written into the specified storage location.
    (c) which perform indicated operations on two fast registers of the machine and have the result in one of the registers
    (d) all of the above

31. The output of the following program will be

```
# include <stdio.h>
int x[ ] = {0,1,2,4};
void s1(int*p1, int*p2)
{
    int temp;
    temp = *p1;
```

```
    *p1=*p2;
    *p2=temp;
}
main ()
{
    int i = 1;
    x[i] = 2;
    s1(&i, &x[i]);
    printf("%d %d \n", i, x[i]);
}
```

(a) 2 1   (b) 2 2
(c) 1 2   (d) None of these

32. Consider the following program

```
#include <stdio.h>
main()
{
int age; char sex;
puts("What is your age ?");
scanf("%d, &age);
puts ( "What is your sex ?");
sex=getchar();
}
```

What happens when the above program is compiled and executed?
(a) Produces syntax error
(b) Accepts age but it does not wait to input sex
(c) Accepts age and sex from standard input
(d) None of these

33. Consider the following program

```
#include <stdio.h>
main ()
{
int x=105,y=0,z=30;
char k[4];
strcpy(k, "FAIL");
if (x/20= =5 && (x*y>100 | | y+z*2<75))
if(x<<2<=256)
strcpy (k,"PASS");
else strcpy (k,"pass");
else strcpy (k, "fail");
}
```

The value of k on execution of the above program will be
(a) FAIL   (b) PASS
(c) pass   (d) None of these

34. Which of the following statements is correct regarding following C program ?

```
main ()
{
int i,,j,*p,*s;
j=j=30;
*(p=&i)*3;
p=(s=p,s=&j,s=&i);
*s+ = *p+5;
```

(a) Produces syntax errors
(b) *s, *p and j are equal
(c) *s, *p and i are equal
(d) None of the above

35. Which of the following function sets first *n* characters of a string to a given character?
(a) strinit()   (b) strnset()
(c) strset()   (d) strcset()

36. If the two strings are identical, then strcmp() function returns
(a) −1   (b) 1
(c) 0   (d) Yes

37. The library function exit() causes an exit from
(a) the functions in which, it occurs
(b) the block in which, it occurs
(c) the loop in which, it occurs
(d) None of these

38. The getch() library function
(a) returns and displays a character on the screen when any key is pressed
(b) returns a character when enter is pressed
(c) returns a character when any key is pressed
(d) None of the above

39. A default argument has a value that
(a) may be supplied by the calling program or function
(b) integers with user defined names

   (c) related data items and variables
   (d) None of these

40. A structure brings together a group of
   (a) integers with user-defined names
   (b) related data items and variables
   (c) items of the same data type
   (d) None of these

41. The && and operators
   (a) combine two numeric values
   (b) compare two numeric values
   (c) compare two Boolean values
   (d) perform none of the above

42. The break statement causes an exit
   (a) only from the innermost switch
   (b) only from the innermost loop
   (c) from the innermost loop or switch
   (d) None of the above

43. The LRU algorithm
   (a) pages out pages that have been used recently
   (b) pages out pages that have not been used recently
   (c) pages out pages that have been least used recently
   (d) pages out the first page in a given area

44. When an array name is passed to a function, the function
   (a) accesses exactly the same array with the same name as the calling program
   (b) refers to the array using the same name as that used by the calling program
   (c) accesses a copy of the array passed by the program
   (d) None of the above

45. Thrashing
   (a) is a natural consequence of virtual memory systems
   (b) can always be avoided by swapping
   (c) always occurs on large computers
   (d) can be caused by poor paging algorithms

46. Supervisor state is
   (a) never used
   (b) entered by programs when they enter the processor
   (c) required to perform any I/O
   (d) only allowed to the operating system

47. The output of
```
main() {
    int i=5, j=5;
    while (j-- >=3) {static int i = 10;
    printf("%d,", i++);}
    printf("%d.",i); }
```
   (a) 10, 11, 12, 1   (b) 5, 6, 7, 8
   (c) 10, 10, 10, 1   (d) None of these

48. The output of
```
main () {
int x, y;
x = 0x0F;
y = 0x0F;
while ( x=y^x) printf ("%d,  %d,",x,y,y--);
printf ("%d.",x); }
```
   (a) 0, 16, 15, 0
   (b) 16, 16, 15, 16
   (c) 0, 16, 15, 15
   (d) 0 e

49. Static int *(*name []) ()
   (a) name is an array of pointers to functions returning pointer to static integer
   (b) name is function returning pointer to array of pointer to static integer
   (c) name is a static array of pointers to functions returning pointer to integer
   (d) None of these

50. The output of
```
main () {
int j = 'b'; switch (j) { case 'a' : putc ('a') ;
continue;
case 'b':putc ('b') ; continue; case 'c' :putc
('e');
continue; default : putc ('d') ; }}
```
   (a) b infinite times

(b) b
(c) bed
(d) none of these

51. What happens when the following C program is executed?

```
#include <stdio.h>
main ()
     FILE *fp1, *fp2; fp1 = fopen("one", "w");
fp2      =      fopen("one",      "w");
fputc('A',fp1);('B',fp2);
fclose (fp1) ; fclose (fp2) ; }
```

(a) Run time error
(b) Results in syntax error - not possible to open same file
(c) One will be created with character 'B'
(d) None of these

52. What is the output of the following code?

```
main() {
puts(concat ("NEWDELHI", "LUCKNOW"); }
char *concat(char *s1, char *s2) {
int l1 = strlen(s1),12 = strlen(s2), i,j;
char s[256] ; strcpy (s, s1);
for (i=l1, j=0; j < 12; j++,i++) s2[j]; s[i] = '\0';
retrun s;}
```

(a) NEW DELHI LUCKNOW
(b) NEWDELHI
(c) NEWDELHI LUCKNOW
(d) None of these

53. Which of the following instruction steps, would be written within the diamond-shaped box, of a flowchart?

(a) S = B - C   (b) IS A<10
(c) PRINT A   (d) DATA X,4Z

54. Consider the following program:

```
main ()
{
    int c – 50;
    for(; c;)
            c--;
    printf("%d\n", c);
}
```

The output of the program will be
(a) -50   (b) 50
(c) 0   (d) None of these

55. What is the output of the following program?

```
#define row 3
#define col 4
int a [row][col] = {1, 2, 3, 4, 5, 6, 7, 8, 9, 10, 11, 12};
main ()
{
    int i, j, k = 99;
    for (i = 0; i < row; i++)
    for (j = 0; j < col; j++)
    if(a[i][j] < k)
    k = a[i][j];
printf("%d\n",k);
}
```

(a) 12   (b) 99
(c) 1   (d) None of these

56. Consider the following program

```
main ()
{
int x = 0, i, j;
for (i=0, j=10; i < 5, j > 0; i += 2, j--)
++x;
printf("%d",x);
}
```

The output of the above program will be
(a) 10
(b) 0
(c) 5
(d) None of the above

57. The output of the following program will be

```
main ()
{
    int a, *ptr,b,c;
    a = 25;
    ptr = &a;
    b = a+30;
    c = *ptr;
    printf("%d,%d,%d", a, b, c);
}
```

(a) 25, 55, 55 (b) 25, 55, 25
(c) 25, 25, 25 (d) None of these

58. Consider the following program fragment:

```
main ()
{
    int a,b,c;
    b = 2;
    a = 2 x (b++);
    c = 2 x (++b);
}
```

The correct values are
(a) $b = 3, c = 6$ (b) $a = 3, c = 8$
(c) $a = 4, c = 6$ (d) $a = 4, c = 8$

59. The output of the following program will be

```
#include <stdio.h>
main ()
{
    int a=10, j=3, i=2;
    test1(a);
    a* = (i+j);
    printf("%d",a);
}
test1(x)
int x;
{
    int k=2;
    x* = k;
    return(x);
}
```

(a) 10 (b) 20
(c) 50 (d) None of these

60.
```
int arr[] = {1,2,3,4};
int count;
incr() {return ++count;}
main()
{
    arr[count++] = incr();
    printf("arr[count = %d\n", arr[count]);
}
```

The value printed by the above program is
(a) 2 (b) 1
(c) 3 (d) None of these

61.
```
#include <stdio.h>
main ()
{
    char ch = 'A';
    while(ch<='F'){
    switch(ch) {
    case 'A' : case 'B': case 'C': case 'D':
    ch++; continue;
    case 'E': case 'F': ch++;
}
putchar(ch);
}
}
```

What will be the output of the above program?
(a) EFG will be displayed
(b) FG will be displayed
(c) ABCDEF will be displayed
(d) None of these

62. In which stage the following code
```
#include<stdio.h>
```
gets replaced by the contents of the file stdio.h
(a) During editing
(b) During linking
(c) During execution
(d) During preprocessing

63. A computer cannot "boot" if it does not have the
(a) Compiler (b) Loader
(c) Operating system (d) Assembler

64. The statement
FILE *fpt;
(a) defines a pointer to pre-defined structure type FILE
(b) defines a pointer to a pre-defined data type FILE DESCRIPTOR
(c) defines a pointer to a user-defined structure type FILE
(d) None of the above

65. Which of the following statements is false?
  (a) the technique of storage compaction involves moving all occupied areas of storage to one end or other of main storage
  (b) compaction does not involve relocation of programs
  (c) compaction is also known as garbage collection
  (d) the system must stop everything while it performs the compaction

66. When one-dimensional character array of unspecified length is assigned an initial value, then
  (a) the length of the string is added to the end of the string
  (b) '10' is added to the end of the string
  (c) an arbitiary character is automatically added to the end of the string
  (d) All of the above

67. When multidimensional arrays are assigned initial value
  (a) Rightmost subscript increases most rapidly
  (b) Rightmost subscript increases least
  (c) Leftmost subscript increases most rapidly
  (d) All of the above

68. What will be the value of r if initial value of i, k and j are 2, −3, −3 with refrence to the following program segment

```
if {(i < 0) | | (j >= 0)}
{
    if (j = = k)
    r = 'T';
}
    else
    if (i = = k)
    r = 'F';
```

  (a) −3   (b) F
  (c) T   (d) 2

69. What is the output of the following program fragment?

```
{ sum = 0;
do {
    scanf ("%d", & i);
    if (i < 0) {
    i = -i;
    ++ flag;
}
sum + = i;
} while (i ! = 0);
}
```

  (a) The sum of (flag-1) number of input number
  (b) The sum of flag number of input numbers
  (c) The sum of absolute values of (flag) number of input numbers
  (d) None of the above

70. Interprocess communication
  (a) is required for all processes
  (b) is usually done via disk drives
  (c) is never necessary
  (d) allows processes to synchronize activity

71. Consider
enum colors {black, blue, siyan, green, red}
Enumeration constants (eg. black, blue) represent
  (a) integer values such that
       black 0

       .

       .

       .
       red 4
  (b) predefined floating point values
  (c) integer values such that
       black -1

       .

       .

       .
       red 3
  (d) None of these

72. Enumeration variables can be used in
  (a) search statement like a integer variable
  (b) preprocessor commands

(c) break statement
(d) All of the above

73. # define preprocessor command can be used for defining
(a) symbolic constants
(b) macros
(c) for loop
(d) both (a) and (c)

74. Which of the following functions is(are) performed by the loader
(a) allocate space in memory for the programs and resolve symbolic references between object decks
(b) adjust all address dependent locations, such as address constants, to correspond to the allocated space.
(c) physically place the machine instructions and data into memory.
(d) All of the above

75. Which of the following addressing modes, facilitates access to an operand whose location is defined relative to the beginning of the data structure in which it appears?
(a) ascending
(b) sorting
(c) index
(d) indirect

76. What will happen if in a C program you assign a value to an array element whose subscript exceeds the size of array?
(a) The element will be set to 0.
(b) The compiler would report an error.
(c) The program may crash if some important data gets overwritten.
(d) The array size would appropriately grow.

77. In C, if you pass an array as an argument to a function, what actually gets passed?
(a) Value of elements in array
(b) First element of the array
(c) Base address of the array
(d) Address of the last element of array

78. ERP is used in talking of
(a) security passes

(b) operating systems
(c) information environment
(d) None of these

79. While running DOS on a PC, which command would be used to duplicate the entire diskette?
(a) COPY
(b) DISKCOPY
(c) CHKDSK
(d) TYPE

80. Memory
(a) is a device that performs a sequence of operations specified by instructions in memory.
(b) is the device where information is stored
(c) is a sequence of instructions
(d) is typically characterized by interactive processing and time-slicing of the CPU's time to allow quick response to each user.

81. In mathematics and computer programming, which is the correct order of mathematical operators ?
(a) Addition, Subtraction, Multiplication, Division
(b) Division, Multiplication, Addition, Subtraction
(c) Multiplication, Addition, Division, Subtraction
(d) Addition, Division, Modulus, Subtraction

82. Select the most appropriate statement of the following
(a) Middle level managers undertake long range planning
(b) Operational managers make unstructured decisions
(c) As the management level goes up the hierarchy, information becomes more and more summarised
(d) None of these

83. A system program that sets up an executable program in main memory ready for execution is

(a) assembler   (b) linker
(c) loader   (d) compiler

84. What is (void*)0?
(a) Representation of NULL pointer
(b) Representation of void pointer
(c) Error
(d) None of above

85. In which header file is the NULL macro defined?
(a) stdio.h
(b) stddef.h
(c) stdio.h and stddef.h
(d) stdlib.h

86. How many bytes are occupied by near, far and huge pointers (DOS)?
(a) near=2 far=4 huge=4
(b) near=4 far=8 huge=8
(c) near=2 far=4 huge=8
(d) near=4 far=4 huge=8

87. What would be the equivalent pointer expression for referring the array element a [i][j][k][l]
(a) ((((a+i)+j)+k)+l)
(b) *(*(*(*(a+i)+j)+k)+l)
(c) (((a+i)+j)+k+l)
(d) ((a+i)+j+k+l)

88. Which of the following are loaded into main memory when the computer is booted?
(a) internal command instructions
(b) external command instructions
(c) utility programs
(d) word processing instructions

89. A typical data processing context, where master files are updated to produce desired output, is known as
(a) Normalisation process
(b) Transaction processing
(c) Validation checking
(d) None of the above

90. Which of the following are tools of SSAD?

(a) DFD   (b) CASE
(c) HIPO   (d) All of the above

91. Which one of the following are a part of the SDLC?
(a) Bench marking
(b) Program specification
(c) Requirement analysis
(d) All of the above

92. The principal of locality of reference justifies the use of
(a) reenterable   (b) non reusable
(c) virtual memory   (d) cache memory

93. The register or main memory location which contains the effective address of the operand is known as
(a) pointer   (b) indexed register
(c) special location   (d) scratch pad

94. If the requirements analysis phase of a software development project is not done properly, then the
(a) output reports will be indecipherable
(b) resulting system will be delivered before time
(c) system may fail to address the real needs of users
(d) All of the above

95. The detailed study / investigation of the present system is frequently referred to as
(a) Feasibility study
(b) System analysis
(c) System planning
(d) None of the above

96. What are the different types of real data type in C ?
(a) float, double
(b) short int, double, long int
(c) float, double, long double
(d) double, long int, float

97. Whether a proposed system can provide right information for the organisation's personnel, falls under the study of

(*a*) Technical feasibility
(*b*) Operational feasibility
(*c*) Economic feasibility
(*d*) All of the above

98. In considering the total cost associated with desired information, cost of data collection, data input and computer processing costs are
(*a*) temporary
(*b*) one time
(*c*) permanent
(*d*) recurring

99. The next major step before system design and after feasibility study is
(*a*) Analysis activity
(*b*) Implementation activity
(*c*) Equipment selection activity
(*d*) None of these

100. If a data dictionary is not included in the systems analysis and design of a software project, then the following task cannot be carried out properly
(*a*) Benchmarking of equipment to be purchased
(*b*) Cross referencing and consistency checks of various data
(*c*) Overall cost benefit analysis of the project
(*d*) None of these

ANSWERS

1	2	3	4	5	6	7	8	9	10
(*c*)	(*c*)	(*b*)	(*a*)	(*c*)	(*a*)	(*c*)	(*b*)	(*b*)	(*d*)
11	12	13	14	15	16	17	18	19	20
(*c*)	(*b*)	(*b*)	(*b*)	(*a*)	(*c*)	(*c*)	(*d*)	(*d*)	(*a*)
21	22	23	24	25	26	27	28	29	30
(*b*)	(*d*)	(*a*)	(*d*)	(*d*)	(*a*)	(*d*)	(*c*)	(*b*)	(*a*)
31	32	33	34	35	36	37	38	39	40
(*a*)	(*b*)	(*c*)	(*a*)	(*b*)	(*c*)	(*d*)	(*b*)	(*a*)	(*b*)
41	42	43	44	45	46	47	48	49	50
(*c*)	(*c*)	(*c*)	(*a*)	(*d*)	(*d*)	(*d*)	(*d*)	(*a*)	(*c*)
51	52	53	54	55	56	57	58	59	60
(*c*)	(*a*)	(*b*)	(*c*)	(*c*)	(*a*)	(*b*)	(*d*)	(*c*)	(*c*)
61	62	63	64	65	66	67	68	69	70
(*b*)	(*d*)	(*c*)	(*a*)	(*b*)	(*b*)	(*a*)	(*b*)	(*c*)	(*d*)
71	72	73	74	75	76	77	78	79	80
(*a*)	(*a*)	(*d*)	(*d*)	(*c*)	(*c*)	(*c*)	(*c*)	(*b*)	(*b*)
81	82	83	84	85	86	87	88	89	90
(*b*)	(*c*)	(*c*)	(*a*)	(*c*)	(*a*)	(*b*)	(*a*)	(*b*)	(*d*)
91	92	93	94	95	96	97	98	99	100
(*d*)	(*d*)	(*a*)	(*c*)	(*b*)	(*c*)	(*b*)	(*d*)	(*a*)	(*b*)

1. A major advantage of systems developed using DBMS as compared to systems using conventional file system is the following
   - (*a*) Conventional file system applications are inflexible
   - (*b*) The DBMS involves simultaneous updates of all data structures to keep the status current
   - (*c*) Ad-hoc queries are not possible in conventional file system applications
   - (*d*) All of the above

2. Removal of functional dependency from a relation falls under the category of
   - (*a*) 3rd form of Normalisation
   - (*b*) 2st form of Normalisation
   - (*c*) 1st form of Normalisation
   - (*d*) None of the above

3. Reason for normalisation is
   - (*a*) the simplification of retrieval e.g., query
   - (*b*) the simplification of maintenance, e.g., updates
   - (*c*) structured data
   - (*d*) All of the above

4. Which of the following is(are) true of the EDP auditors?
   - (*a*) they should have computer expertise
   - (*b*) they will be replaced by traditional auditors in the near future
   - (*c*) two of the above
   - (*d*) currently, there is a very high demand for them, particularly from firms that use personal computers

5. In order to ensure system quality
   - (*a*) unless user needs and software requirements specifications are reviewed, system design should not be initiated
   - (*b*) a proper test plan should be prepared and followed
   - (*c*) inspection should be carried out at pre-specified milestones
   - (*d*) All of the above

6. A lockbox service is used for
   - (*a*) depositing cash when bank is closed
   - (*b*) paying bank customer bills automatically
   - (*c*) storing papers in a bank vault
   - (*d*) depositing payments to bank customers

7. Critical path of the PERT chart is:
   - (*a*) path which takes the longest time to complete the project
   - (*b*) the shortest path
   - (*c*) both of the above
   - (*d*) path which takes the shortest time to complete the project

8. The _____ is a business-oriented data-processing association which publishes a monthly journal, Data Management.
   - (*a*) DPMA
   - (*b*) CDP
   - (*c*) CISA
   - (*d*) None of these

9. _____ are knowledge based system to which present rules are applied to solve a particular problem.
   - (*a*) ES
   - (*b*) AI
   - (*c*) KBS
   - (*d*) Base rule 0

10. How many digits of the DNIC (Data Network Identification Code) identify the country?

COM.Sc.-16

(a) first three   (b) first four
(c) first five   (d) first six

11. Spoken messages may be stored and forwarded by
(a) Voicemail system
(b) Expert System
(c) E-Mail
(d) Videoconferencing

12. A station in a network forwards incoming packets by placing them on its shortest output queue. What routing algorithm is being used?
(a) hot potato routing
(b) flooding
(c) static routing
(d) delta routing

13. When is menu interface a convenient way of user interaction?
(a) When data has to be imported from a spreadsheet
(b) When mouse is used as the main input device
(c) For data processing in a restaurant
(d) When it is difficult for the user to remember all the options available and for typing incomplicated commands

14. The main advantage of normalised relations in relational DBMS is that they
(a) occupy minimal storage
(b) do not suffer from anomalies during delete and update operations
(c) are highly secure
(d) All of the above

15. Which one of the following statements is incorrect?
(a) Current date can be shown in page header as well as page footer
(b) A report format file can show any object within a box
(c) A report format can show vertical lines in the report
(d) None of the above

16. A portfolio management program is
(a) another name for a personal financial management package
(b) never included in other financial management package
(c) used to track the fluctuating value of an investment holding
(d) normally used to track personal budget items and write cheques to pay bills

17. Which of the following condition is used to transmit two packets over a medium at the same time?
(a) Contention   (b) Collision
(c) Synchronous   (d) Asynchronous

18. The computer can potentially be used to monitor most of our actions, thus robbing us of _____
(a) tapping   (b) privacy
(c) back log   (d) security

19. A systems theory of organization sees the firm as a
(a) network of resource flows
(b) system transforming inputs into outputs
(c) physical system managed by a manager using a conceptual system
(d) All of the above

20. _____ decisions are those decisions for which policy standards or guidelines are already established.
(a) programmable   (b) control
(c) predictive reports (d) relevant

21. You have a class A network address 10.0.0.0 with 40 subnets, but are required to add 60 new subnets very soon. You would like to still allow for the largest possible number of host IDs per subnet. Which subnet mask should you assign?
(a) 255.240.0.0   (b) 255.248.0.0
(c) 255.252.0.0   (d) 255.254.0.0

22. What is the default subnet mask for a class C network?

(*a*) 127.0.0.1   (*b*) 255.0.0.0
(*c*) 255.255.0.0   (*d*) 255.255.255.0

23. Which of the following is not a disadvantage of wireless LAN?
(*a*) Slower data transmission
(*b*) higher error rate
(*c*) interference of transmissions from different computers
(*d*) All of the above

24. Which of the following is not an important principle for evaluating the raw data for decision-making:
(*a*) selection   (*b*) pattern
(*c*) everage   (*d*) overview

25. The model curriculum for information-system education suggested by the _______ has a more theoretical and conceptual basis, whereas the model by the _______ is more practical and applied in nature.
(*a*) AI, ES   (*b*) KBS, AI
(*c*) ACM, DPMA   (*d*) SISD, MMD

26. _______ decisions concern the execution of specific tasks to assure that they are carried out efficiently and effectively.
(*a*) tactical   (*b*) strategic
(*c*) operational   (*d*) management

27. The Internet Control Message Protocol (ICMP)
(*a*) allows gateways to send error a control messages to other gateways or hosts
(*b*) provides communication between the Internet Protocol Software on one machine and the Internet Protocol Software on another
(*c*) only reports error conditions to the original source, the source must relate errors to individual application programs and take action to correct the problem
(*d*) All of the above

28. The term 'duplex' refers to the ability of the data receiving stations to echo back a confirming message to the sender. In full duplex data transmission, both the sender and the receiver
(*a*) cannot talk at once
(*b*) can receive and send data simultaneously
(*c*) can send or receive data one at a time
(*d*) can do one way data transmission only

29. Which of the following technique is used for fragment?
(*a*) a technique used in best-effort delivery systems to avoid endlessly looping packets
(*b*) a technique used by protocols in which a lower level protocol accepts a message from a higher level protocol and places it in the data portion of the low level frame
(*c*) one of the pieces that results when an IP gateway divides an IP datagram into smaller pieces for transmission across a network that cannot handle the original datagram size
(*d*) All of the above

30. Error reports are an example of:
(*a*) scheduled reports (*b*) demand reports
(*c*) exception reports (*d*) predictive reports

31. A constraint that does not, affect the feasible solution region is known as
(*a*) redundant constraint
(*b*) unbounded solution
(*c*) slack variable
(*d*) surplus variable

32. Contention is
(*a*) One or more conductors that serve as a common connection for a related group of devices
(*b*) a continuous frequency capable of being modulated or impressed with a second signal
(*c*) the condition when two or more stations attempt to use the same channel at the same time

(*d*) a collection of interconnected functional units that provides a data communications service among stations attached to the network

33. Computer support to the manager has been least in
(*a*) alternative identification
(*b*) alternative selection
(*c*) problem identification
(*d*) alternative evaluation

34. Slack is the calculated time span within which the event must occur:
(*a*) true   (*b*) false
(*c*) cannot be said   (*d*) All of the above

35. The online, softcopy display of a customer's charge account to respond to an inquiry is an example of a(n):
(*a*) regularly scheduled report
(*b*) on-demand report
(*c*) exception report
(*d*) forecasting report

36. In a Bus Passanger Reservation System, which one of the following will be the primary key?
(*a*) The Bus   (*b*) Driver
(*c*) Route   (*d*) None of these

37. A new drug is being tested on Guinea pigs and a computer keeps tag on amount and dates. Which one of the following will the computer be least competent to do?
(*a*) Determine the total dosage individually and collectively
(*b*) Keep a record of each guinea pig, the date and drug dosage
(*c*) Decide weight changes of each guinea pig
(*d*) Record weight changes of each guinea pig

38. What stage of the manufacturing process has been described as "the mapping of function onto form"?

(*a*) Design
(*b*) Distribution
(*c*) project management
(*d*) field service

39. Which kind of planning consists of successive representations of different levels of a plan?
(*a*) hierarchical planning
(*b*) non-hierarchical planning
(*c*) project planning
(*d*) All of the above

40. CAM is used in which industry?
(*a*) Three-wheeler   (*b*) Helicopter
(*c*) Automobile   (*d*) All of the above

41. Data has to be _______ before it can be converted into information.
(*a*) transformed   (*b*) processed
(*c*) changed   (*d*) engineered

42. How does the check digit method capture mistakes that occurs while keying in a code, which incorporates a check digit?
(*a*) The method applies a hashing algorithm to the code entered and if the result is not a single digit, then it concludes the code entered is erroneous
(*b*) The method checks the number of digit keyed in with the maximum permissible number of digits in a code
(*c*) The checking is done completely through hardware
(*d*) Using the method adopted for generating the check digit while code was originally designed, the method computes the check digit again for the non-check digit part of the entered key. If the check digit computed is not equal to the check digit entered, then it indicates an error condition

43. "Back up" refers to
(*a*) job scheduling failure
(*b*) accumulation of programs in the memory
(*c*) delays in production of outputs
(*d*) None of the above

44. Cost of error correction is least at which stage?
- (a) Requirement analysis
- (b) Development
- (c) Design
- (d) Implementation

45. A Digital Signature is used in
- (a) Programming
- (b) Floppy disk marking
- (c) Data Communication
- (d) None of the above

46. The four icons used in building DFD's are
- (a) Flow, process, source / destination, store
- (b) Source, process, destination, store
- (c) Flow, process, source, store
- (d) Flow, process, source / destination, store

47. Which one of the following will ensure accuracy of inputs to a computer?
- (a) OCR
- (b) Scanner
- (c) Check digits
- (d) All of these

48. The type of code, which involves the assignment of a consecutive and unique number to each item is
- (a) group
- (b) sequence
- (c) numeric
- (d) None of these

49. A Structured Decision
- (a) is made after completion of a preplanned series of steps
- (b) is not Routine
- (c) depends upon information not known in advance
- (d) None of these

50. Managers performing strategic and technical roles need
- (a) external information only
- (b) internal information only
- (c) both, internal and external information
- (d) None of these

51. PROLOG is an AI programming language which solves problems with a form of symbolic logic known as predicate calculus. It was developed in 1972 at the University of Marseilles by a team of specialists. Can you name the person who headed this team?
- (a) Alain Colmerauer (b) Nicklaus Wirth
- (c) Seymour Papert (d) John McCarthy

52. Prior to the invention of time sharing, the prevalent method of computer access was:
- (a) batch processing
- (b) telecommunication
- (c) remote access
- (d) All of the above

53. Entities, Attributes and Relationship are associated with
- (a) logical concepts of data
- (b) persons of an organisation
- (c) physical concepts of data
- (d) None of these

54. Transaction Processing is called on-line if the transaction
- (a) is processed as soon as it enters the system
- (b) persons of an organisation
- (c) is processed in discrete lots
- (d) None of these

55. A Distributed Data Processing System
- (a) attempts to capture advantage of both centralised and decentralised processing
- (b) provides slow access to data
- (c) does not allow greater flexibilities
- (d) None of these

56. In Data Processing, Classifying, Calculating, Sorting and Summarizing Data are connected with
- (a) capturing of input data
- (b) managing output results
- (c) manipulating of data
- (d) None of these

57. Prototyping means
- (a) creating, developing and refining a working model of the final operational system

(b) designing the computer system
(c) testing the computer system
(d) None of these

58. Storage devices may be
   (a) direct access type only
   (b) sequential type only
   (c) Either *(a)* or *(b)*
   (d) None of the above

59. Blocking Factors is the
   (a) number of blocks in a file
   (b) number of records grouped in a Block
   (c) ratio between number of records accessed and total number of Records
   (d) None of these

60. The first step in SDLC is
   (a) preliminary investigation and analysis
   (b) database design
   (c) system design
   (d) None of these

61. An aid to System Design should primarily
   (a) help in documentation
   (b) help analyse both data and activities
   (c) generate code
   (d) None of these

62. Peer Review is an aid to
   (a) actions   *(b)* programs
   (c) programming   *(d)* None of these

63. The Strategic Computing Program is a project of the:
   (a) Defense Advanced Research Projects Agency
   (b) National Science Foundation
   (c) Jet Propulsion Laboratory
   (d) All of the above

64. Decision tables link conditions and
   (a) programs   *(b)* tables
   (c) actions   *(d)* None of these

65. Weak AI is
   (a) the embodiment of human intellectual capabilities within a computer.
   (b) a set of computer programs that produce output that would be considered to reflect intelligence if it were generated by humans.
   (c) the study of mental faculties through the use of mental models implemented on a computer.
   (d) All of the above

66. In a Passenger Reservation System, which one of the following is the most critical?
   (a) GUI
   (b) Response time
   (c) Ease of programming
   (d) None of these

67. A software design description document only includes
   (a) DFD   *(b)* ER diagram
   (c) Data dictionary *(d)* *(a)*, *(b)* or *(c)*

68. A Pseudo Code is a
   (a) programming aid
   (b) false logic
   (c) Both *(a)* and *(b)*
   (d) Neither *(a)* nor *(b)*

69. A data dictionary
   (a) defines the data types
   (b) gives the meaning of the data names used in the system
   (c) defines all data elements and structures used in DFD
   (d) None of the above

70. Backup and recovery procedures are necessary to
   (a) control the DBA
   (b) reorganise the disk
   (c) handle contingencies like files getting corrupted or becoming irretrievable
   (d) None of these

71. Which one of the following is an Exception Report?
   (a) Monthly salary sheet
   (b) Value of stocks in hand

(c) Machine replacement report

(d) None of these

72. File conversion is part of

(a) system cut-over

(b) day-to-day activity to DP

(c) system design

(d) None of these

73. Of the following, which one is not a function of a RDBMS?

(a) File and data integrity

(b) Security

(c) Audit trail

(d) None of these

74. Which of the following is not a key component of the evaluation process in building a DSS?

(a) criteria for evaluation

(b) means of measuring system-development time spent on the project

(c) means of monitoring the progress of the DSS

(d) formal review process

75. A model is used to analyse a complex system because it

(a) is closer to reality than the original system

(b) is usually computer-based

(c) contains only the essential features needed and hence easy to manipulate

(d) is aesthetically appealing

76. Structured Analysis and Design uses

(a) prototypes generated using object oriented methods

(b) trained programmers only in the phases

(c) documentation produced on Word Processors

(d) diagrams like DFD's

77. A DBMS is used mainly to

(a) promote decentralised and end user computing

(b) separate management from work

(c) facilitate transmission of files across continents

(d) eliminate data redundancy

78. Modular design of a system means

(a) use of models at each phase of system's life cycle

(b) division of the whole system into a number of units, each of which, is quite cohesive within itself and not too dependent others and also the design and development of the units separately

(c) delivery of a complex system to the customer one piece at a time

(d) use of sophisticated subroutine libraries available in shareware

79. If you are an information-system manager, which organization is most appropriate for your interest?

(a) ACM (b) SIM

(c) ASA (d) IEEE

80. The four major corporate resources are money, materials, information, and

(a) people

(b) icons

(c) information system

(d) on-line

81. The sequence of steps in a system study is

(a) Systems Analysis, System Design, and Systems Implementation

(b) Problem Definition, System Analysis, Programming and Implementation

(c) Problem Definition, System Design, System Analysis, Programming and Implementation

(d) Problem Definition, Systems Analysis, System Design, Programming and Implementation

82. Which one of the following is not a tool of data collection?

(a) Questionaires

(b) Program flowcharts

(c) Interviews

(d) On-site observations

83. Which one of the following tools is not used during systems analysis?

(a) Structured Chart (b) Structured English

(c) Data Flow Diagram (d) Decision Table

84. If a robot can alter its own trajectory in response to external conditions, it is considered to be:

(a) intelligent (b) mobile

(c) open loop (d) non-servo

85. System quality relates to its

(a) maintainability (b) efficiency

(c) reliability (d) All of the above

86. The use of computers in data processing has had several impacts on business. Which of the following is not one of them?

(a) easier business growth

(b) fewer clerical workers

(c) increased data-processing costs

(d) more and better information

87. Most important aspects of System Design focus on

(a) developing end-user information needs

(b) operational feasibility

(c) economic and technical feasibility

(d) All of the above

88. Missing slot covers on a computer can cause?

(a) over heat

(b) power surges

(c) EMI

(d) incomplete path for ESD

89. In order to implement a MIS

(a) E- Mail is required

(b) a computer is mandatory

(c) proper systems and procedures must be in place

(d) None of the above

90. With respect to a network interface card, the term 10/100 refers to

(a) protocol speed

(b) a fiber speed

(c) megabits per seconds

(d) minimum and maximum server speed

91. Encryption is being used primarily with

(a) file retention

(b) transaction entry

(c) computer processing

(d) data communication

92. System specification is mainly concerned with

(a) what functions are to be performed

(b) how functions are performed

(c) both (a) and (b)

(d) None of these

93. Which of the following is(are) true of system analysts?

(a) their responsibility is to analyze and design system software

(b) they may be looked upon as an intermediary between users and programmers

(c) they are heavily involved with the system-development life cycle

(d) both (a) and (c)

94. The primary tool used in structured design is a:

(a) structure chart

(b) data-flow diagram

(c) program flowchart

(d) module

95. Which of the following is not a factor in the failure of the systems developments projects?

(a) size of the company

(b) inadequate user involvement

(c) failure of systems integration

(d) continuation of a project that should have been cancelled

96. A Ring, refers to a record chain, the last of which refers to the first record, in the chain, is called a/an

(a) addressing   (b) location
(c) pointer   (d) loop

97. A computer centre is expressing its inability to make changes to an existing system. This is most probably due to
(a) inability to trace the programmer who developed the system
(b) non-availability of a User's Manual
(c) non-availability of a source code
(d) All of these

98. The phase of System Development associated with creation of test data is
(a) Physical design
(b) System analysis

(c) System acceptance
(d) Logical design

99. To run the old system and the new system at the same time for a specified period, the system implementation approach used is
(a) pilot   (b) phased
(c) parallel   (d) direct

100. Which of the following appropriately explains the desirable characteristic of good system design?
(a) Modular approach
(b) Proper documentation
(c) Conversion
(d) Long discussions

ANSWERS

1	2	3	4	5	6	7	8	9	10
(d)	(b)	(d)	(b)	(d)	(c)	(a)	(d)	(a)	(a)
11	12	13	14	15	16	17	18	19	20
(a)	(a)	(d)	(b)	(d)	(c)	(b)	(b)	(d)	(a)
21	22	23	24	25	26	27	28	29	30
(d)	(d)	(d)	(c)	(c)	(c)	(d)	(b)	(c)	(c)
31	32	33	34	35	36	37	38	39	40
(a)	(c)	(a)	(a)	(b)	(d)	(c)	(a)	(a)	(d)
41	42	43	44	45	46	47	48	49	50
(b)	(d)	(d)	(a)	(c)	(a)	(d)	(c)	(a)	(c)
51	52	53	54	55	56	57	58	59	60
(a)	(a)	(a)	(a)	(a)	(a)	(a)	(c)	(c)	(a)
61	62	63	64	65	66	67	68	69	70
(a)	(b)	(a)	(c)	(c)	(b)	(d)	(a)	(d)	(c)
71	72	73	74	75	76	77	78	79	80
(c)	(a)	(d)	(b)	(c)	(d)	(d)	(b)	(b)	(a)
81	82	83	84	85	86	87	88	89	90
(d)	(b)	(b)	(a)	(d)	(c)	(d)	(a)	(c)	(c)
91	92	93	94	95	96	97	98	99	100
(d)	(c)	(d)	(a)	(a)	(c)	(c)	(c)	(c)	(a)

TEST PAPER 14

1. A parallel run involves
   (a) compiling one program with two different languages
   (b) firing two different applications from different terminals accessing a common database
   (c) the concurrent operation of the existing and newly developed systems
   (d) None of these

2. System Study involves
   (a) study of an existing system
   (b) documenting the existing system
   (c) identifying current deficiencies and establishing new goals
   (d) All of the above

3. A menu driven software is a
   (a) software developed for planning meals at a restaurant
   (b) helps the user reduce errors in data entry
   (c) contains options for the user to indicate his or her choice
   (d) All of these

4. All the following are examples of Physical Security except
   (a) storing tapes and disks not in use in a separate building
   (b) using passwords to access a system
   (c) CCTV
   (d) limiting access to the computer complex

5. Loss of data integrity implies that data is
   (a) outdated
   (b) inconsistent
   (c) repeated
   (d) not suitable for running in an integrated environment

6. In a DBMS, two record types and their relationship are called
   (a) Schema
   (b) Database record
   (c) Set
   (d) Segment

7. In a _____ one module of the new information system is activated at a time.
   (a) System Development Life Cycle
   (b) CASE tool
   (c) Phased Conversion
   (d) Success factors

8. In a hospital database system, the data relationship between the entity 'Patient' and the entity 'ward' will be
   (a) many-to-one
   (b) one-to-many
   (c) one-to-one
   (d) many-to-many

9. An Automatic Teller Machine (ATM) represents
   (a) an on-line banking system
   (b) a combination of batch-cum-on-line system
   (c) a dedicated PC-based system
   (d) None of these

10. The step-by-step instructions that solve a problem are called _____.
    (a) An algorithm
    (b) A list
    (c) A plan
    (d) A sequential structure

11. The primary function of a LAN is
    (a) to extend electronic massaging facility

   (b) to permit access to certain files by every user

   (c) to optimise resource sharing

   (d) All of these

12. Structured English is

   (a) a COBOL statement in the PROCEDURE DIVISION

   (b) a tool for the System Analyst to document the processing procedure using action oriented verbs and terms defined in the data dictionary

   (c) grammatically correct description of the system

   (d) None of the above

13. A report generator is used to

   (a) update files

   (b) print files on paper

   (c) data entry

   (d) All of the above

14. Structured Systems Development Cycle approach includes the following characteristics

   (a) Data Structure   (b) Data Flow

   (c) Top-Down   (d) None of these

15. Each of data files has a _______ that describe the way the data is stored in the file.

   (a) File structure   (b) Records

   (c) Fields   (d) Database

16. Which of the following indicates the maximum number of entities that can be involved in a relationship?

   (a) Minimum cardinality

   (b) Maximum cardinality

   (c) ERD

   (d) Greater Entity Count (GEC)

17. Which one of the following is not a data security measure?

   (a) Allowing only EDP personnel to access any file

   (b) Using retention periods for all files

   (c) Using password for access

   (d) None of these

18. Which type of entity cannot exist in the database unless another type of entity also exists in the database, but does not require that the identifier of that other entity be included as part of its own identifier?

   (a) Weak entity

   (b) Strong entity

   (c) ID-dependent entity

   (d) ID- independent entity

19. In a one-to-many relationship, the entity that is on the one side of the relationship is called a(n) _______ entity.

   (a) parent   (b) child

   (c) instance   (d) subtype

20. A locked file can be

   (a) accessed by only one user

   (b) modified by users with the correct password

   (c) is used to hide sensitive information

   (d) both (b) and (c)

21. Which type of entity represents an actual occurrence of an associated generalized entity?

   (a) Supertype entity   (b) Subtype entity

   (c) Archetype entity   (d) Instance entity

22. With regard to DFD's, which one of the following is incorrect?

   (a) They are System Analyst's tools

   (b) They are different from flowcharts

   (c) They show the sequence of steps

   (d) None of these

23. Which one of the following is not an element in the physical DFD?

   (a) Internal / External entity

   (b) Flow chart

   (c) Processes

   (d) Data flows

24. Which one of the following defies the rules of DFD?

   (a) All data flows must contain data

(b) All data flows must begin and / or end at a process

(c) If two or more documents travel together, each one has to be represented as a separate data flow

(d) Only processes can connect to Data stores

25. The files stored on a secondary stage device are composed of a hierarchy of data. What does a record in a file contain?

(a) Bits   (b) Characters

(c) Data field   (d) Schema

26. What is the name given to the database management system which is able to handle full text data, image data, audio and video?

(a) Full media   (b) Graphics media

(c) Multimedia   (d) Hypertext

27. Which of the following statements, attributed to prototyping, is NOT true?

(a) Always gives faster performance than the actual system

(b) Can accelerate several processes of System Design

(c) It is an active model that end-users can see, feel and experience

(d) Encourages an active end-user participation

28. Hashing procedure is used in

(a) Random files

(b) Indexed sequential files

(c) Sequential files

(d) None of these

29. A DDL

(a) establishes relationships, fields and record types

(b) creates databases

(c) helps in maintaining data in the database

(d) None of these

30. An attribute that names or identifies entity instances is a(n):

(a) entity   (b) attribute

(c) identifier   (d) relationship

31. In order to achieve a good response time from an OTLP, critical requirements are

(a) efficient I/O controller

(b) faster disk transfer

(c) efficient programming

(d) All of these

32. Which one of the following is not an input specification for a Batch System?

(a) Input Record layout

(b) Prototype reports

(c) Expanded Data Dictionary

(d) Source Document Layout

33. Properties that describe the characteristics of entities are called:

(a) entities   (b) attributes

(c) identifiers   (d) relationships

34. In which of the following can many entity instances of one type be related to many entity instances of another type?

(a) One-to-One Relationship

(b) One-to-Many Relationship

(c) Many-to-Many Relationship

(d) Composite Relationship

35. Which of the following is NOT a basic element of all versions of the E-R model?

(a) Entities   (b) Attributes

(c) Relationships   (d) Primary keys

36. In which of the following is a single-entity instance of one type of related to a single-entity instance of another type?

(a) One-to-One Relationship

(b) One-to-Many Relationship

(c) Many-to-Many Relationship

(d) Composite Relationship

37. In development of an application system, which accesses data under a DBMS, the user views the database as a

(a) random storage structure

(*b*) logical structure
(*c*) group of files
(*d*) None of these

38. Entities can be associated with one another in which of the following?
(*a*) Entities
(*b*) Attributes
(*c*) Identifiers
(*d*) Relationships

39. Of the following, which one does not relate to logical design of the system?
(*a*) Output specifications
(*b*) Input specifications
(*c*) File maintenance specifications
(*d*) None of these

40. System Prototyping helps the designer
(*a*) give a demo of the software to the System Manager he or she reports to
(*b*) make the programmers understand how the system will be functioning
(*c*) communicate to the user, quickly, how the system, when developed, will look like and get a feedback
(*d*) None of these

41. A Zero Level DFD describes
(*a*) an overview of processed, inputs and outputs
(*b*) that the System Design cannot be split further
(*c*) the fully blown up System Design
(*d*) None of these

42. Which type of entity has its relationship to another entity determined by an attribute in that other entity called a discriminator?
(*a*) Supertype entity   (*b*) Subtype entity
(*c*) Archetype entity   (*d*) Instance entity

43. The basic objective of systems analysis is to
(*a*) train managers in mathematical analysis
(*b*) understand computer hardware by opening the system unit
(*c*) run a simulation program
(*d*) understand a complex system and modify it in some way

44. One of the main differences between the responsiblities of a System Analyst and a programmer is that
(*a*) a System Analyst is concerned with design of the system whereas a programmer is concerned with computers
(*b*) programmers deal with computer programs whereas a Systems Analyst deals with many more things such as identifying opportunities for computerisation, designing new procedures, selection of equipment etc
(*c*) programmers use lower level languages whereas Systems Analysts use higher level languages
(*d*) programmer's responsibility is to train Systems Analysts in PC usage

45. System support means a
(*a*) battery set that supports computers when the light is off
(*b*) furniture specially designed for holding a computer systems
(*c*) general fund maintained by each organisation towards computer maintenance
(*d*) activity of making modifications and others help as and when needed after a system is made operational

46. An exception report contains data of the following type
(*a*) Unfiltered list of all customer documents
(*b*) Data which violates some specified conditions, value or standard
(*c*) A list of customer orders with ordered quantities greater than one
(*d*) A list of all the transactions already predicted to happen

47. An unstructured problem mean a / an
(*a*) problem in which, the objectives, constraints or relations between variables and solutions procedure cannot be clearly specified

(b) imaginary problem
(c) problem not related to civil engineering
(d) problem with well specified objectives and well specified relations between variables but does not have an efficient solution procedure

48. Which type of entity represents a logical generalization whose actual occurrence is represented by a second, associated entity?
(a) Supertype entity (b) Subtype entity
(c) Archetype entity (d) Instance entity

49. In a one-to-many relationship, the entity that is on the many side of the relationship is called a(n) ________ entity.
(a) parent   (b) child
(c) instance   (d) subtype

50. A data model represents
(a) all types of data and their associations that are relevant to the system
(b) all the processes of the system along with the sequence in which, they are executed
(c) all facts related to the existing system
(d) a sample set of data

51. A data dictionary consists of
(a) all words, which can be referred to during the spellcheck by a word processor
(b) all transactions that have been entered in the system
(c) data about the files and their contents and about the processes used by the system
(d) an indexed sequential file containing the frequency of access of each data item in the system

52. A decision table specifies
(a) a tree showing the causes and effects in a decision process
(b) in the form of a table, the actions to be taken under different conditions for a given process

(c) a list of decisions taken by the top management during the current planning horizon
(d) the consequence of all the possible decisions in a tabular form

53. Back-up procedure helps in restoring
(a) both Application and System software whenever there is a Disk corruption / failure
(b) data files whenever there is a System crash
(c) Both (a) and (b)
(d) None of these

54. A DFD is
(a) mainly used at the system specification stage
(b) the modern version of a flow chart
(c) the primary output of the System Design phase
(d) None of these

55. Which one of the following appropriately explains the desirable characteristic of a good System Design?
(a) Proper Documentation
(b) Modular approach
(c) Neither (a) nor (b)
(d) Both (a) and (b)

56. What name is given to the collection of facts, items of information or data which are related in some way?
(a) Database
(b) Directory information
(c) Information tree
(d) Information provider

57. System specifications are used to
(a) give accurate picture of the system
(b) avoid ambiguity
(c) describe system flow
(d) present all these

58. Which one of the following is not a tool for application prototyping?

(a) Third Generation Language
(b) Screen generators
(c) Report generators
(d) Application generators

59. Which one of the following will not be a major output of the Structured Systems Analysis phase?
(a) Entity Relationship Diagrams
(b) Data Dictionaries
(c) DFD
(d) Prototype Model

60. Structured Programming involves
(a) functional modularisation
(b) decentralised programming
(c) localisation of errors
(d) All of these

61. A System Design is said to be functionally Modular if
(a) each module performs a specific function and can be developed relatively independently by programmers
(b) the system makes extensive use of function keys for maximum user assistance
(c) the system is developed using structured programming through COBOL or PASCAL
(d) the system is able to handle all functions of the application

62. In a large DBMS
(a) each user can "see" only a small part of the entire database
(b) each user can access every subschema
(c) each subschema contains every field in the logical schema
(d) All of the above

63. Internal auditors should review data system design before they are
(a) developed   (b) implemented
(c) modified   (d) All of the above

64. Numerical control:
(a) is a method for controlling the operation of a machine by means of a set of instructions
(b) applies only to milling machines
(c) is a method for producing an exact number of parts per hour
(d) All of the above

65. A technique for displaying applications where complex 3-D geometric are required for the exteror shall of a product is called:
(a) solid modeling   (b) 2-D modeling
(c) 3-D modeling   (d) surface modeling

66. The user communicates directly with the computer through its peripheral devices is known as
(a) On-line processing
(b) Remote-terminal processing
(c) Batch mode processing
(d) Intelligent terminal Processing

67. The approach used in Top-Down Analysis and Design is to
(a) prepare Flow charts after programming has been completed
(b) identify a top-level functions and then, create a hierarchy of lower-level modules and components
(c) identify the top level functions by combining many smaller components into a single entity
(d) None of these

68. Cost-benefit analysis
(a) estimates hardware and software costs
(b) compares the costs, introducing a computer-based system
(c) evaluates the tangible and intangible factors
(d) All of these

69. Which criterion of a real-time system makes it different from an interactive System?
(a) Information transfer error only
(b) Response time limited by strict time constraints

(c) Data gathering from internal environment
(d) None of these

70. A self check digit is useful in detecting
(a) transposition errors only
(b) transcription errors only
(c) random errors only
(d) All the three

71. Which one of the following, is not considered to be a tool to be used in the System Design phase?
(a) Decision Table
(b) DFD
(c) Systems Flowchart
(d) Pie chart

72. A semi-continuous operation means:
(a) the operation is continuous each shift, but stops between shifts
(b) coffee breaks are allowed for the operator
(c) a computer is a required part of the machine
(d) each operation in a sequence is continuous, but subsequent operations in the sequence may be different.

73. A servo controlled robot:
(a) stop only at fixed points on each axis
(b) can accelerate
(c) must be hydraulically driven
(d) must be electrically driven

74. Microprocessor 8085 can address location upto
(a) 32K
(b) 128K
(c) 64K
(d) 1M

75. With 1's complement method, the range of numbers that can be represented using n bits is
(a) a 1 followed by using n−1 zeros to a 0 followed by n−1 ones
(b) -2^{n-1} to 2^{n-1}

(c) a 0 followed by n-1 ones to a 1 followed by n−1 zeros
(d) None of these

76. Using 2's complement method, the range of numbers that can be represented using n bits is
(a) -2^{n-1} to 2^{n-1}
(b) a 1 followed by n−1 zeros to a 0 followed by n−1 1's
(c) a 1 followed by n ones to a 1 followed by n zeros
(d) None of the above

77. When the RET instruction at the end of subroutine is executed,
(a) the information where the stack is initialized is transferred to the stack pointer
(b) the memory address of the RET instruction is transferred to the program counter
(c) two data bytes stored in the top two locations of the stack are transferred to the program counter
(d) two data bytes stored in the top two locations of the stack are transferred to the stack pointer

78. The set of native data types that a particular computer can support is determined by
(a) what software support is required
(b) what functions have been wired into the hardware
(c) the type of hardware company
(d) None of these

79. While considering data structure implementation, the factor/s under consideration is/are
(a) time, space and processor
(b) time and space
(c) time
(d) None of the above

80. Pick out invalid statement from following
Queues can be used for
(a) access to disk storage
(b) the line printer
(c) function call
(d) None of the above

81. p = 1;
for (x=n;x.0;x=x-1)
p = x*p
return(p);
The above set of steps is an example of
(a) Iterative code   (b) Implied function
(c) Recursive code   (d) None of these

82. Pick out invalid statement from following
An algorithm must be
(a) concise and compact
(b) efficient
(c) free of ambiguity
(d) None of these

83. In top down approach
(a) A problem is subdivided into sub problems. Each one is attacked without worrying about the other.
(b) Sub-problems are solved first; then all solutions of sub-problems are put together to solve the main problem.
(c) A problem is tackled from the beginning to the end in one go.
(d) None of these

84. In the bottom up approach
(a) a problem is tackled from beginning to end in one go
(b) a problem is subdivided into subproblems; each one is attacked without worrying about others
(c) sub-problems are solved first; then all solution of sub-problems are put together to solve the main problem
(d) None of these

85. Interrupts which are initiated by an I/O drive are

(a) internal   (b) external
(c) software   (d) all of above

86. In the analysis of algorithms, approximate relationship between the size of the job and the amount of work required to do it is expressed by using
(a) order of magnitude or Big-O
(b) differential equation
(c) central tendency
(d) None of these

87. Which one is better computing time (for the analysis of algorithms)?
(a) $O(2^N)$ (b) $O(N)$
(c) $O(\log_2 N)$ (d) None of these

88. A structured data type made up of finite collections of ordered elements, all of which, are of the same data types, is a / an
(a) file   (b) array
(c) record   (d) None of these

89. Elements of an array are accessed by a / an
(a) mathematical function
(b) accessing functions in built-in data structure
(c) index
(d) None of these

90. An Array is a
(a) linear data structure
(b) complex data structure
(c) non-linear data structure
(d) None of these

91. Row-major order in two dimensional array refers to the following:
(a) All the elements of a row are stored in memory in sequence followed by the next row in sequence and so on
(b) All the elements of a column are stored in memory in sequence followed by the next column in sequence and so on
(c) All the elements of a row are stored in memory in sequence followed by the next column insequence and so on
(d) None of these

92. A data structure in which, an element is added and removed only from only one end, is known as a / an
(a) Array
(b) Stack
(c) Queue
(d) None of these

93. A Stack is a / an
(a) in-built data structure
(b) dynamic data structure
(c) static data structure
(d) None of these

94. In linked list, a node contains at least
(a) node number, data field
(b) node address field, data field
(c) next address field, information field
(d) None of these

95. Which one is not true?
(a) While defining an abstract data type as a mathematical concept, the space and efficiency are not of major concern
(b) An abstract data type is a useful tool for specifying the logical properties of data types
(c) Every abstract data type can be implemented using any programming language
(d) None of these

96. Which is not true?
(a) Recursion may maintain non-useful local variables and temporary variables through a stack
(b) Recursion involves entering and exiting a block
(c) In a recursive process stacking and unstacking local variables is done by a compiler to ensure that no problem arises
(d) None of the above

97. In a queue (where q.rear and q.front are pointer to the two ends of a queue)
(a) if q.rear > q.front, it is empty
(b) the number of total elements is fixed
(c) the number of elements at any time is (q.rear- q.front - 1).
(d) None of the above

98. Implementation of list in dynamic fashion is
(a) the address computation is complex
(b) a set of nodes is not reserved in advance for use
(c) to call upon the system to allocate and free storage may not be time-consuming
(d) None of the above

99. Queue
(a) can be created by setting up an ordinary contiguous array to hold the items
(b) need one pointer to handle addition and deletion of an item
(c) can take care of the delete operation automatically
(d) none of the above

100. A Data Structure
(a) may be helpful to develop efficient algorithms in different phases of data processing
(b) is programming language dependent
(c) need not give relationship between data items
(d) None of these

ANSWERS

1	2	3	4	5	6	7	8	9	10
(c)	(d)	(c)	(b)	(b)	(a)	(c)	(d)	(a)	(a)
11	12	13	14	15	16	17	18	19	20
(d)	(b)	(b)	(d)	(a)	(b)	(d)	(a)	(a)	(a)

21	22	23	24	25	26	27	28	29	30
(d)	(d)	(a)	(c)	(c)	(c)	(d)	(b)	(c)	(c)
31	32	33	34	35	36	37	38	39	40
(d)	(c)	(b)	(c)	(d)	(a)	(d)	(d)	(c)	(c)
41	42	43	44	45	46	47	48	49	50
(a)	(b)	(d)	(b)	(d)	(b)	(a)	(c)	(b)	(a)
51	52	53	54	55	56	57	58	59	60
(c)	(b)	(c)	(a)	(b)	(a)	(d)	(a)	(d)	(a)
61	62	63	64	65	66	67	68	69	70
(a)	(a)	(d)	(a)	(d)	(a)	(b)	(d)	(b)	(d)
71	72	73	74	75	76	77	78	79	80
(d)	(d)	(b)	(c)	(a)	(b)	(c)	(b)	(b)	(c)
81	82	83	84	85	86	87	88	89	90
(a)	(d)	(a)	(c)	(b)	(a)	(c)	(b)	(c)	(a)
91	92	93	94	95	96	97	98	99	100
(a)	(b)	(b)	(c)	(c)	(c)	(d)	(b)	(a)	(a)

1. In a linked list, the logical order of elements
   (a) is determined by their physical arrangement
   (b) is not necessarily equivalent to their physical arrangement
   (c) is same as their physical arrangement
   (d) None of the above

2. Which of the following is meaning of Data scrubbing?
   (a) A process to reject data from the data warehouse and to create the necessary indexes
   (b) A process to load the data in the data warehouse and to create the necessary indexes
   (c) A process to upgrade the quality of data before it is moved into a data warehouse
   (d) A process to upgrade the quality of data after it is moved into a data warehouse

3. The active data warehouse architecture includes which of the following?
   (a) At least one data mart
   (b) Data that can extracted from numerous internal and external sources
   (c) Both (a) & (b)
   (d) None of the above

4. The nth node, in a singly linked list, is accessed via (where n > 1)
   (a) the tail node
   (b) the head node
   (c) (n-1) nodes
   (d) None of these

5. In linked list, the successive elements
   (a) must not occupy contiguous space in memory
   (b) need not occupy contiguous space in memory
   (c) must occupy contiguous space in memory
   (d) None of the above

6. Linear order in linked list is provided through
   (a) the implied position of the node
   (b) index number
   (c) pointer
   (d) None of the above

7. What is the goal of data mining includes ?
   (a) To create a new data warehouse
   (b) To facilitate that data exists
   (c) To analyze data for expected relationships
   (d) To explain some observed event or condition

8. List pointer variable in linked list contains address of the
   (a) current node in the list
   (b) following node in the list
   (c) first node in the list
   (d) None of these

9. Which of the following is operational system?
   (a) A system that is used to run the business in real time and is based on historical data.
   (b) A system that is used to support decision making and is based on current data.
   (c) A system that is used to run the business in real time and is based on current data
   (d) A system that is used to support decision making and is based on historical data.

10. What is data warehouse?
  (*a*) Organized around important subject areas
  (*b*) Contains numerous naming conventions and formats
  (*c*) Can be updated by end users
  (*d*) Contains only current data

11. Because of linear structure of linked list having natural linear ordering, there is similarity between linked list and array in
  (*a*) deletion of a node
  (*b*) insertion of a node
  (*c*) traversal of elements of list
  (*d*) None of the above

12. Searching a linked list requires linked list be created
  (*a*) without underflow condition
  (*b*) in any order
  (*c*) in sorted order only
  (*d*) None of the above

13. Copying all or part of linked list consists of
  (*a*) taking a null string and adding appropriate elements to the list one by one
  (*b*) changing only address of the beginning of the list
  (*c*) taking a null string and putting the address of the beginning of the list
  (*d*) None of the above

14. Deletion of a node in a linked list involves keeping track of the address of the node
  (*a*) which immediately follows the node that is to be deleted
  (*b*) that is to be deleted
  (*c*) which immediately precedes the node that is to be deleted
  (*d*) None of these

15. Which of the following types of tables are snowflake schema?
  (*a*) Fact   (*b*) Dimension
  (*c*) Helper   (*d*) (*a*), (*b*) & (*c*)

16. Which of the following are generic two-level data warehouse architecture?
  (*a*) At least one data mart
  (*b*) Near real-time updates
  (*c*) Data that can extracted from numerous internal and external sources
  (*d*) All of the above

17. Which of the following Fact tables?
  (*a*) Completely denormalized
  (*b*) Completely normalized
  (*c*) Partially denormalized
  (*d*) Partially normalized

18. Polynomials in memory may be maintained through a / an
  (*a*) stack
  (*b*) one-dimensional array
  (*c*) linked list with header node
  (*d*) None of the above

19. Which of the following includes Data transformation ?
  (*a*) Joining data from one source into various sources of data
  (*b*) A process to change data from a summary level to a detailed level
  (*c*) A process to change data from a detailed level to a summary level
  (*d*) Separating data from one source into various sources of data

20. Which of the following Reconciled data ?
  (*a*) Data stored in the various operational systems throughout the organization
  (*b*) Data stored in one operational system in the organization
  (*c*) Current data intended to be the single source for all decision support systems
  (*d*) Data that has been selected and formatted for end-user support applications

21. "Get a node, store new element and insert the new node at the top" refers to insert operation in a non-empty

  (a) stack   (b) array
  (c) queue   (d) None of these

22. String concatenation means
  (a) partitioning a string into two strings
  (b) extracting a substring into two string
  (c) combining two strings
  (d) None of these

23. "Get the value of most recently inserted node and delete the node" refers to operation
  (a) POP   (b) EMPTY
  (c) PUSH   (d) None of these

24. "FRONT = REAR" pointer refers to empty
  (a) array   (b) queue
  (c) stack   (d) None of these

25. Inserting a node after a given node in doubly linked list requires
  (a) two pointer changes
  (b) one pointer changes
  (c) four pointer changes
  (d) None of the above

26. Which of the following is index and load?
  (a) A process to reject data from the data warehouse and to create the necessary indexes
  (b) A process to upgrade the quality of data after it is moved into a data warehouse
  (c) A process to load the data in the data warehouse and to create the necessary indexes
  (d) A process to upgrade the quality of data before it is moved into a data warehouse

27. Memory allocation at the run time is known as
  (a) paging
  (b) dynamic memory allocation
  (c) static memory allocation
  (d) None of the above

28. In memory allocation, the first compile time is known as
  (a) static memory allocation
  (b) paging

  (c) dynamic memory allocation
  (d) None of the above

29. In memory allocation, the first entry, which has a free block equal to or more than the required one is selected through
  (a) first fit method   (b) worst fit method
  (c) best fit method   (d) None of these

30. In memory allocation, an entry, which is smallest amongst all the entries and equals or is bigger than the required one, is selected in the
  (a) worst fit method (b) best fit method
  (c) first fit method   (d) None of these

31. Reduction in wastage due to fragmentation is minimum in
  (a) worst fit method (b) best fit method
  (c) first fit method   (d) None of these

32. Which of the following is extract process ?
  (a) Capturing all of the data contained in various operational systems
  (b) Capturing all of the data contained in various decision support systems
  (c) Capturing a subset of the data contained in various operational systems
  (d) Capturing a subset of the data contained in various decision support systems

33. A star schema has what type of relationship between a dimension and fact table?
  (a) Many-to-one   (b) One-to-one
  (c) One-to-many   (d) All of the above

34. Which of the following is Transient data ?
  (a) Data that are never deleted once they have been added
  (b) Data in which changes to existing records do not cause the previous version of the records to be eliminated
  (c) Data that are never altered or deleted once they have been added
  (d) Data in which changes to existing records cause the previous version of the records to be eliminated

35. Struct address {
char name[40]; struct address *next
  } info;
func(struct address *j;
{ static struct address *i = 0
if(i= =0) i=j;
else i-> next = j;
j-> next = 0;
i=j; }
builds the linked list by placing each element
(a) at the appropriate place in the list
(b) on the end
(c) in the beginning
(d) None of the above

36. struct address {
char name[40]; struct address *next;
} info;
     func(struct address *head);
     { while (head) { printf(head -> name);
head = head -> next; }
}
prints the
(a) name in all elements of linked list starting from the element of the linked list
(b) name in elements of linked list pointed by non-null head
(c) both (a) and (b)
(d) None of the above

37. Which of the following does multifield transformation?
(a) Converts data from one field into multiple fields
(b) Converts data from multiple fields into one field
(c) Converts data from multiple fields into multiple fields
(d) All of the above

38. datatype *s;
datatype *p;
datatype *i;
p = malloc(100); t=p; s = p + (100 / sizeof (datatype)) - sizeof (datatype);

func(datatype j);
    { if (p > s) { printf("Overflow \n"); return;}
      *p = j; p++; j
is referring to the
(a) push operation of stack
(b) push operation of queue
(c) pop operation of stack
(d) None of the above

39. malloc function returns zero value when
(a) memory is successfully allocated
(b) all memory is cleared
(c) allocation error occurs
(d) None of the above

40. Previously allocated memory can be returned to the system by using
(a) calloc()   (b) free()
(c) malloc()   (d) None of these

41. malloc() returns pointer to
(a) structure   (b) integer
(c) character   (d) None of these

42. The function associated with dynamic allocation of memory is
(a) free   (b) malloc
(c) calloc   (d) All of the above

43. You are defining the operational process of your RDBMS. Referring to the scenario which one of the following is a valid ongoing "operational process?"
(a) Operating System requirement
(b) Data dictionary specification
(c) User analysis
(d) Performance monitoring

44. You have been asked to construct a query in the company's RDBMS. You have deployed a Right Outer Join operation.

Referring to the scenario above, what will happen to the final results when there is NO match between the tables?
(a) The right table will return ALL rows
(b) The left table will return ALL rows

(c) Both tables will return NULL
(d) The right table will return NULL

45. Which phase of the data modeling process contains security review?
(a) Storage issue   (b) Data source
(c) Design issue   (d) Structure

46. Which of the following steps is performed first for an in-order traversal of a binary tree?
(a) Processing of the root node
(b) Traversal of the left subtree in postorder
(c) Traversal of the left subtree in inorder
(d) None of the above

47. The part of a compiler that keeps a record of names of variables and their associated attributes/values is known as a
(a) Lexical analyser   (b) Symbol table
(c) Parser   (d) None of these

48. A B-tree of the order n is also called
(a) $n - (n - 2)$ tree   (b) $(n - n) - 1$ tree
(c) $(n - 1) - n$ tree   (d) None of these

49. The pre-order traversal of a binary tree begins with
(a) processing of the root node
(b) traversal of the left subtree in pre-order
(c) traversal of the right subtree in pre-order
(d) None of the above

50. Hashing refers to the process of deriving
(a) a floating point code from a record key
(b) storage address from a record key
(c) a record key from storage address
(d) None of the above

51. If a binary search technique is used for accessing and implementing a symbol table, which of the following statements is true? The ratio of
(a) insertion time to access time for its entries is quite high
(b) search time to insertion time is very high
(c) access time to insertion time is quite high
(d) None of the above

52. If a binary tree is threaded for an inorder traversal order, a NULL right link of any node is replaced by the address of its
(a) successor   (b) root
(c) predecessor   (d) None of these

53. The post-order traversal of a binary tree begins with
(a) the post-order traversal of the left subtree
(b) the post-order traversal of the right subtree
(c) processing of the root node
(d) None of the above

54. If a binary tree is threaded for an in-order traversal order, NULL left link of any node is replaced by the address of its
(a) root   (b) predecessor
(c) successor   (d) None of these

55. Which one of the following is NOT a characteristic of metadata?
(a) Data about data
(b) Describes a data dictionary
(c) Self-describing
(d) All of the above

56. The in-order traversal of some binary tree produced the sequence DBEAFC and the post-order traversal of the same tree produced the sequence DEBFCA. Which one of the following is a correct preorder traversal sequence?
(a) ABEDFC   (b) DBAECF
(c) ABDECF   (d) None of these

57. The inorder traversal of some binary tree produced the sequence DBEAFC and the postorder traversal of the same tree produced the sequence DEBFCA. What will be the total number of nodes in the left sub-tree of the given tree ?
(a) 5   (b) 4
(c) 1   (d) None of these

58. Which one of the following capabilities do you expect to see in a majority of RDBMS extensions to ANSI SQL-92?
(a) Encryption key management
(b) Graphical User Interface Widgets
(c) Thread creation, execution, & coordination
(d) If/Then, for, do/while statements

59. What is the minimum number of keys contained in each non root node of a B-tree of order 11?
(a) 3   (b) 5
(c) 4   (d) None of these

60. The post-order traversal of some binary tree produced the sequence CDBFEA, and the inorder traversal of the same tree produced the sequence CBDAFE. What will be the total number of nodes in its right subtree ?
(a) 2   (b) 4
(c) 3   (d) None of these

61. The postorder traversal of some binary tree produced the sequence CDBFEA and the inorder traversal of the same tree produced the sequence CBDAFE. What will be the total number of nodes in its left subtree?
(a) 5   (b) 2
(c) 3   (d) None of these

62. A mandatory one-to-one relationship indicate?
(a) Self-describing
(b) The tables are not properly indexed
(c) More attributes are needed
(d) More entities are needed

63. The in-order traversal of some binary tree produced the sequence CBDA and the post-order traversal of the same tree produced the sequence CDBA. Which one of the following statements is true for the given tree?
(a) Its both left subtree and right subtree must be non- empty

(b) Its right subtree is empty, and the left subtree contains 3 nodes
(c) Its left subtree is empty, and the total number of nodes in its right subtree is 3
(d) None of the above

64. Which one of the following statements is true in view of a threaded binary tree? It can have
(a) thread links but no structural link
(b) structural links but no thread link
(c) thread links and can also have structural links
(d) None of the above

65. Which of the following terms refers to the balance of a node?
Height of its –
(a) left subtree minus height of its right subtree
(b) left subtree plus height of its right subtree
(c) right subtree minus height of its left subtree
(d) None of the above

66. For maintaining order, insertions in a lexical ordered binary tree can only be performed at
(a) a leaf level
(b) a root node
(c) an intermediate level
(d) None of these

67. Which one of the following statements is true in view of a complete binary tree?
(a) The total number of nodes in the tree has always some power of 2
(b) The out-degree of every node is exactly equal to 2 or 0
(c) The number of nodes at each level is 1 less than some power of 2
(d) None of these

68. Consider the following statements for an AVL tree
(i) Heights of the two subtrees of every node never differ by more than 1

(*ii*) Each node of the tree has a balance of 1, −1, or 0

Which one of the following statement is true?

(*a*) (*i*) is TRUE and (*ii*) is FALSE
(*b*) (*i*) is FALSE and (*ii*) is TRUE
(*c*) (*i*) is FALSE and (*ii*) is FALSE
(*d*) (*i*) is TRUE and (*ii*) is TRUE

69. Which one of the following statements is true in view of threaded binary trees?
(*a*) Deletion from a threaded tree is time consuming but insertion into it is not
(*b*) Both insertions into and deletions from a threaded tree are more time consuming
(*c*) Insertion into a threaded tree is time consuming but deletion from it is not
(*d*) None of the above

70. For performance, you denormalize your database design and create some redundant columns.

Referring to the scenario above, what RDBMS construct can you use to automatically prevent the repeated columns from getting out of sync?
(*a*) Trigger
(*b*) Constraints
(*c*) Stored procedures
(*d*) Cursors

71. You are running a query against a relational database.

Referring to the scenario above, what clause or command do you use in the query to help avoid a costly tablescan?
(*a*) GROUP BY clause
(*b*) FROM clause
(*c*) SHORT clause
(*d*) INDEX command

72. Which one of the following statements is true in view of a lexical ordered binary tree?
(*a*) Its root node contains a key which is lexically greater than most of the keys associated with the nodes of the right subtree
(*b*) Its left subtree contains nodes whose keys are lexically less than the key associated with the root node
(*c*) Its left subtree contains nodes whose keys are lexically greater than the key associated with the root node
(*d*) None of these

73. Which of the following database activities allow for the actual retrieval and use of a database?
(*a*) Logical database design
(*b*) Database implementation
(*c*) Physical database design and definition
(*d*) Enterprise modeling

74. If for the given directed tree out-degree of every node is exactly equal to 2 or 0, and the no. of nodes at level i is 2 raised to the power of $i-1$, the tree is called a / an
(*a*) m-ary tree
(*b*) complete binary tree
(*c*) binary tree
(*d*) None of these

75. While performing the in-order threading of a binary tree, if the left link represents a structural link, then it is
(*a*) replaced with a new thread link
(*b*) left unchanged
(*c*) replaced with a NULL link
(*d*) None of the above

76. While performing inorder threading of a binary tree, if the right link represents a NULL link, then it is
(*a*) left unchanged
(*b*) replaced with a structural link
(*c*) replaced with a new thread link
(*d*) None of the above

77. The three-schema components include all, except:
(*a*) internal schema

(b) programming schema
(c) conceptual schema
(d) external schema

78. Which is not a relevant feature of CASE tools?
(a) The ability to help draw data models using entity-relationship notations
(b) Access to a DB via the Internet
(c) An information repository
(d) The ability to generate code

79. The first step in database development is ?
(a) Database Implementation
(b) Physical database design and definition
(c) Logical database design
(d) Enterprise data modeling

80. In which one of the following trees, must balance of each node be either 1, −1 or 0?
(a) Lexical ordered tree
(b) Threaded tree
(c) AVL tree
(d) None of these

81. Level of any node of a tree is
(a) its distance from the root
(b) height of its right subtree minus height of its subtree
(c) height of its left subtree minus height of its right subtree
(d) None of the above

82. Which of the following statements is true in view of a threaded storage representation of a binary tree?
(a) Its inorder threading is different from its post-order threading
(b) The number of thread links is reduced to zero
(c) The number of NULL links in a threaded tree is very small but it is not zero
(d) None of these

83. Which of the following database activities determines the attributes, entities, and relationships of data?
(a) Logical database design

(b) Conceptual data modeling
(c) Database implementation
(d) Physical database design and definition

84. If graph G has no edges, then corresponding adjacency matrix is
(a) matrix with all 1's
(b) zero matrix
(c) unit matrix
(d) None of these

85. The language developed for string manipulation is
(a) Ada
(b) LISP
(c) SNOBOL
(d) None of these

86. The worst case efficiency of binary search is
(a) $\log_2, n + 1$
(b) n^2
(c) n
(d) None of these

87. Which property is not expected from a good hashing technique?
(a) Easy to program
(b) Produces keys uniformly distributed over the range
(c) Produces no collisions
(d) All properties are expected

88. What is not true for linear collision processing?
(a) It may induce more collision
(b) It is easier to program
(c) It requires space for links
(d) All of the above

89. The Enterprise tier of the three-tiered database architecture includes:
(a) processing HTTP protocol
(b) managing the User-system interface
(c) managing the data
(d) Processing TCP protocol

90. Which of the following are entity type ?
(a) The application software
(b) The System Software
(c) A major category of data about people, place, and things
(d) The business processes the support the mission of an organization

91. A vertex with degree one in a graph is called
   (a) End vertex   (b) Pendant vertex
   (c) Leaf   (d) None of these

92. Which one is not a representation of a graph?
   (a) Adjacency list
   (b) Edge listing
   (c) Adjacency matrix
   (d) All represent graphs

93. In an adjacency matrix parallel edges are given by
   (a) Similar rows
   (b) Similar columns
   (c) Not representable
   (d) None of these

94. If x is the adjacency matrix of a graph then (i, j)th entry of x represents
   (a) the number of edge sequences of length k between ith and jth vertex
   (b) the number of walks of length k between ith and jth vertex
   (c) the number of paths of length k between ith and jth vertex
   (d) None of these

95. Breadth first search
   (a) scans all incident edges before moving to another vertex
   (b) is same as backtracking
   (c) scans adjacent unvisited vertex as soon as is possible
   (d) None of these

96. What is not true about linked list representation for strings?
   (a) It allows dynamic allocation of memory
   (b) Insertion and deletion are easier to handle
   (c) Working with substrings is easy
   (d) All are true

97. Name the sort for which, time is not proportional to n^2
   (a) Bubble sort   (b) Selection sort
   (c) Quick sort   (d) None of these

98. The element at the root of heap is
   (a) smallest
   (b) largest
   (c) dependent upon type of heap it may be smallest or largest
   (d) None of these

99. This sort does not use Divide and Conquer methodology
   (a) Quick sort
   (b) Merge sort
   (c) Bubble sort
   (d) All use divide and conquer methodology

100. Name the sort in which, an array to be sorted is partitioned again and again in such a way that all elements less than or equal to partition elements appear before it and those that are greater appear after it.
   (a) Selection sort   (b) Quick sort
   (c) Merge sort   (d) None of these

ANSWERS

1	2	3	4	5	6	7	8	9	10
(b)	(c)	(c)	(c)	(b)	(c)	(d)	(c)	(c)	(a)
11	12	13	14	15	16	17	18	19	20
(c)	(b)	(a)	(a)	(d)	(c)	(b)	(b)	(c)	(c)
21	22	23	24	25	26	27	28	29	30
(a)	(b)	(a)	(b)	(c)	(c)	(b)	(a)	(a)	(b)

31	32	33	34	35	36	37	38	39	40
(b)	(c)	(c)	(d)	(b)	(a)	(d)	(a)	(a)	(b)
41	42	43	44	45	46	47	48	49	50
(c)	(d)	(d)	(b)	(c)	(c)	(b)	(c)	(a)	(b)
51	52	53	54	55	56	57	58	59	60
(a)	(a)	(a)	(b)	(d)	(c)	(d)	(d)	(b)	(a)
61	62	63	64	65	66	67	68	69	70
(c)	(c)	(b)	(c)	(a)	(a)	(b)	(d)	(b)	(a)
71	72	73	74	75	76	77	78	79	80
(d)	(b)	(b)	(b)	(b)	(c)	(b)	(b)	(d)	(c)
81	82	83	84	85	86	87	88	89	90
(a)	(a)	(b)	(b)	(b)	(a)	(c)	(c)	(c)	(c)
91	92	93	94	95	96	97	98	99	100
(b)	(d)	(c)	(a)	(a)	(c)	(c)	(c)	(c)	(b)

1. The domain of the function log (log sin (x)) is
   (a) $0 < x < \pi$
   (b) $2n\,\pi < x < (2n + 1)\,\pi$, $n \,\varepsilon\, N$
   (c) empty set
   (d) none of the above

2. The system of equation $x + 2y + 3z = 4$; $x + \lambda y + 2z = 3$; $x + 4y + \mu z = 3$ has infinite number of solutions if
   (a) $\lambda = 2$; $\mu = 3$
   (b) $\lambda = 2$; $\mu = 4$
   (c) $3\lambda = 2\mu$
   (d) none of the above

3. Let R be a symmetric and transitive relation on a set A. Then
   (a) R is reflexive and hence an equivalence relation
   (b) R is reflexive and hence an partial order
   (c) R is not reflexive and hence not an equivalence relation
   (d) none of the above

4. The number of elements in the power set of the set $\{\{\{\}\}, 1, \{2, 3\}\}$ is
   (a) 2
   (b) 4
   (c) 8
   (d) 3

5. If $4 \log_9 3 + 9 \log_2 4 = 10 \log_x 81$, then x is
   (a) 2
   (b) e
   (c) 7
   (d) none of the above

6. Ten different letters are given. Five letter words are formed from these given letters. The number of words which have atleast 1 letter repeated is
   (a) 99748
   (b) 87882
   (c) 92182
   (d) 69760

7. The value of the expression $^{47}C_4 + \sum\limits_{j=1}^{5} {}^{(52-j)}C_3$ is equal to
   (a) $47!\,/52!$
   (b) $46!/52!$
   (c) $^{52}C_4$
   (d) $^{52}C_{47}$

8. The rank of the following $(n + 1) \times (n + 1)$ matrix, where a is a real number is
$$\begin{vmatrix} 1 & a & a^2 & \dots & a^n \\ 1 & a & a^2 & \dots & a^n \\ \vdots & \vdots & \vdots & \dots & \vdots \\ 1 & a & a^2 & \dots & a^n \end{vmatrix}$$
   (a) 1
   (b) 2
   (c) n
   (d) dependent on the value of a

9. Let 'S' be the standard deviation of 'n' numbers. If each of the 'n' numbers is multiplied by a constant C, then the new standard deviation will be
   (a) $C \times S$
   (b) $S\sqrt{C}$
   (c) S
   (d) none of the above

10. Which of the following is true?
   (a) MS-DOS does not support multiprogramming
   (b) MS-DOS supports multiprogramming to some extent
   (c) MS-DOS supports multiprogramming fully
   (d) None of the above

11. At a particular time, the value of a counting semaphore is 10. It will become 7 after
   (a) 3 V operations

(b) 3 P operations
(c) 13 P operations and 10 V operations
(d) (b) and (c) only

12. Supervisor call
    (a) is a call made by the supervisor of the system
    (b) is a call with control functions
    (c) are privileged calls that are used to perform resource management functions, which are controlled by the operating system
    (d) is a call made by someone working in root directory

13. Semaphores are used to solve the problem of
    (a) process synchronization
    (b) mutual exclusion
    (c) both the above
    (d) none of the above

14. If the property of locality of reference is well pronounced in a program,
    (a) the number of page faults will be less
    (b) execution will be faster
    (c) both the above
    (d) none of the above

15. At a particular time of computation, the value of a counting semaphore is 7. Then $20P$ operations and 'x' V operations were completed on this semaphore. If the final value of the semaphore is 5, x will be
    (a) 15   (b) 22
    (c) 18   (d) 13

16. The length of the longest pole that can be made inside a hall of length 18m, breadth 6m and height 4.5m is
    (a) 17.5m   (b) 19.5m
    (c) 20m   (d) 18.25m

17. Six x's have to be placed in the squares in the adjacent figure, such that each row contains at least one x. This can be done in

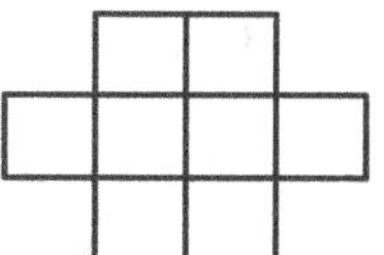

(a) 160 ways
(b) 180 ways
(c) 170 ways
(d) 26 ways

18. Out of 100 students, 10 students used to drink milk (M), coffee (C) and tea (T); 20 M and C; 30 C and T; 25 M and T; 12 M only; 5 C only and 8 T only. The number of students who did not drink any of these is
    (a) 18   (b) 24
    (c) 20   (d) 16

19. Given the relation R = {(1, 2), (2, 3)}. The minimum number of ordered pairs that must be added to this set so that the enlarged relation is reflexive, symmetric and transitive is
    (a) 4   (b) 5
    (c) 6   (d) 7

20. A box contains 2 black, 4 white and 3 red balls. One ball is drawn at random from the box and kept aside. From the remaining balls in the box, another ball is drawn at random and kept beside the first. This process is repeated till all the balls are drawn from the box. The probability that the balls drawn are in the sequence 2 black, 4 white, and 3 red is
    (a) 1/1260   (b) 17/1260
    (c) 7/1260   (d) 13/1260

21. Consider the grammar

        S   → ABSc | Abc
        BA → AB
        Bb → bb
        Ab → ab
        Aa → aa

    Which of the following sentences can be derived by this grammar?
    (a) abc   (b) aab
    (c) abcc   (d) abbc

22. The language generated by the above grammar is the set of all strings, made up of a, b, c, such that

(*a*) the number of *a*'s, *b*'s, and *c*'s will be equal
(*b*) *a*'s always precede *b*'s
(*c*) *b*'s always precede *c*'s
(*d*) the number of *a*'s *b*'s and *c*'s are same and the *a*'s precede *b*'s, which precede *c*'s

23. In an incompletely specified automata
(*a*) no edge should be labeled epsilon
(*b*) from any given state, there can't be any token leading to two different states
(*c*) some states have no transition on some tokens
(*d*) `start` state may not be there

24. The main difference between a DFSA and an NDFSA is
(*a*) in DFSA, ε transition may be present
(*b*) in NDFSA, ε transitions may be present
(*c*) in DFSA, from any given state, there can't be any alphabet leading to two different states
(*d*) No difference

25. The following grammar is
$$S \rightarrow a\alpha b \mid b\alpha c \mid aB$$
$$S \rightarrow aS \mid b$$
$$S \rightarrow \alpha bb \mid ab$$
$$b\alpha \rightarrow bdb \mid b$$
(*a*) context free   (*b*) regular
(*c*) context sensitive   (*d*) LR(k)

26. A CFG is said to be in Chosky Normal form (CNF), if all the productions are of the form $A \rightarrow BC$ or $A \rightarrow a$. Let G be a CFG in CNF. To derive a string of terminals of length *x*, the number of production to be used is
(*a*) $2x - 1$ (*b*) $2x$
(*c*) $2x + 1$ (*d*) 2^x

27. Let *g*, *h* belong to a group G. If O (*h*) is 2, then $O(ghg^{-1})$ is
(*a*) 0   (*b*) 1
(*c*) 2   (*d*) 4

28. At any time, the total number of persons on earth who have shaken hands an odd number of times has to be
(*a*) an even number   (*b*) an odd number
(*c*) a prime number   (*d*) a perfect square

29. Which of the following is/are irrational numbers?
(*a*) $\sqrt{2}$
(*b*) *e*
(*c*) both of the above
(*d*) none of the above

30. The function $f(x) = |x/(x + 1)|$
(*a*) is less than 1, for all *x*
(*b*) equals $f(-x)$
(*c*) equal $1 - f(1/x)$
(*d*) none of the above

31. Integer division results in
(*a*) truncation   (*b*) rounding
(*c*) overflow   (*d*) none of the above

32. which of the following comments about EOF are true?
(*a*) Its value is defined within `stdio.h`
(*b*) Its value is implementation dependent
(*c*) Its value should not equal the integer equivalent of any character
(*d*) all of the above

33. The value of an automatic variable that is declared but not initialized will be
(*a*) 0   (*b*) −1
(*c*) unpredictable   (*d*) none of the above

34. Choose the correct answers.
(*a*) An identifier may start with an underscore
(*b*) An identifier may end with an underscore
(*c*) The number of significant characters in an identifier is implementation dependent
(*d*) all of the above

35. Choose the correct answers.
(*a*) Constant expressions are evaluated at compile time

(*b*) String constants can be concatenated at compile time

(*c*) Size of array should be known at compile time

(*d*) Allof the above

36. Pre-emptive scheduling is the strategy of temporarily suspending a running process
(*a*) before the CPU time slice expires
(*b*) to allow starving processes to run
(*c*) when it requests I/O
(*d*) none of the above

37. Mutual exclusion problem occurs between
(*a*) two disjoint processes that do not interact
(*b*) processes that share resources
(*c*) processes that do not use the same resource
(*d*) none of the above

38. Sector interleaving in disks is done by
(*a*) the disk manufacturer
(*b*) the disk controller cord
(*c*) the operating system
(*d*) none of the above

39. Memory protection is of no use in a
(*a*) single user system
(*b*) non-multiprogramming system
(*c*) non-multitasking system
(*d*) none of the above

40. Some computer systems support dual mode operation—the user mode and the supervisor or monitor mode. These refer to the modes
(*a*) by which user programs handle their data
(*b*) by which the operating system executes user programs
(*c*) in which the processor and the associated hardware operate
(*d*) of memory access

41. two procedures both of which treat the other as a called procedure and itself the callee, are called as
(*a*) master-slave routines
(*b*) sub-sub-routines
(*c*) co-routines
(*d*) ambiguous master-slave routines

42. Choose the true statements about the linkage loaders.
(*a*) The input to it consists of a set of object programs that are to be linked together
(*b*) pass1 assigns addresses to all external symbols
(*c*) pass 2 performs loading, relocating and linking
(*d*) All (*a*), (*b*), (*c*)

43. The entity-relationship model comes under
(*a*) object based logical model
(*b*) record based logical model
(*c*) physical data model
(*d*) None of the above

44. Third normal form is inadequate in situation where the relation
(*a*) Has multiple candidate key
(*b*) Has candidate keys that are composite
(*c*) Has overloaded candidate keys
(*d*) All of the above

45. Redundancy is dangerous as it is a potential threat to data
(*a*) Integrity
(*b*) Consistency
(*c*) Both of the above
(*d*) None of the above

46. Representing the syntax by a grammar is advantageous because
(*a*) it is accurate
(*b*) automation becomes easy
(*c*) intermediate code can be generated easily and efficiently
(*d*) all of the above

47. CFG can be recognized by a,
(*a*) push-down automata
(*b*) 2-way linear bounded automata
(*c*) finite state automata
(*d*) none of the above

48. CSG can be recognized by
   (a) push-down automata
   (b) 2-way linear bounded automata
   (c) both of the above
   (d) none of the above

49. Choose the correct statements.
   (a) Sentence of a grammar is a sentential form without any terminals
   (b) A sentence of a grammar should be derivable from the `start` state
   (c) a sentence of a grammar should be frontier of a derivation tree, in which the root node has the `start` state as the label
   (d) (b) and (c) only

50. A grammar
   (a) can have a non-terminal A that can't derive any string of terminals
   (b) can have a non-terminal A that can be present in any sentential form
   (c) both of the above
   (d) none of the above

51. Which of the following is the most general phase-structured grammar?
   (a) Regular   (b) Context-free
   (c) Context-sensitive (d) None of these

52. In a context-sensitive grammar,
   (a) number of grammar symbols on the left hand side of a production can't be greater than the number of grammar symbols on the right hand side
   (b) number of grammar symbols on the left hand side of a production can't be greater than the number of terminals on the right hand side
   (c) number of grammar symbols on the left hand side of a production can't be greater than the number of non-terminals on the right hand side
   (d) all of the above

53. In a context-free grammar,
   (a) ε can't be the right hand side of any production
   (b) terminal symbols can't be present in the left hand side of any production
   (c) the number of grammar symbols in the left hand side is not greater than the number of grammar symbols in the right hand side
   (d) all of the above

54. If w is a string of terminals and A, B are two non-terminals, then which of the following are right-linear grammars?
   (a) $A \rightarrow Bw$ (b) $A \rightarrow Bw/w$
   (c) $A \rightarrow Bw\,|\,w$ (d) None of these

55. If a is a terminal and S, A, B are three non-terminal, then which of the following are regular grammars?
   (a) $S \rightarrow \varepsilon$ (b) $A \rightarrow abB\,|\,aB$
       $A \rightarrow aS\,|\,b$ (d) $A \rightarrow aB\,|\,a$
   (c) $A \rightarrow Ba\,|\,Bab$ $B \rightarrow bA\,|\,b$

56. Choose the correct answers.
   (a) Casting refers to implicit type conversion
   (b) Coercion refers to implicit type conversion
   (c) Casting refers to explicit type conversion
   (d) (b) and (c) only

57. Consider the following program fragment.
```
char c = 'a';
while (c++ <= 'z')
putchar(xxx);
```
If the required output is abcd ... xyz, then xxx should be
   (a) c+1   (b) c
   (c) c−1   (d) −−c

58. Choose the correct answers.
   (a) C provides no input-output features
   (b) C borrowed most of its ideas from BCPL
   (c) C provides no features to manipulate composite objects
   (d) all of the above

59. If y is of integer type then the expressions
```
3 * (y  - 8) / 9 and (y - 8) /
9 * 3
```
(a) must yield the same value
(b) must yield different values
(c) may or may not yield the same value
(d) none of the above

60. If y is of integer type then the expressions
```
3 * (y  - 8) / 9 and (y - 8) /
9 * 3
```
yield the same value if
(a) y is an even number
(b) y is an odd number
(c) y - 8 is an integral multiple of 9
(d) y - 8 is an integral multiple of 3

61. Which of the following definitions generates the same language as L, where
$L = \{x^n y^n, n \geq 1\}.$
 I. $E \rightarrow xEy \mid xy$
 II. $xy \mid x^+ xyy^+$
III. $x^+ y^+$
(a) I only
(b) I and II
(c) II and III
(d) II only

62. A finite state machine with the following state table has a single input x and a single output z.

Present state	Next state, z	
	x = 1	x = 0
A	D, 0	B, 0
B	B, 1	C, 1
C	B, 0	D, 1
D	B, 1	C, 0

If the initial state is unknown, then the shortest input sequence to reach the final state C is
(a) 01
(b) 10
(c) 101
(d) 110

63. Let $A = \{0, 1\}$ and $L = A^*$. Let $R = \{0^n 1^n, n > 0\}$, then the languages $L \cup R$ and R are respectively

(a) regular, regular
(b) not regular, regular
(c) regular, not regular
(d) not regular, not regular

64. Which of the following is not possible algorithmically?
(a) Regular grammar to context free grammar
(b) Non-deterministic FSA to deterministic FSA
(c) Non-deterministic PDA to deterministic PDA
(d) Non-deterministic Turing machine to deterministic Turing machine

65. An FSM can be used to add two given integers. Tis is
(a) true
(b) false
(c) may be true
(d) none of the above

66. The const feature can be applied to
(a) an identifier
(b) an array
(c) an array argument
(d) all of the above

67. Which of the following operators takes only integer operands?
(a) +
(b) ×
(c) /
(d) %

68. In an expression involving || operator, evaluation
(a) will be stopped if one of its components evaluates to false
(b) will be stopped if one of its components evaluates to true
(c) takes places from left to right
(d) (b) and (c) only

69. The cost of developing a compiler
(a) is proportional to the complexity of the source language
(b) is proportional to the complexity of the architecture of the target machine

(c) is proportional to the flexibility of the available instruction set
(d) all of the above

70. An ideal compiler should
(a) take less time for compiling
(b) be written in a high level language
(c) produce object code that is smaller in size and executes faster
(d) all of the above

71. Which of the following options correctly relates / and % ?
(a) b = (a/b) *b + a % b
(b) a = (a/b) *b + a % b
(c) b = (a % b) *b + a/b
(d) a = (a % b) *b + a/b

72. Literal means
(a) a string
(b) a string constant
(c) a character
(d) an alphabet

73. Length of the string "correct" is
(a) 7
(b) 8
(c) 6
(d) Implementation dependant

74. Which of the following are true regardless of the implementation?
(a) `sizeof(short)` equals `sizeof(int)`
(b) `sizeof(int)` equals `sizeof(unsigned)`
(c) `sizeof(double)` is not less than `sizeof(float)`
(d) (b) and (c) only

75. Coercion
(a) takes place across assignment operator
(b) takes place if an operator has operands of different data types
(c) both of the above
(d) none of the above

76. An optimizing compiler
(a) is optimized to occupy less space
(b) is optimized to take less time for execution

(c) optimizes the code
(d) none of the above

77. In a compiler, grouping of characters into tokens is done by
(a) scanner
(b) parser
(c) code generator
(d) code optimizer

78. Whether a given pattern constitutes a token or not
(a) depends on the source language
(b) depends on the target language
(c) depends on the compiler
(d) none of the above comments is true

79. A grammar will be meaningless
(a) if terminal set and non-terminal set are not disjoint
(b) if the left hand side of a production is a single terminal
(c) if the left hand side of a production has no non-terminal
(d) all of the above

80. Which of the following grammars are not phase-structured?
(a) Regular
(b) Context-free
(c) Context-sensitive
(d) None of these

81. Critical region is
(a) a part of the operating system which is not allowed to be accessed by any process
(b) a set of instructions that access common shared resource which exclude one another in time
(c) the portion of the main memory which can be accessed only by one process at a time
(d) none of the above

82. Kernel is
(a) considered as the critical part of the operating system
(b) the software which monitors the operating system

(c) the set of primitive functions upon which the rest of operating system functions are built up

(d) none of the above

83. With a single resource, deadlock occurs

(a) if there are more than two processes competing for that resource

(b) if there are only two process competing for that resource

(c) if there is a single process competing for that resource

(d) none of the above

84. Necessary conditions for deadlock are

(a) nonpreemption and circular wait

(b) Mutual exclusion and partial allocation

(c) both (a) and (b)

(d) none of the above

85. In a time-sharing operating system, when the time slot given to a process is completed, the process goes from the Running state to the

(a) BLOCKED state

(b) READY state

(c) SUSPENDED state

(d) TERMINATED state

86. The range of the function $f(x) = x^2 / (1 + x^2)$ is

(a) $(-\infty, +\infty)$

(b) $(0, \infty)$

(c) $(-\infty, 0]$

(d) $[0, 1)$

87. In calculating the mean and variance of 10 readings, a student wrongly used 52 instead of the correct figure 25. If the mean he obtained was 45, then the correct mean is

(a) 47.3

(b) 43.7

(c) 42.3

(d) impossible to find

88. Refer Qn. 87. If the variance he obtained was 16, then the correct variance is

(a) 43.8

(b) 47.3

(c) 42.3

(d) impossible to find

89. If $^nC_{r-1} = 36$; $^nC_r = 84$ and $^nC_{r+1} = 126$, then the value of 'r' is

(a) 9

(b) 6

(c) 5

(d) 3

90. In the interval $[0, \pi]$, the equation $x = \cos(x)$ has

(a) no solution

(b) exactly one solution

(c) exactly two solution

(d) an infinite number of solutions

91. Disk scheduling involves deciding

(a) which disk should be accessed next

(b) the order in which disk access requests must be serviced

(c) the physical location where files should be accessed in the disk

(d) none of the above

92. Which of the following is/are not assembler directive(s)?

(a) START

(b) LOAD

(c) END

(d) BYTE

93. Which of the following remarks about the assembler are true?

(a) It translates mnemonic instruction into machine code

(b) The instruction formats, addressing modes, etc., are of direct concern in assembler design

(c) Design of an assembler is independent of the source language

(d) Both (a) and (b) only

94. A programming language is to be designed to run on a machine that does not have a big memory. The language should

(a) prefer a 2 pass compiler to a 1 pass compiler

(b) prefer an interpreter to a compiler

(c) not support recursion

(d) all of the above

95. Which of the following about the loader is/are incorrect?

(a) Loader brings object program into memory for execution

    (b) Linkage editors perform linking after loading

    (c) Dynamic linking schemes delay linking until execution time

    (d) All of the above

96. A top-down parser generates
    (a) left-most derivation
    (b) right-most derivation
    (c) right-most derivation in reverse
    (d) left-most derivation in reverse

97. A bottom-up parser generates
    (a) left-most derivation
    (b) right-most derivation
    (c) right-most derivation in reverse
    (d) left-most derivation in reverse

98. A given grammar is said to be ambiguous if
    (a) two or more production have the same non-terminal on the left hand side
    (b) a derivation tree has more than one associated sentence
    (c) there is a sentence with more than one derivation tree corresponding to it
    (d) brackets are not present in the grammar

99. The grammar $E \rightarrow E + E \rightarrow E*E \mid a$, is
    (a) ambiguous
    (b) unambiguous
    (c) ambiguous or not depends on the given sentence
    (d) none of the above

100. Choose the correct statement.
    (a) Language corresponding to a given grammar, is the set of all strings that can be generated by the given grammar
    (b) A given language is ambiguous if no unambiguous grammar exists for it
    (c) Two different grammars may generate the same language
    (d) All of the above

ANSWERS

1	2	3	4	5	6	7	8	9	10
(c)	(d)	(c)	(c)	(d)	(d)	(c)	(a)	(a)	(b)
11	**12**	**13**	**14**	**15**	**16**	**17**	**18**	**19**	**20**
(d)	(c)	(c)	(c)	(c)	(b)	(d)	(c)	(d)	(a)
21	**22**	**23**	**24**	**25**	**26**	**27**	**28**	**29**	**30**
(a)	(d)	(c)	(c)	(c)	(a)	(c)	(a)	(c)	(d)
31	**32**	**33**	**34**	**35**	**36**	**37**	**38**	**39**	**40**
(a)	(d)	(c)	(d)	(d)	(a)	(b)	(c)	(d)	(c)
41	**42**	**43**	**44**	**45**	**46**	**47**	**48**	**49**	**50**
(c)	(d)	(a)	(d)	(c)	(d)	(c)	(b)	(d)	(c)
51	**52**	**53**	**54**	**55**	**56**	**57**	**58**	**59**	**60**
(c)	(d)	(b)	(c)	(d)	(d)	(c)	(d)	(c)	(c)
61	**62**	**63**	**64**	**65**	**66**	**67**	**68**	**69**	**70**
(a)	(b)	(c)	(c)	(b)	(d)	(d)	(d)	(d)	(d)
71	**72**	**73**	**74**	**75**	**76**	**77**	**78**	**79**	**80**
(b)	(b)	(a)	(d)	(c)	(c)	(a)	(a)	(d)	(d)
81	**82**	**83**	**84**	**85**	**86**	**87**	**88**	**89**	**90**
(b)	(c)	(d)	(c)	(b)	(d)	(c)	(a)	(d)	(b)
91	**92**	**93**	**94**	**95**	**96**	**97**	**98**	**99**	**100**
(b)	(b)	(d)	(d)	(b)	(a)	(c)	(c)	(a)	(d)

1. The following program fragment
```
unsigned i = 1;
int  j  = -4;
printf ("%u", i + j);
```
prints
(a) garbage
(b) −3
(c) an integer that changes from machine to machine
(d) none of the above

2. Pick the correct answers.
Universal TM influenced the concept of
(a) stored-program computers
(b) interpretive implementation of programming languages
(c) computability
(d) all of the above

3. The number of internal states of a UTM should be atleast
(a) 1
(b) 2
(c) 3
(d) 4

4. The number of symbols necessary to simulate a TM with m symbols and n states is
(a) $m + n$
(b) $8\ mn + 4\ m$
(c) mn
(d) $4\ mn + m$

5. Any TM with m symbols and n states can be simulated by another TM with just 2 symbols and less than
(a) $8\ mn$ states
(b) $4\ mn + 8$ states
(c) $8\ mn + 4$ states
(d) mn states

6. The statement—"A TM can't solve halting problem" is
(a) true
(b) false
(c) still an open question
(d) none of the above

7. If there exists a TM which when applied to any problem in the class, terminates if the correct answer is yes and may or may not terminate otherwise, is said to be
(a) stable
(b) unsolvable
(c) partially solvable
(d) unstable

8. The number states of the FSM, required to simulate the behaviour of a computer, with a memory capable of storing 'm' words, each of length 'n' bits is
(a) $m \times 2^n$
(b) 2^{mn}
(c) 2^{m+n}
(d) none of the above

9. The vernacular language English, if considered a formal language, is a
(a) regular language
(b) context free language
(c) context sensitive language
(d) none of the above

10. P, Q, R are three languages. If P and R are regular and if PQ = R, then
(a) Q has to be regular
(b) Q cannot be regular
(c) Q need not be regular
(d) Q has to be a CFL

11. The sequence of events that happen during a typical fetch operation is
(a) PC → Mar → Memory → MDR → IR
(b) PC → Memory → MDR → IR
(c) PC → Memory → IR
(d) PC → MAR → Memory → IR

12. Let A be a finite set of size 'n'. The number of elements in the power set of $A \times A$ is

(a) 2^{2^n} (b) 2^{n^2}
(c) $(2^n)^2$ (d) $(2^2)^n$

13. Probability of an event A happening is 0.4. Probability that in 3 independent trials, event A happens atleast once is

(a) 0.064   (b) 0.144
(c) 0.784   (d) 0.4

14. If x, y are two real numbers such that $x > 0$ and $xy = 1$, then $x + y$ can't be less than

(a) 1.5   (b) 1.9
(c) 1.75   (d) 2.0

15. Let $f(x + y) = f(x) + f(y)$, for all x, y. If $f(x)$ is continuous at $x = 0$, then

(a) f is continuous at all points
(b) the number of points of discontinuity of f can't be infinite
(c) the number of points of discontinuity of f must be infinite
(d) none of the above

16. $f(x)$ and $g(x)$ are two functions differentiable in [0, 1]. such that $f(0) = 2$; $g(0) = 0$; $f(1) = 6$; $g(1) = 2$. Then

(a) there must exist a constant C in (0, 1), such that $f'(C) = 2g'(C)$
(b) there must exist a constant C in [0, 1], such that $f'(C) = 2\,g'(C)$
(c) there must exist a constant C in (0, 1), such that $2\,f'(C) = g'(C)$
(d) there must exist a constant C in [0, 1], such that $2f'(C) = g'(C)$

17. Let f be a one-to-one function with domain $\{x, y, z\}$ and range $\{1, 2, 3\}$. It is given that exactly one of the following statements is true and the remaining 2 are false:

$$f(x) = 1;\ f(y) \neq 1;\ f(z) \neq 2$$

The $f^{-1}(1)$ equals
(a) 2   (b) x
(c) y (d) z

18. Let f be a twice differentiable function such that

$f''(x) = -f(x)$ and $f'(x) = g(x)$; $h(x) = (f(x))^2 + (g(x))^2$. If $h(5) = 11$, then $h(10)$ is
(a) 8   (b) 9
(c) 10   (d) 11

19. If A and B are two events such that $P(A) > 0$ and $P(B) \neq 1$, then $P(\overline{A}/\overline{B})$ equals

(a) $(1 - P(A \cup B))/P(\overline{B})$
(b) $(1 - P(A \cup B))/P(B)$
(c) $(1 - P(A \cap B))/P(\overline{B})$
(d) $(1 - P(A \cap B))/P(B)$

20. i^i, where i is $\sqrt{-1}$, is
(a) a pure imaginary number
(b) a complex number
(c) an integer
(d) a real number

21. Let $f(x + y) = f(x)\,f(y)$, for all x, y. If $f(5) = 2$ and $f'(0) = 3$, Then $f'(5)$ is equal to
(a) 1   (b) 5
(c) 6   (d) −1

22. In numerical methods, accuracy means
(a) the number of significant figures representing a quantity
(b) the spread in repeated readings of an instrument in measuring a particular physical quantity
(c) the proximity of an approximate number or measurement to the true value it is supposed to represent
(d) all of the above

23. Suppose A_1, A_2, ... A_{30} are 30 sets, each with 5 elements, and B_1, B_2, ...B_n are 'n' sets, each with 3 elements.

Let $\quad \bigcup\limits_{i=1}^{30} A_i = \bigcup\limits_{i=1}^{n} B_j = S.$

Each element of S, belongs to exactly 10 of the A_i's and to exactly 9 of the B_j's. Then 'n' is

(a) 25 (b) 45
(c) 40 (d) 20

24. Which of the following remarks about an ill-conditioned system of equations are true?
(a) Small change in coefficient will result in large change in solution
(b) A wide range of solutions can approximately satisfy the equations
(c) If slope of two lines are almost same, they make up an ill-conditioned system of equations
(d) All of the above

25. If the cube roots of unity are 1, 2, w^2, then the roots of the equation $(x - 1)^3 + 8 = 0$, are
(a) $-1, 1 + 2\ w, 1 + 2\ w^2$
(b) $1, 1 - 2\ w, 1 - 2\ w^2$
(c) $-1, 1 - 2\ w, 1 - 2\ w^2$
(d) $-1, -1 + 2\ w, -1 + 2\ w^2$

26. If p, q, r are three real numbers, then
(a) max (p, q) < max (p, q, r)
(b) max (p, q) = $(p + q + |\ p - q\ |)/2$
(c) max (p, q) < min (p, q, r)
(d) none of the above

27. The number of 1's in the binary representation of $(3 \times 4096 + 15 \times 256 + 5 \times 16 + 3)$ is
(a) 8 (b) 9
(c) 10 (d) 12

28. A determinant is chosen at random from the set of all determinants of order 2 with each element either 0 or 1 only. The probability that the value of the chosen determinant is positive is
(a) 1/2 (b) 2/7
(c) 3/16 (d) 7/16

29. The number of permutations of 'n' different things taken not more than 'r' at a time, with repetitions being allowed, is
(a) $(n^r - 1)/(n - 1)$ (b) $(n^r - 1)/(n - 1)!$
(c) $n(n^r - 1)/(n - 1)$ (d) $(n^r - 1)/n\ !$

30. A relation R is defined in N × N, such that (a, b) R (c, d) iff $a + d = b + c$. The relation R is
(a) reflexive but not transitive
(b) reflexive and transitive, but not symmetric
(c) an equivalence relation
(d) a partial order

31. Consider the grammar
```
S   →   PQ  |  SQ  |  PS
P   →   x
Q   →   y
```
To get a string of n terminals, the number of productions to be used is
(a) n^2 (b) $n + 1$
(c) $2\ n$ (d) $2n - 1$

32. Choose the correct statements.
A class of languages that is closed under
(a) union and complementation has to be closed under intersection
(b) intersection and complementation has to be closed under union
(c) union and complementation has to be closed under union
(d) both (a) and (b) only

33. Choose the correct statements.
(a) An FSM with 1 stack is more powerful than an FSM with no stack
(b) An FSM with 2 stacks is more powerful than a FSM with 1 stack
(c) An FSM with 3 stacks is more powerful than an FSM with 2 stacks
(d) Both (a) and (b) only

34. Choose the correct statements.
(a) An FSM with 2 stacks is as powerful as a TM
(b) DFSM and NDFSM have the same power
(c) A DFSM with 1 stack and an NDFSM with 1 stack have the same power
(d) Both (a) and (b) only are correct

35. Bounded minimalization is a technique for
(a) proving whether a primitive recursive function is Turning computable or not

(b) proving whether a primitive recursive function is a total function or not

(c) generating primitive recursive functions

(d) generating partial recursive functions

36. Choose the correct statements.

(a) Set of recursively enumerable languages is closed under union

(b) If a language and its complement are both regular, then the language must be recursive

(c) Recursive languages are closed under complementation

(d) All of the above

37. Select the statement that are incorrect about the macroprocessor.

(a) The general features such as macro expansion, use of keyword parameters are machine dependent

(b) Macro invocation given the name of the macro being invoked and arguments to be used

(c) Macro definition is also referred to as macro call

(d) Both (a) and (c) only

38. Transfer of information to and from the main memory takes place in terms of

(a) bits
(b) bytes
(c) words
(d) nibbles

39. The output of the lexical analyser is

(a) a set of regular expressions

(b) syntax tree

(c) set of tokens

(d) string of characters

40. An interpreter is preferred over a compiler

(a) when efficient use of computer resources is the consideration

(b) during program development phase

(c) when storage space is to be minimised

(d) both (b) and (c) only

41. The first operating system used in micro-processors is

(a) Zenix
(b) DOS
(c) CP/M
(d) Multics

42. Which of the following remarks about PLA is/are true?

(a) It produces product of sum as the output

(b) It produces sum of products as the output

(c) It is dedicated for a particular operation

(d) All of the above

43. Any given truth table

(a) can be represented by a Karnaugh map

(b) can be represented by a sum of product of boolean expressions

(c) can be represented by a product of sum of boolean expression

(d) all of the above

44. A number system uses 20 as the radix. The excess code that is necessary for its equivalent binary coded representation is

(a) 4
(b) 5
(c) 6
(d) 7

45. Choose the correct statements.

(a) Bus is a group of information carrying wires

(b) Bus is needed to achieve reasonable speed of operation

(c) Bus can carry data or address

(d) All of the above

46. The advantage of MOS devices over bipolar devices is

(a) it allows higher bit densities and also cost effective

(b) it is easy to fabricate

(c) its higher-impedance

(d) all of the above

47. The boolean expression $X + X'Y$ equals

(a) $X + Y$
(b) $X + XY$
(c) $Y + YX$
(d) $X'Y + Y'X$

48. $(X + Y) + Z = X + (Y + Z)$

(a) shows that the boolean operator OR is associative

(b) implies the associativity of the boolean operator AND
(c) both of the above
(d) none of the above

49. Which of the following are registers?
(a) Accumulator (b) Stack pointer
(c) Program counter (d) All of the above

50. Which of the following remarks about BCD are true?
(a) It is a 8–4–2–1 weighted code
(b) $(12345678)_{10}$ needs 4 bytes in BCD representation
(c) Conversion to and from the decimal system can be done easily
(d) All of the above

51. Which of the following comments about the Program Counter (PC) are true?
(a) It is a register
(b) It is a cell in ROM
(c) During execution of the current instruction, its content changes
(d) Both (a) and (c) only

52. If $(123)_5 = (x3)_y$, then the number of possible values of x is
(a) 4 (b) 1
(c) 3 (d) 2

53. If $(12x)_3 = (123)_x$, then the value of x is
(a) 3 (b) 3 or 4
(c) 2 (d) none of the above

54. Choose the correct statements.
(a) By scanning a bit pattern, one can say whether it represents data or not
(b) Whether a given piece of information is a data or not depends on the particular application
(c) Positive numbers can't be represented in 2's complement form
(d) Both (b) and (c) only

55. Which of the following does not need extra hardware for DRAM refreshing?

(a) 8085 (b) Motorola-6800
(c) Z-80 (d) None of these

56. A + B can be implemented by
(a) NAND gates alone
(b) NOR gates alone
(c) AND gates alone
(d) Both (a) and (b) only

57. Bipolar devices are desirable in the fabrication of which of the following components?
(a) main memory
(b) cache memory
(c) micro program memory
(d) both (b) and (c) only

58. Which of the following is the programmable internal timer?
(a) 8251 (b) 8250
(c) 8253 (d) 8275

59. The idea of cache memory is based
(a) on the property of locality of reference
(b) on the fact that only a small portion of a program is referenced relatively frequently
(c) on the fact that references generally tend to cluster
(d) all of the above

60. Which of the following weights makes the complement operation easier in BCD form?
(a) 8-4-2-1 (b) Excess-3
(c) 2-4-2-1 (d) 3-2-1-0

61. If $\log_5 10 = \log_7 x \log_n m$, then the values of x, m, n are
(a) 10, 7, 5 (b) −1, 2, 3
(c) 7, 5, 3 (d) 7, 5, 8

62. If $\sqrt{5} + \sqrt{7} + i$ is one of the roots of the equation $f(x) = 0$ with rational coefficients, then the degree of the given equation can't be less than
(a) 5 (b) 6
(c) 7 (d) 8

63. Printing a character as an integer
(a) results in the printing of a negative integer
(b) always prints a positive integer
(c) prints a value that is implementation dependent
(d) none of the above

64. Pick the operators that associate from the left.
(a) +
(b) ,
(c) %
(d) all of the above

65. Pick the operators that associate from the right.
(a) ++
(b) +=
(c) =
(d) all of the above

66. `x - = y + 1;` means
(a) `x = x - y + 1`
(b) `x = -x - y - 1`
(c) `x = -x + y + 1`
(d) `x = x - y - 1`

67. Which of the following comments about the ++ operator are correct?
(a) It is a unary operator
(b) The operand can come before or after the operator
(c) It cannot be applied to an expression
(d) All of the above

68. When a variable of data type `double` is converted into `float`
(a) rounding takes place
(b) truncation takes place
(c) the lower order bits are dropped
(d) none of the above

69. The expression `5 - 2 - 3 * 5 - 2` will evaluate to 18, if
(a) − is left associative and * has precedence over −
(b) − is right associative and * has precedence over −
(c) − is right associative and − has precedence over *

(d) − is left associative and − has precedence over*

70. `printf ("%c", 100);`
(a) prints 100
(b) prints the ASCII equivalent of 100
(c) prints garbage
(d) none of the above

71. The program fragment
```
int  i = 263;
putchar (i);
```
(a) prints 263
(b) prints the ASCII equivalent of 263
(c) rings the bell
(d) prints garbage

72. Which of the following comments regarding the reading of a string, using `scanf` (with `%s` option) and `gets`, is true?
(a) Both can be used interchangeably
(b) `Scanf` is delimited by end of line, while `gets` is not
(c) `Scanf` is delimited by blank space, while `gets` is not
(d) None of the above

73. The following statement
```
printf ("%f", 9/5);
```
prints
(a) 1.8
(b) 1.0
(c) 2.0
(d) none of the above

74. The statement
```
printf ("%f", (float) 9/5);
```
prints
(a) 1.8
(b) 1.0
(c) 2.0
(d) none of the above

75. Which of the following are not keywords in C?
(a) `printf`
(b) `main`
(c) `IF`
(d) all of the above

76. The operators ., ||, <, = if arranged in the ascending order of precedence reads
(a) . , || , < , =
(b) = , <, || , .

(c) = , || , < , .
(d) < , || , = , .

77. Pick the operators whose meaning is context dependent.
(a) *
(b) #
(c) &
(d) all of the above

78. Pick the operators that associate from the left.
(a) &&
(b) ||
(c) ,
(d) all of the above

79. int x, y = 2, z, a;

```
x = (y *= 2) + (z = a = y);
printf ("%d", x);
```

(a) prints 7
(b) prints 6
(c) Prints 8
(d) is syntactically wrong

80. In n has the value 3, then the output of the statement `printf ("%d %d", n++, ++n);`
(a) is 3   5
(b) is 4   5
(c) is 4   4
(d) is implementation dependent

81. Which of the following is not primitive recursive but computable?
(a) Carnot function
(b) Riemann function
(c) Bounded function
(d) Ackermann function

82. Which of the following is not primitive recursive but partially recursive?
(a) Carnot function
(b) Riemann function
(c) Bounded function
(d) Ackermann function

83. Choose the correct statements.
(a) A total recursive function is also a partial recursive function
(b) A partial recursive function is also a total recursive function

(c) A partial recursive function is also a primitive recursive function
(d) All of the above are correct

84. If there exists a language L, for which there exists a TM, T, that accepts every word in L and either rejects or loops for every word that is not in L, is said to be
(a) recursive
(b) recursively enumerable
(c) NP-HARD
(d) none of the above

85. Choose the correct statements.
(a) $L = \{a^n b^n a^n \mid n = 1, 2, 3 \ldots\}$ is recursively enumerable
(b) Recursive languages are closed under union
(c) Every recursive language is recursively enumerable
(d) All of the above on correct

86. When exceptional situation occurs outside the CPU the `H/W` signal given is
(a) `reset`
(b) `interrupt`
(c) `hold`
(d) `wait`

87. The root directory of a disk should be placed
(a) at a fixed address in main memory
(b) at a fixed location on the disk
(c) anywhere on the disk
(d) at a fixed location on the system disk

88. Efficient use of addressing modes
(a) speeds up execution
(b) reduces the number of instructions
(c) reduces the size of instructions
(d) all of the above

89. The correct sequence of time delays that happen during a data transfer from a disk to memory is
(a) seek time, latency time and transfer time
(b) seek time, access time and transfer time
(c) latency time, seek time and transfer time

   (d) latency time, access time and transfer time

90. Writing a software in assembly language is preferred to writing in a high level language when
   (a) optimal use of the hardware resources available is of primary concern
   (b) programmer's productivity is important
   (c) portability is important
   (d) none of the above

91. a compiler- compiler is a/an
   (a) compiler which compiles a compiler program
   (b) software tool used in automatic generation of a compiler
   (c) compiler written in the same language it compiles
   (d) another name for cross compiler

92. A compiler which allows only the modified section of the source code to be recompiled is called as
   (a) incremental compiler
   (b) reconfigurable compiler
   (c) dynamic compiler
   (d) selective compiler

93. Which of the following system software resides in main memory always?
   (a) Text editor
   (b) Assembler
   (c) Linker
   (d) Loader

94. In a two pass assembler the pseudo-code EQU is to be evaluated during
   (a) pass 1
   (b) pass 2
   (c) not evaluated by the assembler
   (d) none of the above

95. Effective address got by index mode will be the same as that of register indirect mode
   (a) when the index register has the value 0
   (b) when the index register has the value 1

   (c) when the index register has the value – 1
   (d) can never be the same

96. Indexing can be done with which of the following addressing modes?
   (a) Relative
   (b) Direct
   (c) Immediate
   (d) Both (a) and (b) only

97. Which of the following are the advantages of 2's complement over 1's complement?
   (a) Easy to implement using digital components
   (b) Subtraction can be done by a single addition
   (c) It has only one zero
   (d) Both (a) and (c) only

98. Pick the functions which are completely performed in pass 1.
   (a) Updating the location counter
   (b) Processing of EQU pseudo-op
   (c) Processing of DS pseudo-op
   (d) All of the above

99. Pick the functions which are performed in pass 2.
   (a) Creating the proper address mode, using the base table
   (b) Updating the location counter
   (c) Generation of object code using machine operation table
   (d) Both (a) and (c) only

100. Pick the correct statement(s) about LTORG.
   (a) It is a pseudo-op
   (b) It is used to load the object program in some specified memory, which is given in the operand field
   (c) It creates a literal pool that contains all the literal operands used since the previous LTROG
   (d) None of the above

ANSWERS

1	2	3	4	5	6	7	8	9	10
(c)	(d)	(b)	(d)	(a)	(a)	(c)	(b)	(b)	(c)
11	12	13	14	15	16	17	18	19	20
(a)	(b)	(c)	(d)	(a)	(a)	(c)	(d)	(a)	(d)
21	22	23	24	25	26	27	28	29	30
(c)	(c)	(b)	(d)	(c)	(b)	(c)	(c)	(c)	(c)
31	32	33	34	35	36	37	38	39	40
(d)	(d)	(d)	(d)	(c)	(d)	(d)	(c)	(c)	(d)
41	42	43	44	45	46	47	48	49	50
(c)	(b)	(d)	(c)	(d)	(d)	(a)	(c)	(d)	(d)
51	52	53	54	55	56	57	58	59	60
(d)	(d)	(d)	(d)	(c)	(d)	(d)	(c)	(d)	(c)
61	62	63	64	65	66	67	68	69	70
(a)	(d)	(c)	(d)	(d)	(d)	(d)	(a)	(c)	(b)
71	72	73	74	75	76	77	78	79	80
(c)	(c)	(d)	(a)	(d)	(c)	(d)	(d)	(c)	(d)
81	82	83	84	85	86	87	88	89	90
(d)	(d)	(a)	(b)	(d)	(b)	(b)	(d)	(a)	(a)
91	92	93	94	95	96	97	98	99	100
(b)	(a)	(d)	(a)	(a)	(d)	(d)	(d)	(d)	(a)

1. The following program fragment
```
int a = 4, b = 6;
printf ("%d", a == b);
```
(a) outputs an error message
(b) prints 0
(c) prints 1
(d) none of the above

2. The following program fragment
```
int a = 4, b = 6;
printf ("%d", a != b);
```
(a) outputs an error message
(b) prints 0
(c) prints a non-zero value
(d) none of the above

3. The following program fragment
```
int a = 4, b = 6;
printf ("%d", a = b);
```
(a) outputs an error message
(b) prints 0
(c) prints 1
(d) none of the above

4. A possible output of the following program fragment
```
for(i = getchar();; 1 -
getchar())
if (i == '1') break;
else putchar (i);
```
is
(a) mi
(b) mil
(c) mill
(d) none of the above

5. A computer system has 6 tape drives, with 'n' processes competing for them. Each process may need 3 tape drives. The maximum value of 'n' for which the system is guaranteed to be deadlock free is
(a) 2
(b) 3
(c) 4
(d) 1

6. Which of the following symbol table implementation, makes efficient use of memory?
(a) List
(b) Search tree
(c) Hash table
(d) Self-organization list

7. Access time of the symbol table will be logarithmic, if it is implemented by
(a) linear list
(b) search tree
(c) hash table
(d) self-organizing list

8. An ideal compiler should
(a) detect error
(b) detect and repair error
(c) detect, repair and correct error
(d) none of the above

9. Which of the following is not a source of error?
(a) Faulty design specification
(b) Faulty algorithm
(c) Compiler themselves
(d) None of the above

10. Any transcription error can be repaired by
(a) insertion alone
(b) deletion alone
(c) insertion and deletion alone
(d) replacement alone

11. $1 - x^2/2\ ! + x^4/4\ ! - ... + (-1)^n\ x^{2n}/2n\ ! + ...$ is the expansion of
(a) e^x
(b) $\log x$
(c) $\cos x$
(d) $\sin x$

12. If the following program fragment (assume negative numbers are stored in 2's complement form)

```
unsigned  i = 1;
int    j = -4 ;
printf ("%u", i + j);
```

prints x, then `printf("%d", 8* sizeof (int));`

outputs (log in the answers are to the base two)
(a) an unpredictable value
(b) `8* log(x + 3)`
(c) `log(x + 3)`
(d) `log8(x + 3)`

13. Choose the statements that are syntactically correct.
(a) `/*  Is  /*  this  a  valid*/ comment*/`
(b) `for(;;);`
(c) `return;`
(d) both (b) and (c) only

14. The following program fragment

```
for(i = 3;   i < 15 ; i   += 3);
    printf ("%d",  i);
```

results in
(a) a syntax error
(b) an execution error
(c) printing of 12
(d) printing of 15

15. For `(i = 1;  i < 5; ++i)`

```
if  (i == 3) continue;

else printf ("%d", i);
```

results in the printing of
(a) 1 2 4 5
(b) 1 2 4
(c) 2 4 5
(d) none of the above

16. Dirty bit is used to show the
(a) page with corrupted data
(b) the wrong page in the memory
(c) page that is modified after being loaded into cache memory
(d) page that is less frequently accessed

17. Fence register is used for
(a) CPU protection
(b) memory protection
(c) file protection
(d) all of the above

18. Which of the following is a service not supported by the operating system?
(a) Protection
(b) Accounting
(c) Compilation
(d) I/O operation

19. The first-fit, best-fit and the worst-fit algorithm can be used for
(a) contiguous allocation of memory
(b) linked allocation of memory
(c) indexed allocation of memory
(d) all of the above

20. Which of the following are single-user operating systems?
(a) MS-DOS
(b) XENIX
(c) Both of the above
(d) None of the above

21. Any given boolean expression can be implemented by using
(a) only NAND gates
(b) only NOR gates
(c) only OR gates
(d) both (a) and (b) only

22. To get boolean expression in the product of sum form, from a given Karnaugh map
(a) don't care conditions should not be present
(b) don't care conditions, if present, should be taken as zeroes
(c) one should cover all the 0's present and complement the resulting expression

    (*d*) one should cover all the 1's present and complement the resulting expression

23. The boolean expression $AB + AB' + A'C + AC$ is independent of the boolean variable
    (*a*) A
    (*b*) B
    (*c*) C
    (*d*) none of the above

24. The minimum number of gates required to implement the boolean expression $AB + AB' + A'C$ is
    (*a*) 1 AND gate and 1 OR gate
    (*b*) 2 NAND gates
    (*c*) 3 AND gates and 2 OR gates
    (*d*) none of the above

25. Property of locality of reference may fail, if a program has
    (*a*) many conditional jumps
    (*b*) many unconditional jumps
    (*c*) many operands
    (*d*) all of the above

26. The number of columns in a state table for a sequential circuit with '*m*' flip-flops and '*n*' input is
    (*a*) $m + n$
    (*b*) $m + 2n$
    (*c*) $2m + n$
    (*d*) $2m + 2n$

27. A computer uses trinary system instead of the traditional binary system. An '*n*' bit string in the binary system will occupy
    (*a*) $3 + n$ trinary digits
    (*b*) $2n/3$ trinary digits
    (*c*) $n\log_2 3$ trinary digits
    (*d*) $n\log_3 2$ trinary digits

28. The boolean expression $A'BE + BCDE + BC'D'E + A'B'DE' + B'C'DE'$ can be simplified to $BE + B'DE'$, if the don't care conditions are
    (*a*) $ABCDE + AB'CDE'$
    (*b*) $ABCD + AB'CDE' + ABCDE$
    (*c*) $ABC'DE + AB'CDE' + ABCD'E$
    (*d*) none of the above

29. The decimal equivalent of the binary number 101: 101 is

    (*a*) 5.6249
    (*b*) 5.625
    (*c*) 5.5
    (*d*) 5.25

30. Which of the following does not have 8 data lines?
    (*a*) 8085
    (*b*) 8086
    (*c*) 8088
    (*d*) Z-80

31. Choose the correct statements.
    (*a*) if two graphs $G1$ and $G2$ are isomorphic, then they should have the same number of vertices and edges
    (*b*) if two graphs have the same number of nodes and edges, they have to be isomorphic
    (*c*) loops can't be present in an isomorphic graph
    (*d*) none of the above

32. In any undirected graph,
    (*a*) the sum of degrees of all the nodes must be even
    (*b*) the sum of degrees of all the nodes is twice the number of edges
    (*c*) the sum of degrees of all the nodes must be odd
    (*d*) both (*a*) and (*b*) only

33. $(PVQ) \wedge (P \rightarrow R) \wedge (Q \rightarrow S)$ is equivalent to
    (*a*) $S \wedge R$
    (*b*) $S \rightarrow R$
    (*c*) SVR
    (*d*) none of the above

34. Which of the following are tautologies?
    (*a*) $((PVQ) \wedge Q) \leftrightarrow Q$
    (*b*) $(PV(P \rightarrow Q)) \rightarrow P$
    (*c*) $((PVQ) \wedge P) \rightarrow Q$
    (*d*) None of the above

35. Identify the valid conclusion from the premises $P \vee Q$, $Q \rightarrow R$, $P \rightarrow M$, $\neg M$
    (*a*) $P \wedge (Q \vee R)$
    (*b*) $P \wedge (Q \wedge R)$
    (*c*) $R \wedge (P \vee Q)$
    (*d*) None of these

36. Three address codes involves
    (*a*) exactly 3 address
    (*b*) at the most 3 address
    (*c*) no unary operators
    (*d*) none of the above

37. Symbol table can be used for
    (a) checking type compatibility
    (b) suppressing duplication of error messages
    (c) storage allocation
    (d) all of the above

38. The best way to compare the different implementations of symbol table is to compare the time required to
    (a) add a new name
    (b) make an inquiry
    (c) add a new name and make an inquiry
    (d) none of the above

39. Which of the following symbol table implementation is based on the property of locality of reference?
    (a) Linear list
    (b) Search tree
    (c) Hash table
    (d) Self-organization list

40. Which of the following symbol table implementation is best suited if access time is to be minimum?
    (a) Linear list
    (b) Search tree
    (c) Hash table
    (d) Self-organization list

41. In a system that does not support swapping,
    (a) the compiler normally binds symbolic addresses (variables) to relocatable addresses
    (b) the compiler normally binds symbolic addresses to physical addresses
    (c) the loader binds relocatable addresses to symbolic addresses
    (d) binding of symbolic addresses to physical addresses normally takes place during execution

42. To obtain better memory utilization, dynamic loading is used. With dynamic loading, a routine is not loaded until it is called for. For implementing dynamic loading,
    (a) special support from hardware is essential
    (b) special support from operating system is essential
    (c) special support from both hardware and operating system are essential
    (d) user programs can implement dynamic loading without any special support from the operating system or the hardware

43. Which of the following is true?
    (a) The linkage editor is used to edit programs which have to be later linked together
    (b) The linkage editor links object modules during compiling or assembling
    (c) The linkage editor links object modules and resolves external references between them before loading
    (d) The linkage editor resolves external references between the object modules during execution time

44. Two finite state machines are said to be equivalent if
    (a) they have the same number of states
    (b) they have the same number of edges
    (c) they have the same number of states and edges
    (d) they recognize the same set of tokens

45. If two finite state machines are equivalent, they should have the same number of
    (a) states   (b) edges
    (c) states and edges (d) none of the above

46. T is a graph with 'n' vertices. T is connected and has exactly $n - 1$ edges, then
    (a) T contains no cycles
    (b) every pair of vertices in T is connected by exactly one path
    (c) the addition of a new edge will create a cycle
    (d) all of the above

47. If one has to obtain the roots of $x^2 - 2x + \log$ 2 = 0 to four decimal places, log 2 should be given to the accuracy of approximately
(a) 6×10^{-5} (b) 7×10^{-6}
(c) 8×10^{-5} (d) 9×10^{-7}

48. Choose the incorrect statement(s).
(a) The determinant of a matrix equals the sum of its eigen values
(b) A matrix satisfies its characteristic equation
(c) The sum of the principal diagonal elements of a matrix equals the sum of its eigen values
(d) All of the above are incorrect

49. A is a square matrix of order 'n' and its determinant value is 5. If all the elements are multiplied by 2, its determinant value becomes 40. Then 'n' is
(a) 2   (b) 3
(c) 4   (d) 5

50. In a computer an n digit integer $a_n\, a_{n-1} \ldots a_1$ is represented as $a_n\, a_{n-1} \ldots a_{r+1}\, 00 \ldots 0$. The error e is
(a) $0 \le e \le 10^{r-1}$ (b) $1 \le e \le 10^r - 1$
(c) $0 \le e \le 10^{r-1} - 1$ (d) $0 \le e \le 10^{r+1} - 1$

51. If two finite states machine M and N are isomorphic, then
(a) M can be transformed to N, merely re-labelling its states
(b) M can be transformed to N, merely re-labelling its edges
(c) M can be transformed to N, merely re-labelling its states and edges
(d) none of the above

52. In a syntax directed translation scheme, if the value of an attribute of a node is a function of the values of the attributes of its children, then it is called a
(a) synthesized attribute
(b) inherited attribute
(c) canonical attribute
(d) none of the above

53. Synthesized attribute can be easily simulated by a
(a) LL grammar
(b) ambiguous grammar
(c) LR grammar
(d) none of the above

54. For which of the following situations, inherited attribute is a natural choice
(a) evaluation of arithmetic expressions
(b) keeping track of variable declaration
(c) both of the above
(d) none of the above

55. The graph depicting the inter-dependencies of the attributes of different nodes in a parse tree is called
(a) flow graph
(b) dependency graph
(c) Karnaugh's graph
(d) Steffi graph

56. Which of the following logic families, is well suited for high-speed operation?
(a) TTL   (b) ECL
(c) MOS   (d) CMOS

57. The function performed by the following arrangement of JK flip-flops is

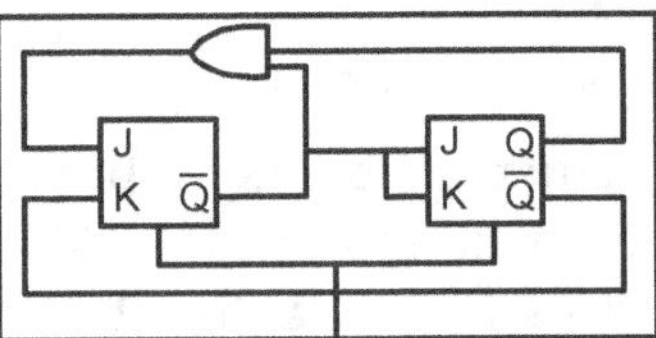

(a) Shift register   (b) Mod-3 counter
(c) Mod-2 counter   (d) none of the above

58. Negative numbers can't be represented in
(a) signed magnitude form
(b) 1's complement form
(c) 2's complement form
(d) none of the above

59. The addressing mode used in an instruction of the form ADD x y, is
(a) absolute   (b) immediate
(c) indirect   (d) index

60. The combination circuit in Fig. 2 can be replaced by a single
- (*a*) OR gate
- (*b*) XOR gate
- (*c*) NOR gate
- (*d*) AND gate

61. In Round Robin CPU scheduling, as the time quantum is increased, the average turn around time
- (*a*) increases
- (*b*) decreases
- (*c*) remains constant
- (*d*) varies irregularly

62. In a multiprogramming environment,
- (*a*) the processor executes more than one process at a time
- (*b*) the programs are developed by more than one person
- (*c*) more than one process is resident in the memory
- (*d*) a single user can execute many programs in the same time

63. Which of the following is/are true?
- (*a*) A re-entrant procedure can be called any number of times
- (*b*) A re-entrant procedure can be called even before the procedure has not returned from its previous call
- (*c*) Re-entrant procedures cannot be called recursively
- (*d*) None of the above are true

64. In a paged memory, the page hit ratio is 0.35. The time required to access a page in secondary memory is equal to 100 ns. The time required to access a page in primary memory is 10 ns. The average time required to access a page is
- (*a*) 3.0 ns
- (*b*) 68.0 ns
- (*c*) 68.5 ns
- (*d*) 78.5 ns

65. A state is safe if the system can allocate resources to each process (up to its maximum) in some order and still avoid deadlock.

Which of the following is/are true?
- (*a*) Deadlocked state is unsafe
- (*b*) Unsafe state may lead to a deadlock situation
- (*c*) Unsafe state must lead to a deadlock situation
- (*d*) both (*a*) and (*b*) only

66. Let A = {1, 2, 3}. Which of the following relations are functions (mappings)?
- (*a*) {(1, 2), (2, 3), (1, 3)}
- (*b*) {(1, 2), (2, 2), (3, 2)}
- (*c*) {(1, 2), (2, 1), (3, 3)}
- (*d*) both (*b*) and (*c*) only

67. Consider the mapping $f : X \rightarrow Y$. f is a bijection if and only if
- (*a*) $f(x) = f(y) \Rightarrow x = y$, for all x, y
- (*b*) range of f is Y
- (*c*) both (*a*) and (*b*) are true
- (*d*) the co-domain equals the range

68. For a function to be invertible, it has to be
- (*a*) one-one
- (*b*) onto
- (*c*) both one-one and onto
- (*d*) none of the above

69. The advantages of Partial pivoting in the solution of a system of equations are
- (*a*) division by zero can be avoided
- (*b*) round-off errors can be minimized
- (*c*) ill-conditioned system can be handled efficiently
- (*d*) all of the above

70. Choose the correct statements.
- (*a*) any 7 integers chosen from 1 to 12 should have atleast 2 of them summing up to 13
- (*b*) any 11 integers chosen from 1 to 20 should have atleast 2 numbers, such that one is a multiple of the other
- (*c*) 10 integers, 1 to 10 arranged at random in a circle should have atleast 3 successive numbers summing up to greater than 16
- (*d*) all of the above

71. The size of the virtual memory depends on
(a) the size of the data bus
(b) the size of the main memory
(c) the size of the address bus
(d) none of the above

72. In a multi-user operating system, 20 requests are made to use a particular resource per hour, on an average. The probability that no requests are made in 45 minutes is
(a) e^{-15}
(b) e^{-5}
(c) $1 - e^{-5}$
(d) $1 - e^{-10}$

73. In which of the following scheduling policies does context switching never take place?
(a) Round-robin
(b) Shortest job first
(c) Pre-emptive
(d) All of the above

74. In which of the following directory systems, is it possible to have multiple complete paths for a file, starting from the root directory?
(a) Single level directory
(b) Two level directory
(c) Tree structured directory
(d) Acyclic graph directory

75. Suppose that a process is in 'BLOCKED' state waiting for some I/O service. When the service is completed, it goes to the
(a) RUNNING state
(b) READY state
(c) SUSPENDED state
(d) TERMINATED state

76. Which of the following comments about half adder are true?
(a) It adds 2 bits
(b) It is called so because a full adder involves two half-adders
(c) It does half the work of a full adder
(d) Both (a) and (b) only

77. The binary equivalent of the decimal number 0.4375 is
(a) 0.0111
(b) 0.1011
(c) 0.1100
(d) 0.1010

78. The boolean expression $(A + C)(AB' + AC)(A'C' + B')$ can be simplified to
(a) AB
(b) $AB + A'C$
(c) $A'B + BC$
(d) $AB + BC$

79. A byte addressable computer has a memory capacity of 2^m kbytes and can perform 2^n operations. An instruction involving 3 operands and one operator needs a maximum of
(a) $3\,m$ bits
(b) $3\,m + n$ bits
(c) $m + n$ bits
(d) none of the above

80. In the previous problem, if the computer is word addressable with the word size being 8 bytes then the answer will be
(a) $3\,m$ bits
(b) $3\,m + n$ bits
(c) $m + n$ bits
(d) none of the above

81. $(10110011100011110000)_2$ in base 32 is
(a) 22 14 7 16
(b) 11 9 23 31
(c) 11 9 7 16
(d) 11 14 23 16

82. The XOR operator + is
(a) commutative
(b) associative
(c) both of the above
(d) none of the above

83. Bubble memories are preferable to floppy disks because
(a) of their higher transfer rate
(b) cost needed to store a bit is less
(c) they consume less power
(d) both (b) and (c) only

84. Error detection at the data link level is achieved by
(a) Bit stuffing
(b) Cyclic redundancy codes
(c) Hamming codes
(d) Equalization

85. The topology with highest reliability is
(a) Bus
(b) Star
(c) Ring
(d) Mesh

86. Choose the correct statements.
  (a) Topological sort can be used to obtain an evaluation order of a dependency graph
  (b) Evaluation order for a dependency graph dictates the order in which the semantic rules are done
  (c) Code generation depends on the oder in which the semantic actions are performed
  (d) only (b) and (c) are correct

87. A syntax tree
  (a) is another name for a parse tree
  (b) is a condensed form of parse tree
  (c) should have keywords as leaves
  (d) none of the above

88. Syntax directed translation scheme is desirable because
  (a) it is based on the syntax
  (b) its description is independent of any implementation
  (c) it is easy to modify
  (d) all of the above

89. Which of the following is not an intermediate code form?
  (a) Postfix notation
  (b) Syntax trees
  (c) Three address codes
  (d) Quadruples

90. Three address codes can be implemented by
  (a) indirect triples
  (b) direct triples
  (c) both of the above
  (d) none of the above

91. Choose the correct answers.

  The set {1, 2, 3} is equal to
  (a) {2, 1, 3}   (b) {3, 2, 1}
  (c) {1, 2, 3, 4}   (d) All of the above

92. Let A = {1, {2}, 3}.

  Choose the correct answers.

  (a) $1 \in A$ (b) {2} A
  (c) $\phi \in A$ (d) None of these

93. Choose the correct answers.
  If A, B, C are three sets, then
  (a) $A \cup (B \cap C) = (A \cup B) \cap (A \cup C)$
  (b) $(A - B) - C = (A - C) - (B - C)$
  (c) $(A \times B) \times C = A \times (B \times C)$
  (d) Both (a) and (b) are correct

94. In the set of integers, a relation R is defined as aRb, if and only if $b = |a|$. This relation is
  (a) reflexive   (b) irreflexive
  (c) symmetric   (d) anti-symmetric

95. Let S = {1, 2, 3, 4}. A relation R defined in S as, R = {(1, 2), (4, 3), (2, 2), (2, 1), (3, 1)} is
  (a) transitive   (b) symmetric
  (c) anti-symmetric   (d) none of the above

96. The following program fragment
```
if (a = 0)
printf("a is zero");
else
printf("a is not zero");
```
results in the printing of
  (a) a is zero
  (b) a is not zero
  (c) nothing
  (d) garbage

97. The following program fragment
```
if(a   = 7)
printf("a is seven");
else
printf("a is not seven");
```
results in the printing of
  (a) a is seven
  (b) a is not seven
  (c) nothing
  (d) garbage

98. The following program fragment
```
int k = -7;
printf("%d",   0 < !k);
```
  (a) prints 0

    (b) prints a non-zero value
    (c) is illegal
    (d) prints an unpredictable value

99. The following loop

```
for(putchar ('c'); putchar
('a'); putchar ('r'))
putchar ('t');
```

outputs

(a) a syntax error

(b) `cartrt`

(c) `catrat`

(d) `catratratratrat...`

100. The following loop

```
for(i = 1, j = 10; i < 6; ++ i,
    - -j)
print("%d %d", i, j);
```

prints

(a) 1 10 2 9 3 8 4 7 5 6

(b) 1 2 3 4 5 10 9 8 7 6

(c) 1 1 1 1 1 9 9 9 9 9

(d) none of the above

ANSWERS

1	2	3	4	5	6	7	8	9	10
(b)	(c)	(d)	(a)	(a)	(a)	(b)	(c)	(d)	(c)
11	**12**	**13**	**14**	**15**	**16**	**17**	**18**	**19**	**20**
(c)	(c)	(d)	(d)	(b)	(c)	(b)	(c)	(a)	(c)
21	**22**	**23**	**24**	**25**	**26**	**27**	**28**	**29**	**30**
(d)	(c)	(b)	(d)	(d)	(c)	(d)	(c)	(b)	(b)
31	**32**	**33**	**34**	**35**	**36**	**37**	**38**	**39**	**40**
(a)	(d)	(c)	(a)	(c)	(b)	(d)	(c)	(d)	(c)
41	**42**	**43**	**44**	**45**	**46**	**47**	**48**	**49**	**50**
(a)	(d)	(c)	(d)	(d)	(d)	(c)	(a)	(b)	(a)
51	**52**	**53**	**54**	**55**	**56**	**57**	**58**	**59**	**60**
(a)	(a)	(c)	(b)	(b)	(b)	(b)	(d)	(a)	(a)
61	**62**	**63**	**64**	**65**	**66**	**67**	**68**	**69**	**70**
(d)	(c)	(b)	(c)	(d)	(d)	(c)	(c)	(d)	(d)
71	**72**	**73**	**74**	**75**	**76**	**77**	**78**	**79**	**80**
(c)	(d)	(b)	(d)	(b)	(d)	(a)	(a)	(d)	(d)
81	**82**	**83**	**84**	**85**	**86**	**87**	**88**	**89**	**90**
(a)	(c)	(d)	(b)	(d)	(d)	(b)	(d)	(d)	(b)
91	**92**	**93**	**94**	**95**	**96**	**97**	**98**	**99**	**100**
(d)	(a)	(d)	(d)	(d)	(b)	(a)	(a)	(d)	(a)

1. Let A be a set having 'n' elements. The number of binary operations that can be defined on A is

(a) n^{n^2} (b) 2^{n^n}

(c) n^{2^n} (d) 2^{2^n}

2. The values of x and y, if $(x567)_8 + (2yx5)_8 = (71yx)_8$ is

(a) 4, 3 (b) 3, 3
(c) 4, 4 (d) 4, 5

3. A decimal number has 25 digits. The number of bits needed for its equivalent binary representation is, approximately,

(a) 50 (b) 60
(c) 70 (d) 75

4. The number of instructions needed to add 'n' numbers and store the result in memory using only one address instructions is

(a) n (b) $n - 1$
(c) $n + 1$ (d) independent of n

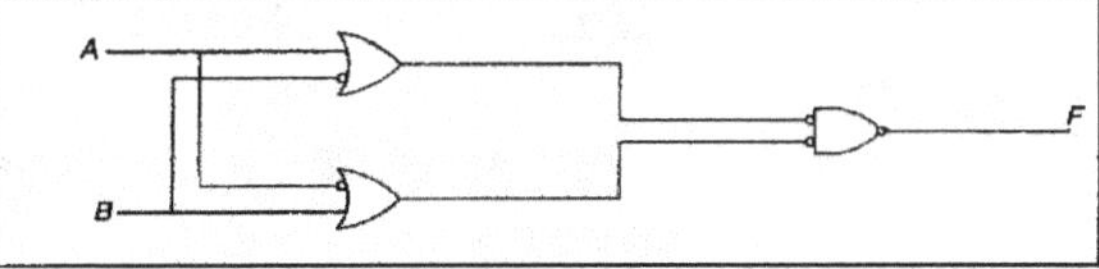

Fig. 1

5. The boolean expression corresponding to the circuit in Fig 1.
(a) is a tautology]
(b) is an inconsistency
(c) is independent of A
(d) none of the above

6. The clock of a micro-processor can be divided by 5 using a

(a) 3 bit counter (b) 5 bit counter
(c) mod 5 counter (d) mod 3 counter

7. The minimal cover for the maximal compatibility calsses {ae, acd, ad, bd} is

(a) ae, acd, ad (b) acd, ad, bd
(c) ae, acd, bd (d) ae, ad, bd

8. The values of a, x, y if 47x80 is the 10's complement of yaya0 are

(a) 4, 3, 2 (b) 5, 4, 4
(c) 3, 4, 5 (d) 2, 4, 5

9. The reasons for the presence of ALE pin in 8085, but not in 6800 is that
(a) 8085 uses I/O mapped I/O, whereas 6800 uses memory mapped I/O
(b) 8085 has 5 interrupt lines, whereas 6800 has only 2
(c) 8085 has multiplexed bus, whereas 6800 doesn't have
(d) none of the above

10. If memory access takes 20ns with cache and 110 ns without it, then the hit-ratio, (cache uses a 10 ns memory) is,
(a) 93% (b) 90%
(c) 87% (d) 88%

11. If `switch` feature is used, then
(a) `default` case must be present
(b) `default` case, if used, should be the last case
(c) `'default'` case, if used, can be placed anywhere
(d) none of the above

COM.Sc.-23

12. Addressing capability of 8086/88 is
    (*a*) 64 K   (*b*) 512 K
    (*c*) 2 MB   (*d*) 1 MB

13. The following circuit produces the output sequence

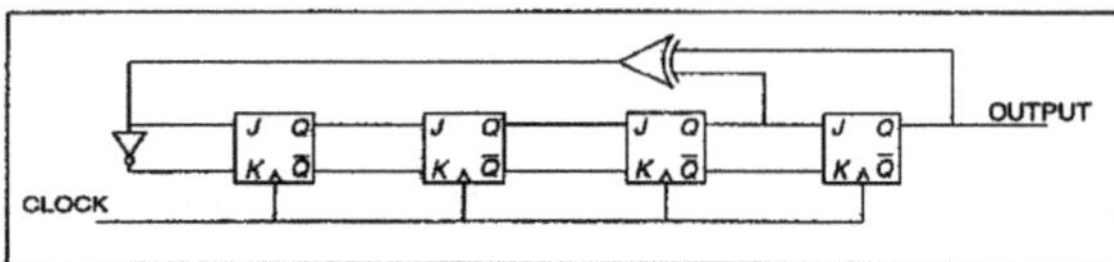

Fig. 2

    (*a*) 1111 1111 0000 0000
    (*b*) 1111 0000 1111 000
    (*c*) 1111 0001 0011 010
    (*d*) 1010 1010 1010 1010

14. Which of the following units can be used to measure the speed of a computer?
    (*a*) SYPS   (*b*) MIPS
    (*c*) BAUD   (*d*) None of these

15. if A + B = C (+ stands for the XOR operator), then
    (*a*) A + B = B
    (*b*) B + C = A
    (*c*) A + B + C = 0
    (*d*) all of the above

16. Choose the correct answers.
    (*a*) 0 stands for a false condition
    (*b*) Non-zero value stands for a false condition
    (*c*) 1 stands for a false condition
    (*d*) Anything that is not 1, stands for a false condition

17. Which of the following comments about `for` loop are correct?
    (*a*) Index value is retained outside the loop
    (*b*) Index value can be changed from within the loop
    (*c*) `goto` can be used to jump, out of the loop
    (*d*) All of the above

18. Which of the following comments about `for` loop are correct?

19. Choose the correct answers.
    (*a*) `for` loops can be nested
    (*b*) Nested `for` loop may use the same index
    (*c*) Both of the above
    (*d*) None of the above

20. Consider the following program fragment

```
if (a > b)
    if (b > c)
        s1;
    else    s2;
```
s2 will be executed if
    (*a*) a <= b
    (*b*) b > c
    (*c*) b <= c and a <= b
    (*d*) a > b and b <= c

21. Which of the following comments about peep-hole optimization are true?
    (*a*) It is applied to a small part of the code
    (*b*) It can be used to optimize intermediate code
    (*c*) To get the best out of this, it has to be applied repeatedly
    (*d*) All of the above

22. Shift-reduce parsers are
    (*a*) top-down parsers
    (*b*) bottom-up parsers
    (*c*) may be top-down or bottom-up
    (*d*) none of the above

23. Recursive descent parsing is an example of
    (*a*) top-down parsing
    (*b*) bottom-up parsing

The (a)-(d) options for question 18 continue in the right column context:
    (*a*) Using `break` is equivalent to using `goto`—the statement inmmediately following the loop
    (*b*) Continue is used to by-pass the remainder of the current pass of the loop.
    (*c*) If comma operator is used, then the value returned is the value of the right operand.
    (*d*) All of the above

(c) predictive parsing
(d) none of the above

24. In operator precedence parsing, precedence relations are defined
(a) for all pair of terminals
(b) to delimit the handle
(c) only for a certain pair of terminals
(d) both (b) and (c) only

25. For parsing arithmetic expressions, involving (,) , + and −, the precedence relation between − and −, will be <, if
(a) we are talking of unary minus
(b) minus is right associative
(c) minus is left associative
(d) both (a) and (b) only

26. For the previous problem, the precedence relation between) and (will be
(a) > (b) <
(c) = (d) undefined

27. In the previous question, for 5-digit accuracy, if $|x| < \pi/2$, the number of terms in the series that should be considered is
(a) 5 (b) 7
(c) 9 (d) 10

28. If a = 9, b = 5 and c = 3, then the following expression `(a − a/b * b%c) > a%b%c` is
(a) true (b) false
(c) invalid (d) 0

29. In a `for` loop, if the condition is missing then
(a) it is assumed to be present and taken to be false
(b) it is assumed to be present and taken to be true
(c) it results in a syntax error
(d) execution will be terminated abruptly

30. In a `for` loop if the condition is missing, then infinite looping can be avoided by a
(a) `goto` statement
(b) `break` statement

(c) `return` statement
(d) all of the above

31. Changing the right hand side of the constraints and the coefficient of the cost function
(a) can't destroy the optimality of the solution
(b) can't destroy the feasibility of the solution
(c) can destroy the optimality and feasibility of the solution
(d) none of the above

32. The following program
```
main()
{int i = 5;
   if (i == 5) return;
   else printf("i is not
five");
   printf("over");}
```
results in
(a) a syntax error
(b) an execution error
(c) printing of `over`
(d) execution termination, without printing anything

33. The following program fragment
```
int i = 5;
do  {putchar(i + 100);
printf("%d", i --);}
while (i);
```
results in the printing of
(a) i5h5g3f2e1 (b) i4h3g2fle0
(c) an error message (d) none of the above

34. The following program fragment
```
int i = 107, x = 5;
   printf((x      >      7)?
"÷d":"÷c",i);
```
results In
(a) an execution error
(b) a syntax error
(c) printing of `k`
(d) none of the above

35. Replacing $>$ by $<$ in the previous question results in
   (a) printing of 107   (b) a syntax error
   (c) printing of k   (d) none of the above

36. Which of the following optimization techniques are typically applied on loops?
   (a) Removal of invariant computation
   (b) Elimination of induction variables
   (c) Both of the above
   (d) None of the above

37. The technique of replacing run time computations by compile time computations is called
   (a) constant folding
   (b) code hoisting
   (c) peephole optimization
   (d) invariant computation

38. The graph that shows the basic blocks and their successor relationship is called
   (a) control graph
   (b) flow graph
   (c) DAG
   (d) Hamiltonian graph

39. Reduction in strength means
   (a) replacing run time computation by compile time computation
   (b) removing loop invariant computation
   (c) removing common sub-expressions
   (d) replacing a costly operation by a relatively cheaper one

40. A basic block can be analyzed by
   (a) a DAG
   (b) a graph which may involve cycles
   (c) flow-graph
   (d) none of the above

41. Hamming distance is
   (a) a theoretical way of measuring errors
   (b) a technique for assigning codes to a set of items known to occur with a given probability

   (c) a technique for optimizing the intermediate code
   (d) none of the above

42. Error repair may
   (a) increase the number of errors
   (b) generate spurious error messages
   (c) mask subsequent errors
   (d) all of the above

43. A parser with the valid prefix property is advantageous because
   (a) it detects error as soon as possible
   (b) it detects errors as an when they occur
   (c) it limits the amount of erroneous output passed to the next phase
   (d) both (a) and (c) only

44. The advantage of panic mode of error recovery is that
   (a) it is simple to implement
   (b) it is very effective
   (c) it always gets into an infinite loop
   (d) none of the above

45. To recover from an error, the operator precedence parser may
   (a) insert symbols onto the stack
   (b) insert symbols onto the input
   (c) delete symbols from the stack
   (d) all of the above

46. Revised simplex method
   (a) is conceptually same as the simplex method
   (b) is a version of simplex method ideal for implementation in computer
   (c) a version of simplex method ideal for sensitivity analysis
   (d) both (a) and (b) only

47. The dual simplex method
   (a) starts with a feasible but super-optimal solution
   (b) starts with a feasible but sub-optimal solution

(c) starts with a infeasible but super-optimal solution

(d) starts with a infeasible but sub-optimal solution

48. Which of the following simplex based techniques are ideal for sensitivity analysis?
(a) Revised simplex method
(b) Parametric programming
(c) Dual simplex method
(d) Both (b) and (c) only

49. Choose the correct statements.
(a) It is computationally advantageous to solve a given LPP in its dual form, if the number of constraints in the primal form is more than the number of variables.
(b) The cost of the (primal) objective function corresponding to a feasible solution can't be greater than the cost of the (dual) objective function corresponding to any of its feasible solution.
(c) It is computationally advantageous to solve a given LPP in its dual form, if the number of variables in the primal form is more than the number of constraints.
(d) The cost of the (primal) objective function corresponding to a non-feasible solution can't be less than the cost of the (dual) objective function corresponding to any of its feasible solution.

50. Choose the correct statement(s).
(a) Addition of a new constraint to an LPP always improve the optimal value
(b) Addition of a new variable can never decrease the optimal value
(c) Addition of a new constraint can never decrease the optimal value
(d) Addition of a new variable can never improve the optimal value

51. The following loop
```
while(printf("%d", printf ("az")))
printf ("by");
```

(a) prints `azbybybyby...`
(b) prints `azbyazbyazbyazby...`
(c) results in a syntax error
(d) none of the above

52. The following statements
```
for(i = 3; i < 15; i += 3)
{ printf("%d ", i);
++i;
}
```

will result in the printing of
(a) 3 6 9 12
(b) 3 6 9 12 15
(c) 3 7 11
(d) 3 7 11 15

53. Which of the following methods gives the least error when e^x is integrated from 0 to 0.4?
(a) Trapezoidal rule with the interval width as 0.2
(b) Trapezoidal rule with the interval width as 0.1
(c) Simpson's 1/3 rule with the interval width as 0.1
(d) Simpson's 1/3 rule with the interval width as 0.2

54. Which of the following laws doesn't hold good in finite precision floating point arithmetic?
(a) $a \times b = b \times a$
(b) $(a + b) + c = a + (b + c)$
(c) $a \times (b + c) = a \times b + a \times c$
(d) both (b) and (c) only

55. Surplus variables are usually introduced in an LPP model
(a) if the demand is less than the available resource
(b) if the available resource is less than the demand
(c) if the demand is same as the available resource
(d) all of the above

56. The ideal choice for interrupt oriented applications is
(a) Z-80
(b) Motorola-6800
(c) 8085
(d) 8008

57. Choose the correct statement.
    (*a*) Any software can be simulated by hardware
    (*b*) Any hardware can be simulated by software
    (*c*) Firmware is nothing but hardware implementation of software
    (*d*) All of the above are correct

58. Which of the following is always true?
    (*a*) A compiled program uses more memory than an interpreted program
    (*b*) A compiler converts a program to a lower level language for execution
    (*c*) A compiler takes less memory than an interpreter
    (*d*) Compiled programs take more time for execution than interpreted programs.

59. In a two pass assembler the object code generation is done during the
    (*a*) second pass
    (*b*) first pass
    (*c*) zeroeth pass
    (*d*) not done by assembler

60. In a two pass assembler, adding literals to literal table and address resolution of local symbols are done during
    (*a*) first pass and second respectively
    (*b*) both second pass
    (*c*) second pass and first respectively
    (*d*) both first pass

61. ud-chaining is useful for
    (*a*) determining whether a particular definition is used anywhere or not
    (*b*) constant folding
    (*c*) checking whether a variable is used, without prior assignment
    (*d*) all of the above

62. Which of the following concepts can be used to identify loops?
    (*a*) Dominators
    (*b*) Reducible graphs
    (*c*) Depth first ordering
    (*d*) All of the above

63. Which of the following are not loop optimization techniques
    (*a*) jamming
    (*b*) unrolling
    (*c*) induction variable elimination
    (*d*) none of the above

64. Running time of a program depends on
    (*a*) the way the registers are used
    (*b*) the order in which computations are performed
    (*c*) the way the addressing modes are used
    (*d*) all of the above

65. du-chaining
    (*a*) stands for use definition chaining
    (*b*) is useful for copy propagation removal
    (*c*) is useful for induction variable removal
    (*d*) both of the above

66. In an LPP model in its standard form, three of the constraints are

$$x_1 + x_2 \leq 2$$
$$2 x_1 + 2 x_2 \leq 3$$
$$3 x_1 + 3 x_2 \leq 8$$

Removal of which of the constraints will not affect the optimality?
    (*a*) II and III   (*b*) I and II
    (*c*) I and III   (*d*) I only

67. An LPP having 2 optimal solutions
    (*a*) must have more than 3 constraints
    (*b*) must have more than 2 optimal solutions
    (*c*) must have even number of constraints
    (*d*) none of the above

68. The number of iterations taken by simplex method for solving an LPP in its standard form, with '*m*' equations and '*n*' unknowns ($m < n$) can't exceed
    (*a*) m_{C_n} (*b*) m_{P_n}
    (*c*) n_{C_m} (*d*) n_{P_m}

69. In the solution of an LPP using simplex method, the current cost of the objective function must
 (a) increase in the next iteration
 (b) can't decrease in the next iteration
 (c) correspond to one of the corners of the convex region bound by the constraining equations
 (d) both (b) and (c) only

70. If the cost of the objective function (of an LPP in its standard form) which corresponds to one of the corners of the convex region bound by the constraints, is greater than the cost corresponding to all its adjacent corners, then
 (a) it is the optimal solution
 (b) simplex method enters a cycle
 (c) simplex method moves onto one of the adjacent corners
 (d) simplex method doesn't terminate

71. Pick the class of interrupt with lowest priority.
 (a) Supervisor call interrupt (SVC)
 (b) Program interrupt
 (c) I/O interrupt
 (d) Timer interrupt

72. The delay between job submission and job completion is called
 (a) turnaround time   (b) in-process time
 (c) response time   (d) waiting time

73. Which of the following techniques is preferable for transferring large amount of data to and from a memory in a short time?
 (a) Programmed I/O
 (b) Interrupt-driven I/O
 (c) DMA
 (d) None of the above

74. Privileged instructions can be executed
 (a) only in monitor mode
 (b) only in user mode
 (c) both in user and monitor mode
 (d) none of the above

75. The first pass of a simple 2-pass assembler
 (a) allocates spaces for the literals
 (b) computes the total length of the program
 (c) builds the symbol table for the symbols and their values
 (d) both (b) and (c) only

76. The data transfer rate of a double density floppy disk system is about
 (a) K bits/sec   (b) 50 Kbits/sec
 (c) 500 Kbits/sec   (d) 5000 K bits/sec

77. A linker is given object modules for a set of programs that were compiled separately. What information need not be included in an object module?
 (a) Object code
 (b) Relocation bits
 (c) Names and locations of all external symbols defined in the object module
 (d) Absolute addresses of internal symbols

78. Consider the statement
```
static char hello[]="hello";
```
The output of `printf("%s\n", hello);` will be same as that of
 (a) `puts("hello");`
 (b) `puts(hello);`
 (c) `printf("%s\n", "hello");`
 (d) all of the above

79. If storage class is missing in the array definition, by `default` it will be taken to be
 (a) automatic
 (b) external
 (c) static
 (d) either automatic or external depending on the place of occurrence.

80. The following program fragment
```
int  x[5][5], i, j;
for (i = 0; i < 5; ++i)
    for (j = 0; j < 5 ; j++)
    x[i][j] = x[j][i];
```

(a) transposes the given matrix x
(b) makes the given matri x, symmetric
(c) doesn't alter the matrix x
(d) none of the above

81. Pick the machine dependent operating system features.
(a) Interrupt processing
(b) File processing
(c) Job scheduling
(d) All of the above

82. Pick the machine independent operating system features.
(a) I/O supervision
(b) Interrupt processing
(c) Management of real memory
(d) Job scheduling

83. Pick the machine independent step(s) that can be used to optimise the memory requirement of a program.
(a) Eliminating loop invariant computations
(b) Code hoisting
(c) Elimination of common sub-expressions
(d) All of the above

84. When an attempt to divide by zeo is made what interrupt is generated?
(a) Supervisor call interrupt (SVC)
(b) Program interrupt
(c) I/O interrupt
(d) Timer interrupt

85. Pick the class of interrupt with highest priority.
(a) Supervisor call interrupt (SVC)
(b) Program interrupt
(c) I/O interrupt
(d) Timer interrupt

86. Initialization cannot be a part of the definition if the storage class of the array is
(a) static   (b) external
(c) automatic   (d) none of the above

87. Consider the array definition
```
int num [10] = {3, 3, 3};
```
Pick the correct answers.

(a) This is invalid if it comes within a function
(b) The value of num [8] is 3
(c) The value of num [3] is 3
(d) None of the above

88. Pick the correct answers.
(a) During array declaration, no storage is set aside
(b) Array definition precedes array declaration
(c) Array declaration precedes array definition
(d) Both (a) and (b) only are correct

89. While passing an array as an actual argument, the function call must have
(a) the array name with empty brackets
(b) the array name with its size
(c) the array name alone
(d) none of the above

90. The following program
```
main ( )
{
    static int a[] = {7, 8, 9};
    printf("%d", a[2] = 2[a] +
a[2];
}
```
(a) results in bus error
(b) results in segmentation violation error
(c) will not compile successfully
(d) none of the above

91. In which of the following instruction bus idle situation occurs?
(a) EI   (b) DAD rp
(c) INX H   (d) DAA

92. Any instruction should have atleast
(a) 2 operands   (b) 1 operand
(c) 3 operands   (d) none of the above

93. Consider the following circuit
In order to make it a tautology the '?' marked box should be replaced by
(a) OR gate   (b) AND gate
(c) NOR gate   (d) All of the above

94. Pick the machine independent phase(s) of the compiler.
  (a) Syntax analysis
  (b) Intermediate code generation
  (c) Lexical analysis
  (d) All of the above

95. Which of the following statement(s) about loading is/are true?
  (a) Modification records are used for specifying program relocation in relative addressing mode instructions
  (b) Modification records are best suited for specifying program relocation in direct addressing and fixed instruction format
  (c) Text record uses a relocation bit associated with each word of the object code in direct addressing and fixed instruction format
  (d) Only (a) and (c) are true

96. Which of the following operation(s) is/are not closed as regards to computers?
  (a) Addition   (b) Substraction
  (c) Multiplication   (d) All of the above

97. If $(11x1y)_8 = (12c9)_{16}$ (c stands for decimal 12), then the values of x and y are
  (a) 5, 1   (b) 7, 5
  (c) 5, 7   (d) none of the above

98. The total number of possible boolean functions involving 'n' boolean variables is
  (a) infinitely many   (b) n^n
  (c) n^2 (d) none of the above

99. Which of the following architecture is/are not suitable for realising SIMD?
  (a) Vector processor (b) Array processor
  (c) Von Neumann   (d) All of the above

100. How many $2-$ input multiplexers are required to construct a $2^{10}-$ input multiplexer?
  (a) 1023   (b) 31
  (c) 10   (d) 127

ANSWERS

1	2	3	4	5	6	7	8	9	10
(a)	(a)	(d)	(c)	(a)	(c)	(c)	(d)	(c)	(b)
11	**12**	**13**	**14**	**15**	**16**	**17**	**18**	**19**	**20**
(c)	(d)	(c)	(b)	(d)	(a)	(d)	(d)	(a)	(d)
21	**22**	**23**	**24**	**25**	**26**	**27**	**28**	**29**	**30**
(d)	(b)	(a)	(d)	(d)	(d)	(c)	(a)	(b)	(d)
31	**32**	**33**	**34**	**35**	**36**	**37**	**38**	**39**	**40**
(c)	(d)	(a)	(c)	(a)	(c)	(a)	(b)	(d)	(a)
41	**42**	**43**	**44**	**45**	**46**	**47**	**48**	**49**	**50**
(a)	(d)	(d)	(a)	(d)	(d)	(c)	(d)	(a)	(b)
51	**52**	**53**	**54**	**55**	**56**	**57**	**58**	**59**	**60**
(d)	(b)	(c)	(d)	(b)	(c)	(d)	(b)	(a)	(d)
61	**62**	**63**	**64**	**65**	**66**	**67**	**68**	**69**	**70**
(d)	(d)	(d)	(d)	(c)	(c)	(b)	(c)	(d)	(a)
71	**72**	**73**	**74**	**75**	**76**	**77**	**78**	**79**	**80**
(c)	(a)	(c)	(a)	(d)	(a)	(d)	(d)	(d)	(h)
81	**82**	**83**	**84**	**85**	**86**	**87**	**88**	**89**	**90**
(a)	(c)	(d)	(b)	(a)	(c)	(a)	(d)	(c)	(d)
91	**92**	**93**	**94**	**95**	**96**	**97**	**98**	**99**	**100**
(b)	(d)	(c)	(d)	(d)	(d)	(d)	(d)	(c)	(a)

1. The set $\{a^n b^n \mid n = 1, 2, 3 \ldots\}$ can be generated by the CFG
   (a) S → ab | aSb
   (b) S → aaSbb | ab
   (c) S → ab | aSb | E
   (d) None of the above

2. Choose the correct statements.
   (a) Some regular languages can't be generated by any CFG
   (b) Any regular language has an equivalent CFG
   (c) Some non-regular languages can't be generated by any CFG
   (d) Only (b) and (c) are correct

3. Which of the following CFG's can't be simulated by an FSM?
   (a) S → Sa | a   (b) S → abX
                                    X → cY
                                    Y → d | aX
   (c) S → aSb | ab   (d) None of these

4. Which of the following is true?
   (a) Overlays are used to increase the size of physical memory
   (b) Overlays are used to increase the logical address space
   (c) When overlays are used, the size of a process is not limited to the size of physical memory
   (d) Overlays are used whenever the physical address space is smaller than the logical address space

5. In partitioned memory allocation scheme,
   (a) the best fit algorithm is always better than the first fit algorithm
   (b) the first fit algorithm is always better than the best fit algorithm
   (c) the superiority of the first fit and best-fit algorithms depend on the sequence of memory requests
   (d) none of the above

6. A process refers to 5 pages, A, B, C, D and E in the following order A; B; C; D; A; B; E; A; B; C; D; E. If the page replacement algorithm is FIFO, the number of page transfer with an empty internal store of 3 frames is
   (a) 8   (b) 10
   (c) 9   (d) 7

7. Distributed systems should
   (a) meet prescribed time constraints
   (b) aim better resource sharing
   (c) aim better system utilization
   (d) aim low system overhead

8. The main function of shared memory is
   (a) to use primary memory efficiently
   (b) to do intra process communication
   (c) to do inter process communication
   (d) none of the above

9. In real-time operating systems, which of the following is the most suitable scheduling scheme?
   (a) round-robin
   (b) first-come-first-served
   (c) pre-emptive scheduling
   (d) random scheduling

10. In Question number 6, if the number of available page frames is increased to 4 then

(a) the number of page transfers decreases
(b) the number of page transfers increases
(c) the number of page transfer remains the same
(d) none of the above

11. Cascading termination refers to
(a) termination of all child processes before the parent terminates normally
(b) termination of all child processes before the parent terminates abnormally
(c) termination of all child processes before the parent terminates normally or abnormally
(d) none of the above

12. For implementing a multiprogramming operating system,
(a) special support from processor is essential
(b) special support from processor is not essential
(c) cache memory must be available
(d) more than one processor must be available

13. Consider a system having 'm' resources of the same type. These resources are shared by 3 processes A, B, C, which have peak time demands of 3, 4, 6 respectively. The minimum value of 'm' that ensures that deadlock will never occur is
(a) 11   (b) 12
(c) 13   (d) 14

14. A system has 3 processes sharing 4 resources. If each process needs a maximum of 2 units then
(a) deadlock can never occur
(b) deadlock may occur
(c) deadlock has to occur
(d) none of the above

15. 'm' processes share 'n' resources of the same type. The maximum need of each process doesn't exceed 'n' and the sum all the their maximum needs is always less than $m + n$. In this set up

(a) deadlock can never occur
(b) deadlock may occur
(c) deadlock has to occur
(d) none of the above

16. Choose the correct statement(s).
(a) Macro definitions cannot appear within another macro definitions in assembly language programs.
(b) Overlaying is used to run a program which is longer than the address space of a computer
(c) Virtual memory can be used to accomodate a program which is longer than the address space of a computer
(d) It is possible to write interrupt service routines in a high level language

17. A software is to be developed for a system which has a small memory. The software should
(a) use recursion wherever possible
(b) avoid using recursion
(c) use macros instead of functions
(d) all of the above

*Directions :*The next three questions are based on the following memory configurations.

ADDRESS	VALUE
1	5
5	7
7	11
10	13

Register R

5

18. `ADD 6(immediate) TO R(indirect)` gives the value
(a) 20   (b) 7
(c) 10   (d) 13

19. If the effective address of X is got by auto-increment mode and the effective address of Y by auto-decrement mode then the instruction `ADD X TO Y`, gives the value
(a) 16   (b) 14
(c) 20   (d) 10

20. If the instruction ADD A TO B gives 16, then the addressing mode for A, B will be
(a) register (direct) and auto-increment indirect respectively
(b) register (indirect) and auto-increment indirect respectively
(c) register (direct) and auto-increment direct respectively
(d) register (indirect) and auto-increment indirect respectively

21. The intersection of a CFL and regular language
(a) need not be regular
(b) need not be context free
(c) is always regular
(d) none of the above

22. A PDM behaves like an FSM when the number of auxiliary memory it has, is
(a) 0
(b) 1
(c) 2
(d) none of the above

23. A PDM behaves like a TM when the number of auxiliary memory it has, is
(a) 0
(b) 1 or more
(c) 2 or more
(d) none of the above

24. Choose the correct statements.
(a) The power of DFSM and NDFSM are same
(b) The power of DFSM and NDFSM are different
(c) The power of DPDM and NDPDM are different
(d) Both (a) and (c) are correct

25. Which of the following is accepted by an NDPDM, but not by a DPDM?
(a) All strings in which a given symbol is present atleast twice
(b) Even palindromes (i.e., palindromes made up of even number of symbols)
(c) Strings ending with a particular alphabet
(d) Name of the above

26. Which of the following interrupt is both level and edge sensitive?
(a) RST 5.5
(b) INTR
(c) RST 7.5
(d) TRAP

27. The difference between 80486 and 80386 is/are
(a) presence of floating point co-processor
(b) presence of memory controller
(c) presence of 8 K cache on chip
(d) all of the above

28. The addressing mode used in the instruction PUSH B is
(a) direct
(b) register
(c) register indirect
(d) immediate

29. The most relevant addressing mode to write position independent code is
(a) direct mode
(b) indirect mode
(c) relative mode
(d) indexed mode

30. Which of the following are CISC machines?
(a) IBM 360
(b) 80386
(c) 68030
(d) all of the above

31. If the cache needs an access time of 20 ns and the main memory 120 ns, then the average access time of a CPU is (assume hit-ratio is 80%)
(a) 30 ns
(b) 40 ns
(c) 35 ns
(d) 45 ns

32. The number of clock cycles necessary to complete 1 fetch cycle in 8085 (excluding wait state) is
(a) 3 or 4
(b) 4 or 5
(c) 4 or 6
(d) 3 or 5

33. The seek time of a disk is 30 ms. It rotates at the rate of 30 rotations per second. Each track has a capacity of 300 words. The access time is, approximately,
(a) 47 ms
(b) 50 ms
(c) 60 ms
(d) 62 ms

34. Motorola's 68040 is comparable to
(a) 8085
(b) 80286
(c) 80386
(d) 80486

35. The possible number of boolean functions of 3 variables x, y and z such that
$$f(x, y, z) = f(x', y', z') \text{ is}$$
(a) 8   (b) 16
(c) 64   (d) 32

36. Parallel printer uses
(a) RS-232C interface
(b) centronics interface
(c) hand-shake mode
(d) both (b) and (c) only

37. A micro-programmed control unit
(a) is faster than a hard-wired control unit
(b) facilitates easy implementation of new instructions
(c) is useful when very small programs are to be run
(d) usually refers to the control unit of a microprocessor

38. Which of the following are typical characteristics of a RISC machine?
(a) Instruction taking multiple cycles
(b) Highly pipelined
(c) Instructions interpreted by micro-programs
(d) None of the above

39. The working of a staircase switch is a typical example of the logical operation
(a) OR   (b) NOR
(c) Exclusive–OR   (d) Exclusive–NOR

40. The exponent of a floating point number is represented in excess-N code so that
(a) the dynamic range is large
(b) the precision is high
(c) the smallest number is represented by all zeroes
(d) overflow is avoided

41. On receiving an `interrupt` from an I/O device, the CPU
(a) halts for a predetermined time
(b) hands over control of address bus and data bus to the interrupting device

(c) branches off to the 'interrupt' service routine immediately
(d) branches off to the 'interrupt' service routine after completion of the current instruction

42. CFG is not closed under
(a) union   (b) Kleene star
(c) complementation (d) product

43. The set $A = \{a^n\, b^n\, a^n \mid n = 1, 2, 3 \ldots\}$ is an example of a grammar that is
(a) regular   (b) context free
(c) not context free   (d) none of the above

44. Let $L1 = \{a^n\, b^n\, a^m \mid n,\ m = 1, 2, 3\ldots\}$
$$L2 = \{a^n\, b^m\, a^m \mid n, m = 1, 2, 3\ldots\}$$
$$L3 = \{a^n\, b^n\, a^n \mid n = 1, 2, 3\ldots\}$$

Choose the correct answers.
(a) $L3 = L1 \cap L2$
(b) $L1$ and $L2$ are CFL but $L3$ is not CFL
(c) $L1$ and $L2$ are not CFL but $L3$ is CFL
(d) Both (a) and (b) are correct

45. $L = \{a^n\, b^n\, a^n \mid n = 1, 2, 3 \ldots\}$ is an example of a language that is
(a) context free
(b) not context free
(c) context free but whose complement is CF
(d) none of the above

46. Which of the following rules regarding the addition of 2 given numbers is correct, if negative numbers are represented in 2's complement form?
(a) Add `sign` bit and discard `carry`, if any
(b) Add `sign` bit and add `carry`, if any
(c) Don't add `sign` bit and discard `carry`, if any
(d) Don't add `sign` bit and add `carry`, if any

47. When `INTR` is encountered, the processor branches to the memory location which is

(a) determined by the 'call address' instruction issued by the I/O device
(b) determined by the 'RST n' instruction issued by the I/O device
(c) all of the above
(d) none of the above

48. The advantage of a single bus over a multi-bus is the
(a) flexibility in attaching peripheral devices
(b) high operating speed
(c) all of the above
(d) none of the above

49. The number of possible boolean functions that can be defined for n boolean variables over n-valued boolean algebra is
(a) 2^{2^n}
(b) 2^{n^2}
(c) n^{2^n}
(d) n^{n^n}

50. The ASCII code 56, represents the character
(a) V
(b) 8
(c) a
(d) carriage return

51. YACC builds up
(a) SLR parsing table
(b) canonical LR parsing table
(c) LALR parsing table
(d) none of the above

52. Choose the correct statements.
(a) LL (k) grammar has to be CFG
(b) LI (k) grammar has to be unambiguous
(c) LL (k) grammars cannot have left recursive non-terminals
(d) All are correct

53. Consider an ε-free CFG. If for every pair of productions $A \rightarrow u$ and $A \rightarrow v$
(a) if $\mathrm{FIRST}(u) \cap \mathrm{FIRST}(v)$ is empty then the CFG has to be LL (1)
(b) if the CFG is LL (1) then $\mathrm{FIRST}(u)$ § $\mathrm{FIRST}(v)$ is not empty
(c) if $\mathrm{FIRST}(u) \cap \mathrm{FIRST}(v)$ is empty then the CFG cannot be LL (1)
(d) none of the above

54. LR (k) grammar
(a) can only examine a maximum of k input symbols
(b) can be used to identify hanldles
(c) can to used to identify the production associated with a handle
(d) all of the above

55. The set of all viable prefixes of right sentential form of a given grammar
(a) can be recognized by a finite state machine
(b) cannot be recognized by a finite state machine
(c) cannot be used to control an LR (k) parser
(d) none of the above

Directions: FIRST_k (x), where x is a string, is the set of all leading terminal strings of length k or less, in the strings derivable from x.

FOLLOK_k (A), where A is a non-terminal, is the set of all derivable terminal strings of length k or less, that can follow A in some left-most sentential form.

The next three questions are based on the above definition.

56. Consider the grammar
$$E \rightarrow TE'$$
$$E' \rightarrow +\ TE'\ \mid\ \varepsilon$$
$$T \rightarrow +\ FT'$$
$$T' \rightarrow *FT'\ \mid\ \varepsilon$$
$$F \rightarrow (E)\ \mid\ id$$

FIRST_1 (E) will be same as that of
(a) FIRST_1 (T)
(b) FIRST_1 (F)
(c) all of the above
(d) none of the above

57. FOLLOW_1 (F) is
(a) {+, *,), $}
(b) {+,), $}
(c) {*,), $}
(d) {+, (,), *}

58. The switch feature
(a) can always be replaced by a nested `if-then-else` clause
(b) connot enhance logical clarity

(c) can't always be replaced by a nested `if-then-else` clause

(d) none of the above

59. break statement can be simulated by using

(a) `goto`

(b) `return`

(c) `exit`

(d) any to the above features

60. The following statement

```
if (2 < 1)
    ;
else
    x = (2 < 0) ? printf("one")
        : printf("four");

    printf ("%d", x);
```

(a) prints nothing

(b) results in a syntax error

(c) prints four 0

(d) none of the above

61. The following program fragment

```
int x = 4, y = x, i;
for (i = 1; i <   4; ++i)
x += x;
```

(a) finds 8 `*` y

(b) finds y `*` (1 + 2 + 3 + 4)

(c) finds y `*` 4

(d) finds y `*` y

62. Using `goto` inside `for` loop is equivalent to using

(a) `continue`

(b) `break`

(c) `return`

(d) none of the above

63. Choose the correct statements.

(a) All the elements of the array should be of the same data type and storage class

(b) The number of subscripts determines the dimension of the array

(c) In an array definition, the subscript can be any expression yielding a non-zero integer value

(d) Both (a) and (b) are correct

64. Let A be the set of all non-singular matrices over real numbers and let * be the matrix multiplication operator. Then,

(a) A is closed under * but <A, *> is not a semi-group

(b) <A, *> is a semi-group but not a monoid

(c) <A, *> is a monoid but not a group

(d) <A, *> is a group but not an abelian group

65. Newton-Raphson method

(a) is not efficient in handling multiple roots

(b) should not be preferred if the graph of the curve is almost parallel to the x-axis, in the vicinity of the root

(c) should not be preferred if there is a point of inflexion in the vicinity of the root

(d) all of the above

66. If the proposition $\neg P \Rightarrow Q$ is true, then the truth value of the proportion $\neg PV (P \Rightarrow Q)$, is

(a) true

(b) multi-valued

(c) false

(d) cannot be determined

67. The number of divisors of 600 (including 1 and 600) is

(a) 24

(b) 22

(c) 23

(d) 25

68. The determinant value of the matrix

$$\begin{pmatrix} 1 & 2 & 3 \\ 4 & 5 & 6 \\ 5 & 7 & 9 \end{pmatrix}$$ is

(a) 12

(b) 16

(c) 42

(d) none of the above

69. Which of the following elementary operations may effect the rank of a matrix?

(a) Scalar multiplication

(b) Adding two rows

(c) Adding a row with the scalar multiple of another row

(d) None of the above

70. Generation of intermediate code based on an abstract machine model is useful in compilers because
(a) it makes implementation of lexical and syntax analysis easier
(b) syntax-directed translations can be written for intermediate code generation
(c) it enhances the portability of the front end of the compiler.
(d) it is not possible to generate code for real machines directly from high level language programs

71. Merging states with a common core may produce ...., conflicts and does not produce .... conflicts in an LALR parser
(a) reduce-reduce; shift-reduce
(b) shift-reduce; reduce-reduce
(c) shift-reduce; shift-reduce
(d) none of the above

72. For a CFG, `FOLLOW(A)` is the set of all terminals that can immediately appear to the right of the non-terminal A in some sentential form. We define two sets `LFOLLOW(A)` and `RFOL-LOW(A)` by replacing the word sentential by "Left most sentential" and "Right most sentential" respectively in the definition of `FOLLOW(A)`.

Choose the correct statement(s).
(a) `FOLLOW(A)` and `LFOLLOW(A)` may be different
(b) `FOLLOW(A)` and `RFOLLOW(A)` are always the same
(c) Both the above are correct
(d) All the three are different

73. In some programming language, an identifier is permitted to be a letter followed by any number of letters or digits. If L and D denote the set of letters and digits respectively, which of the following expressions defines an identifier?
(a) $(L \cup D)^+$
(b) $L.(L \cup D)^*$
(c) $(L.D)^*$
(d) $L.(L.D)^*$

74. A shift reduce parser carries out the actions specified within braces immediately after reducing with the corresponding rule of grammar

```
S → xxW { print "1" }
S → y { print "2" }
W → Sz { print "3" }
```

What is the translation of xxxxyzz using the syntax directed translation scheme described by the above rules.
(a) 23131   (b) 11233
(c) 11231   (d) 33211

75. Which of the following features cannot be captured by CFG?
(a) Syntax of `if-then-else` statements
(b) Syntax of recursive procedures
(c) Wheter a variable is declared before its use
(d) Matching nested parenthesis

76. The 'k', in LR (k) cannot be
(a) 0   (b) 1
(c) 2   (d) none of the above

Directions: The next three questions are based on the following grammar

```
E → E/X | X
X → T – X | X*T | T
T → T + F | F
F → (E) | id
```
(id stands for identifier)

77. This grammar is
(a) unambiguous
(b) ambiguous
(c) context-free
(d) both (a) and (c) only

78. The above grammar is used to generate all valid arithmetic expressions in a hypothetical language in which
(a) / associates from the left
(b) * associative from the left
(c) + associative from the left
(d) all of the above

79. The above grammar is used to generate all valid arithemetic expressions in a hypothetical language in which
(a) + has the highest precedence
(b) * has the highest precedence
(c) − has the highest precedence
(d) / has the highest precedence

80. Back-patching is useful for handling
(a) conditional jumps
(b) unconditional jumps
(c) backward references
(d) forward references

81. CSG can be recognized by a
(a) FSM
(b) DPDM
(c) NDPDM
(d) linearly bounded memory machine

82. The following CFG
$$S \rightarrow aS \mid bS \mid a \mid b$$
is equivalent to the regular expression
(a) $(a+b) * (a+b)$
(b) $(a+b)^+$
(c) $(a+b)(a+b)^*$
(d) all of the above

83. Any string of terminals that can be generated by the following CFG
$$S \rightarrow XY$$
$$X \rightarrow aX \mid bX \mid a$$
$$Y \rightarrow Ya \mid Yb \mid a$$
(a) has atleast one b
(b) should end in a 'a'
(c) has no consecutive a's or b's
(d) has atleast two a's

84. The following CFG
$$S \rightarrow aB \mid bA$$
$$A \rightarrow b \mid aS \mid bAA$$
$$B \rightarrow b \mid bS \mid aBB$$
generates strings of terminals that have
(a) equal number of a's and b's
(b) odd number of a's and odd number b's
(c) even number of a's and even number of b's
(d) odd number a's and even number of a's

85. To prove set $A = L(G)$,
(a) it is enough to prove that an arbitrary member of A can be generated by grammar G
(b) it is enough to prove that an arbitrary string generated by G, belongs to set A
(c) both the above comments (a) and (b) are to be proved
(d) either of the above comments (a) or (b) is to be proved

86. 'Aging' is
(a) keeping track of cache contents
(b) keeping track of what pages are currently residing in the memory
(c) keeping track of how many times a given page is referenced
(d) increasing the priority of jobs to ensure termination in a finite time

87. LR stands for
(a) left to right
(b) left to right reduction
(c) right to left
(d) left to right and right-most derivation in reverse

88. LR parsers are attractive because
(a) it can be constructed to recognize CFG corresponding to almost all programming constructs
(b) it detects error as and when they occur
(c) all of the above
(d) none of the above

89. Which of the following is the most powerful parser?
(a) SLR
(b) LALR
(c) Canonical LR
(d) Operator-precedence

90. Choose the correct statements.
(a) There are CFG's that are LR
(b) An ambiguous grammar can never be LR
(c) An ambiguous grammar can be LR
(d) Any CFG has to be LR

91. Consider the following program fragment

```
if (a > b) printf("a > b");
else printf("else part");
    printf("a <= b");
```

a <= b will be printed if

(a) a > b
(b) a < b
(c) a == b
(d) all of the above

92. Consider the following flow chart.

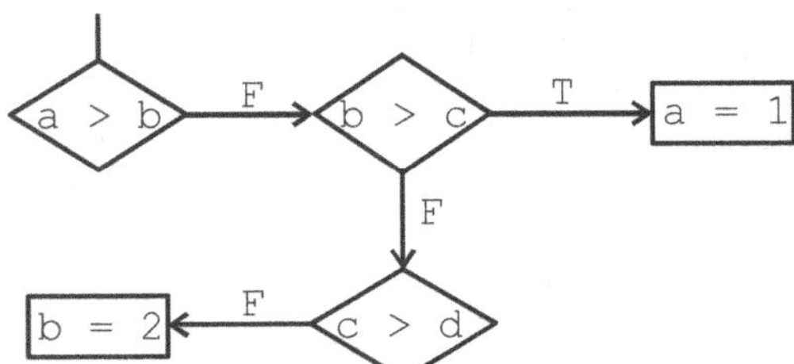

Which of the following is equivalent to the above flow chart?

```
(a) if (a > b)
    if (b > c)
    a = 1;
    else if (c > d)
    b = 2;

(b) if (a <= b)
    if (b > c)
    a = 1;
    else if (c > d)
    b = 2;

(c) if (a > b)
    ;
    else if (b > c)
    a = 1;
    else if (c <= d)
    b = 2;

(d) if (a > b)
    ;
    else if (b > c)
    a = 1;
    if (c < d) ;
    else b = 2;
```

93. The body of the following `for` loop

```
for (putchar ('a'); putchar
(0); putchar('c'))
putchar ('b');
```

will be executed

(a) 0 times
(b) 1 time
(c) infinitely many times
(d) will not be executed because of syntax error

94. The following statement

```
if (a > b)
```

```
if (c > b)
    printf ("one");
    else
    if (c == a) printf("two");
    else printf ("three");
    else printf ("four");
```

(a) results in a syntax error
(b) prints four if c <= b
(c) prints two if c <= b
(d) prints four if a <= b

95. The above statement can never print

(a) one
(b) two
(c) three
(d) four

96. In the bisection method for finding the roots of an equation, the approximate relative error is always

(a) greater than the relative error
(b) equal to the relative error
(c) less than the relative error
(d) none of the above

97. Trapezoidal rule gives the exact solution when the curve is

(a) concave towards the base line
(b) convex towards the base line
(c) a straight line
(d) none of the above

98. If a function $y' = f(x)$ has an inverse function, then $f(x)$ can't be

(a) symmetric about x-axis
(b) an odd function
(c) symmetric about y-axis
(d) none of the above

99. For what value of c, will the vector $i + cj$ be orthogonal to $2i - j$?

(a) 0
(b) 1
(c) 2
(d) 3

100. The solution of the differential equation $y'' + 3y' + 2y = 0$, is of the form

(a) $C_1e^x + C_2e^{2x}$
(b) $C_1e^{-x} + C_2e^{3x}$
(c) $C_1e^{-x} + C_2e^{-2x}$
(d) $C_1e^{-2x} + C_2e^{-x}$

ANSWERS

1	2	3	4	5	6	7	8	9	10
(a)	(d)	(c)	(c)	(c)	(c)	(b)	(c)	(c)	(b)
11	**12**	**13**	**14**	**15**	**16**	**17**	**18**	**19**	**20**
(c)	(b)	(a)	(a)	(a)	(c)	(b)	(d)	(b)	(a)
21	**22**	**23**	**24**	**25**	**26**	**27**	**28**	**29**	**30**
(c)	(a)	(c)	(d)	(b)	(d)	(d)	(c)	(c)	(d)
31	**32**	**33**	**34**	**35**	**36**	**37**	**38**	**39**	**40**
(b)	(c)	(a)	(d)	(b)	(d)	(b)	(b)	(c)	(c)
41	**42**	**43**	**44**	**45**	**46**	**47**	**48**	**49**	**50**
(d)	(c)	(c)	(d)	(b)	(a)	(c)	(a)	(d)	(b)
51	**52**	**53**	**54**	**55**	**56**	**57**	**58**	**59**	**60**
(c)	(d)	(a)	(d)	(a)	(c)	(a)	(a)	(a)	(d)
61	**62**	**63**	**64**	**65**	**66**	**67**	**68**	**69**	**70**
(a)	(d)	(d)	(d)	(d)	(d)	(a)	(d)	(d)	(c)
71	**72**	**73**	**74**	**75**	**76**	**77**	**78**	**79**	**80**
(a)	(c)	(b)	(a)	(c)	(d)	(d)	(d)	(a)	(d)
81	**82**	**83**	**84**	**85**	**86**	**87**	**88**	**89**	**90**
(d)	(d)	(d)	(a)	(c)	(d)	(d)	(a)	(c)	(b)
91	**92**	**93**	**94**	**95**	**96**	**97**	**98**	**99**	**100**
(d)	(c)	(a)	(d)	(b)	(a)	(c)	(c)	(c)	(c)

YOUR SPACE